# gulfshore delights

**a collection of recipes**

**from the**

**Florida Gulfshore**

*Cover design and illustrations by*
Connie Kittinger Whiteside

The purpose of the Junior League of Fort Myers, Florida, Inc., is exclusively educational and charitable and is to promote voluntarism, to develop the potential of its members for voluntary participation in community affairs, and to demonstrate the effectiveness of trained volunteers.

The proceeds realized from the sale of **Gulfshore Delights** will be returned to the community through projects of The Junior League of Fort Myers, Florida, Inc.

Additional copies may be obtained by addressing:

**GULFSHORE DELIGHTS**
The Junior League of Fort Myers, FL, Inc.
P.O. Box 6774
Fort Myers, Florida 33911-6774

**Gulfshore Delights** may be obtained for fundraising projects or by retail outlets at special rates. Write above address for further information.

For your convenience, order blanks are included in the back of the book.

First Edition

| First Printing | 15,000 copies | October, 1984 |
| Second Printing | 15,000 copies | December, 1985 |
| Third Printing | 10,000 copies | July, 1989 |

The Library of Congress Catalog Number: 84-80560
International Standard Book Number: 0-9613314-0-2
Printed in the United States of America by:
S.C. Toof & Company
Memphis, Tennessee

# INTRODUCTION

Fort Myers was established as a military post during the Seminole Indian wars in 1850. Situated beside the broad Caloosahatchee River, the soul of Fort Myers follows its river a few short miles to the Gulf of Mexico. It is the Gulf which dominates the life of our people, providing leisure activities, jobs, panoramic vistas, and the bountiful supply of seafood enjoyed by all.

Do not believe, however, that **Gulfshore Delights** is only a seafood cookbook. Southwest Florida is also cattle country—one quick stop at the Trading Post, 30 miles to the east in LaBelle, will prove that fact. Our tomato, strawberry and pepper fields are the truck garden for the nation during the winter months. Our citrus and other tropical fruits are second to none. The quality of the ingredients so readily available is an inspiration to the willing cook. Many of our recipes are original.

By the same token there is no one country or style of cooking which predominates in **Gulfshore Delights**. From France to the Bahamas, from Greece to the Keys, we have striven to bring you consistently fine recipes that can readily be followed by even the novice cook. For those who have fallen in love with our Gulfshore life, there are ample tropical recipes throughout the book.

The pencil sketches found at chapter dividers throughout the book are intended as a visual reminder of the beauty of Southwest Florida —both natural and man-made. The gentle but rapidly disappearing manatee, the stately royal palm, the Sanibel Lighthouse are but representative of the hundreds of other items and scenes we might have selected as easily as we did these. To those of you who have visited with us, we hope they will bring back fond memories and that you will return soon. To those who have never been to our delightful Gulfshore, please come. And to those who reside here, take a moment to reflect upon the beauty which surrounds you.

# COOKBOOK COMMITTEE

Chairman. . . . . . . . . . . . . . . . . . Susan Harrison

Assistant Chairman. . . . . . . . . . . . . . . . . Marie Taschner

Editor. . . . . . . . . . . . . . . . . . . . . . Orpah Travis

Cover design and illustrations. . . . . . . . . . Connie Whiteside

Layout design. . . . . . . . . . . . . . . . . . Susie Henderson

Testing Captains. . . . . . . . . . . . . . . . . Beverly Fuller
Nancy Green
Susan Kyle
Julie Peters
Diann Seals
Annie Bea Sisler
Mary Squires

Sustaining Advisor. . . . . . . . . . . . . . . . . Judy Dees

Typists. . . . . . . . . . . . . . . . . . . . . . Babs Kendziorski
Judy McIver

Committee

| | | |
|---|---|---|
| Jane Ball | Sara Morrison | Maggie Reese |
| Kathleen Belcastro | Annette Morroni | Mary Shorack |
| Winnie Bruek | Judy O'Halloran | Dawn Simmons |
| Marilyn Johansen | Beverly Pierce | Bunny Terry |

## ABOUT THE ARTIST

Connie Kittinger Whiteside is a resident of Fort Myers and an active member of the Junior League. Connie comes from three generations of artists and has her B.F.A. from Stratford College. She studied graphic arts in Florence, Italy and has done master's work at the University of South Florida and Harvard University. She has taught art in the public school system and now does free-lance work. Connie was selected as the 1983 Lee County Celebrated Woman in Fine Arts by the Celebration of Women.

"In attempting to render the warmth and charm of Fort Myers in these pencil drawings, I was once again reminded how glad I am Southwest Florida is where my children will grow up. Its beauty is felt as well as seen and it is hoped this book will help you experience both."

# TABLE OF CONTENTS

# WINE

*Tom and Linda Uhler have had an interest in fine food and wines since before moving to Florida from their native Pennsylvania in the early 1970's. Through visits to the winemaking areas of America and Europe and through founding the local chapter of Les Amis du Vin (The Friends of Wine), an international wine society, their appreciation has grown. They are the proprietors of The Wine Merchant and Delectables at Royal Palm Square in Fort Myers.*

*The wines listed beneath many of the recipes are the Uhlers' suggestions for a pleasant and compatible accompaniment to the individual recipes.*

Wine can be an important ingredient in your menu planning. Not only does wine add a festive air to any occasion, wine complements food. Both wine and food taste better in each others' company.

When planning meals that will include wine, questions might arise as to which wines to serve. Generations of wine drinkers have followed some established guidelines for the pairings of wines and foods. While these rules can be changed according to one's personal tastes, it would be foolish to ignore them. Red wines usually accompany red meats and white wines make good partners for fish and fowl. Generally, white wines are served before reds, dry wines before sweet wines, and lighter wines before heavier wines. If your selection of wines includes one that has some impressive attributes, plan to serve it last so it does not overshadow any wines which might follow it.

Champagne or a German Kabinett or Spätlese makes a delightful apéritif. A crisp dry wine such as a French Chablis, Muscadet or Champagne is required for rich foods or those with cream sauces. Sautéed or grilled fish and fowl are best with a more highly flavored white; a Chardonnay, a white Burgundy or a Sauvignon Blanc would be a good choice. Red meats such as beef or lamb are best paired with a Cabernet Sauvignon, a red Burgundy or Bordeaux, or a Pinot Noir. Zinfandel, Chianti and Barolo are perfect with spicier foods. When serving roast turkey or chicken, select almost any dry wine. While many people do not think of wine as an accompaniment to dessert, there are quite a few wines that are a wonderful way to end a meal. Among these are Auslese or Beerenauslese Rieslings and sweet Sauternes.

Cheeses are as diverse as wines and there are many pleasing combinations of the two. Possibilities include a mature red Bordeaux, Burgundy or Cabernet Sauvignon with a mild cheese and a Zinfandel, Côte Rôtie or Barolo with a more strongly flavored one.

Wine and food do form a perfect marriage—most of the time. The combination of a vinegar-based salad dressing and wine will be an unpleasant one for our taste buds. Everyone's favorite, chocolate, is also best consumed without wine.

How much wine should be planned for serving? For a multi-course dinner three-fourths of a bottle should be allowed per person. If wine is also served as an apéritif, another one-fourth bottle could be added for each guest. At first this might seem excessive, but note that most of this amount is being consumed with a substantial quantity of food. If less food is planned, the amount of wine should be decreased accordingly. When serving hors d'oeuvres in a party situation, allow a maximum of one-half bottle of wine for each guest.

The characteristics of a wine are enhanced when the wine is served at the proper temperature. Sparkling wines are best at forty-five degrees (refrigerator temperature), white wines at fifty to fifty-five degrees, and red wines at sixty-five degrees. To achieve this with a red wine, place the bottle in the refrigerator for fifteen to twenty minutes before serving. Refrigerate wine on the day you plan to serve it as extended refrigeration tends to dull wine. To chill a wine quickly, immerse the bottle in an ice and water mixture for twenty to thirty minutes.

Does wine have to breathe for a time before it is served? The current consensus in the wine world is no. Open a bottle of wine when you are ready to drink it—and enjoy.

If you have an older red wine, you might notice a sediment in the bottle. This is perfectly normal, but it is best to decant the wine by pouring the wine off of the sediment so there is a clear wine in your glass. When a wine is to be decanted, the bottle should stand upright for a day before serving. Handling the bottle gently, uncork it. Place a light under the neck of the bottle. Pour evenly and steadily into a clean carafe stopping when the sediment (which will appear as a dark line) reaches the neck.

The proper glass will add to the enjoyment of a wine. A glass with no color or decoration is best. A balloon shape is preferred for still wines and a flute shape for sparkling wines. The saucer-shaped glass often used for serving champagne is not satisfactory because the wine loses its sparkle too quickly.

It is fun (and convenient) to have a small wine "cellar" in your home. The perfect location for this "cellar" is dark, free of vibration and has a constant temperature. The ideal temperature would be fifty-five to sixty-five degrees, but a dark closet or pantry with no temperature fluctuations is fine for short term storage. Because of the heat and bright light, a wine rack in your kitchen is not a good idea, no matter how attractive. When storing wine, the bottles should lie on their sides in order to keep the corks moist; if a cork dries out, it can allow air to enter the bottle which will spoil the wine.

Much mystique has developed about wine. This can make wine seem intimidating. Remember, however, that one rule is the most important: Drink the wine you enjoy, enjoy the wine you drink.

*—Tom and Linda Uhler*

appetizers and beverages

# Appetizers and Beverages

## APPETIZERS

### CHEESES

### DIPS

### MEATS

### SEAFOOD

### STUFFED

### VEGETABLES

## BEVERAGES

### ALCOHOLIC

### NON-ALCOHOLIC

*Found elsewhere in the book.

## SANIBEL LIGHTHOUSE

*This majestic sentinel has been standing its silent watch over the southeastern tip of Sanibel Island, known as Point Ybel, for over 100 years. Its symmetrical grace and beauty combined with its lush tropical setting make it surely the most photographed and painted landmark in Southwest Florida.*

# Cheese and Chutney Spread

**May prepare ahead**                                    **10-12 servings**

1 8-ounce package cream
   cheese, softened
8 ounces cheddar cheese,
   shredded
1 teaspoon garlic powder
½ teaspoon salt
2 tablespoons vermouth
1 5-ounce jar chutney
4 to 5 green onions, thinly
   sliced

Mix cream cheese, cheddar cheese, garlic powder, salt and vermouth. Spread on an 8-inch plate. Mixture will be about 1 inch thick. Refrigerate.

Just before serving, spread chutney on top of cheese and sprinkle with onion. Serve with crackers.

# Cheese Ball
*One of the best cheese balls ever*

**Must prepare ahead**                                    **8-10 servings**

4 3-ounce packages cream
   cheese
1 5-ounce jar Old English
   cheese spread
1 4-ounce package bleu cheese
3 tablespoons chopped onion
2 tablespoons chopped parsley
1 cup finely chopped pecans,
   divided
paprika
chopped parsley for garnish,
   optional

Let cheeses soften to room temperature. Mix with fork until well blended. Combine onion, parsley and ½ cup nuts; add to cheese mixture, blending well. Cover and chill until firm. Shape into a ball and roll in remaining nuts. Sprinkle with paprika and additional parsley, if desired. Chill.

Place in center of large tray. Serve with crackers.

# Cheese Puffs

May prepare ahead                                    2 dozen

4 ounces cream cheese,
  softened
¾ teaspoon grated onion
¼ cup mayonnaise
1 tablespoon chopped chives
⅛ teaspoon cayenne pepper
4 tablespoons grated Parmesan
  cheese
party rye bread

In mixing bowl, combine cream cheese, onion, mayonnaise, chives, pepper and Parmesan cheese. Mix well. Spread on party rye bread. Bake at 350 degrees for 15 minutes or until done.

Cheese puffs may be assembled and frozen. Do not thaw before baking.

# Mozzarella en Carrozza

May prepare partially ahead                          4 servings

8 slices thin-sliced firm white
  or Italian bread, crusts
  removed
½ pound sliced mozzarella
  cheese
6 flat anchovy filets, mashed,
  optional
freshly ground black pepper
2 eggs, beaten
½ cup milk
bread crumbs
3 tablespoons olive oil
3 tablespoons vegetable oil

Optional Garnishes:
parsley
pepperoncini
roasted red peppers
pimentos

WINE: Chianti Classico
      or Valpolicella

Divide cheese evenly among four slices of bread. Dot with mashed anchovies. Sprinkle lightly with pepper. Cover with remaining slices of bread. Beat eggs and milk in a shallow bowl. Dip sandwiches in egg mixture and then in bread crumbs.

Heat cooking oils until fragrant; fry sandwiches until golden brown on both sides and cheese melts. Drain on paper towels. Cut into triangles and arrange on serving plates.

Garnish with parsley or, for an Italian touch, with pepperoncini and roasted red peppers or pimentos.

# Fried Cheese Logs

**May prepare partially ahead**

**4-6 servings**

1 8-ounce package Monterey
   Jack cheese
2 eggs, beaten
1 cup Italian seasoned dry
   bread crumbs
vegetable oil

Cut cheese into bite-size "logs." Dip each piece in eggs, then roll in bread crumbs. Fry in hot oil until lightly browned. Serve hot.

WINE: Bulgarian Cabernet
      Sauvignon or Chianti

# Olive-Cheese Tidbits

**Must prepare partially ahead**

**4 dozen**

½ cup butter, softened
1 5-ounce jar Old English
   cheese spread, softened
1¼ cups flour
¼ teaspoon salt, optional
48 small stuffed green olives,
   drained and dried well

Cut butter and cheese into flour. Add salt if desired. Form dough into 48 small balls that can be patted out into 1½-inch rounds. Place an olive in the center of each and form dough around olive, sealing well. Refrigerate overnight.

Bake in preheated 400 degree oven 15 minutes or until brown. Serve hot.

*Do not discard moldy cheese; cut off mold and use the remaining cheese.*

# Spicy Cream Cheese Topper
*Perfect for unexpected guests*

**May prepare ahead**                                      **6 cups**

1 16-ounce jar apricot
  preserves
1 16-ounce jar pineapple
  preserves
1 12-ounce jar apple jelly
1 1-ounce can dry mustard
1 6-ounce bottle prepared
  horseradish

Mix all ingredients. Pour into glass jars and store covered in refrigerator. Keeps up to two months.

To serve, pour 1½ cups of the mixture over an 8-ounce bar of cream cheese. Serve with crackers.

# Tuna-Pimento Cheese Spread

**Must prepare ahead**                                      **12 servings**

1 6½ to 7-ounce can tuna,
  drained
10 ounces extra-sharp cheddar
  cheese, grated
1 medium onion, chopped
1 4-ounce jar diced pimento,
  undrained
1 cup mayonnaise
paprika, optional
dried parsley, optional

Mix tuna, cheese, onion, pimento and mayonnaise. Mound on plate and sprinkle with paprika and parsley, if desired. Chill.

Serve with party rye or party pumpernickel.

*A simple, quick hors d'oeuvre is an 8-ounce bar of cream cheese covered with your favorite sauce, chutney or preserves and topped with sautéed sesame seeds.*

# Guacamole Pie

May prepare ahead

8-12 servings

Guacamole:
1 small onion, finely chopped
1 medium tomato, peeled,
 seeded and finely chopped
2 very ripe avocados, peeled
 and pitted
2 teaspoons chili powder
1 teaspoon salt
2 teaspoons vinegar

Combine chopped onion and tomato and rub to a paste with a
wooden spoon. Cream avocados
with wooden spoon; add onion and
tomato mixture. Add chili powder,
salt and vinegar. Beat lightly.

Pie:
1½ cups refried beans, slightly
 heated
1¼ cups guacamole (above)
¾ cup sour cream
½ cup grated sharp cheddar
 cheese
¼ cup chopped black olives

Assemble the following in layers in
an 8-inch pie plate: refried beans,
guacamole, sour cream, cheese and
olives. Refrigerate if not served immediately. Serve as a dip with large
corn chips.

# Hot Artichoke Dip
*Fantastic*

May prepare partially ahead

8-10 servings

2 14-ounce cans artichoke
 hearts, squeezed, drained
 and finely chopped
¼ to ½ teaspoon garlic powder
6 to 8 green onion tops,
 chopped
12 ounces sliced bacon, cooked
 and crumbled
1 cup grated Parmesan cheese
½ cup mayonnaise
paprika

Preheat oven to 350 degrees. Mix
artichoke hearts, garlic powder,
onions, bacon, cheese and mayonnaise; put in 2-quart ovenproof
dish. Bake uncovered 20 minutes.
Sprinkle with paprika. Serve with
tortilla chips, corn chips or crackers.

# Hot Beef Dip

**May prepare partially ahead**                                    **8 servings**

1 8-ounce carton sour cream
2 3-ounce packages cream
  cheese, softened
¼ cup mayonnaise
1 cup chopped pecans, divided
1 2½-ounce jar dried beef,
  chopped

Preheat oven to 350 degrees. Blend sour cream and cream cheese in a small bowl or food processor. Add mayonnaise. Stir in ¾ cup pecans and beef. Transfer mixture to an ovenproof crock. Top mixture with remaining pecans. Bake uncovered 15 minutes or until heated through. Serve hot with assorted crackers.

# Pizza Crab Dip
*Receives many compliments and is so easy*

**Must prepare ahead**                                    **8-10 servings**

12 ounces cream cheese,
  softened
2 tablespoons Worcestershire
  sauce
1 small onion, grated
pinch of garlic salt
1 tablespoon lemon juice
2 tablespoons mayonnaise
6 ounces seafood cocktail sauce
  or chili sauce
6 ounces minced crabmeat
  (canned or fresh), drained
chopped parsley

Blend cream cheese, Worcestershire sauce, onion, garlic salt, lemon juice and mayonnaise; spread on a 10-inch plate. Spread cocktail sauce on cream cheese mixture; sprinkle crabmeat then parsley on top. Refrigerate 24 hours. If liquid forms around edge, drain off before serving. Serve with crackers.

# Spinach Dip

May prepare ahead                                    1½ cups

1 10-ounce package frozen
   chopped spinach, thawed
¾ cup mayonnaise
¼ cup finely chopped green
   onion
¼ cup dried parsley
½ teaspoon dill weed
2 teaspoons Salad Supreme
   seasoning

Drain thawed spinach well, then roll and squeeze in paper towels to get out all the moisture. It is important to have spinach entirely free of moisture! Add remaining ingredients and mix well. Serve with crackers.

# Vegetable Dip

Must prepare ahead                                   2½ cups

1 cup mayonnaise
½ cup sour cream
¼ cup white vinegar
1½ teaspoons lemon juice
1 tablespoon anchovy paste
½ cup chopped fresh parsley
¼ cup finely chopped
   scallions with some green
   tops
4 ounces bleu cheese, crumbled

Mix all ingredients. Chill. Serve with fresh vegetables.

*Place stale chips or crackers in a microwave oven on high for 45 to 60 seconds to recrisp.*

# Crab and Cheese Dip

May prepare partially ahead

8-10 servings

1 cup fresh, frozen or canned
    crabmeat*, drained
1 cup mayonnaise
1 cup chopped onion
1 cup shredded cheddar,
    Monterey Jack or Muenster
    cheese (or combination)

*May substitute one 14-ounce
can artichoke hearts, drained
and chopped.

Preheat oven to 350 degrees. Mix all ingredients; pour into a 1-quart casserole. Bake uncovered 15 minutes or until hot and bubbly. Stir once while baking. Serve with taco chips or melba rounds.

May be mixed and refrigerated until ready to bake.

# Raw Vegetable Dip
*Also makes a tasty, unusual salad dressing*

Must prepare ahead

2 cups

1 tablespoon finely chopped
    fresh dill weed
2 scallions, finely chopped
1 tablespoon chopped parsley
1 cup mayonnaise
1 cup sour cream
1 teaspoon seasoned salt

Mix all ingredients. Cover bowl and refrigerate at least 24 hours before serving. May be refrigerated several days. Serve with crisp raw vegetables.

# Baked Clams Oregano

May prepare partially ahead                                              2 dozen

24 fresh clams in shells
2 tablespoons fresh lemon
   juice
¼ cup freshly grated Parmesan
   cheese
¼ cup seasoned bread crumbs
¼ cup finely chopped fresh
   parsley
2 garlic cloves, crushed
1 teaspoon oregano
½ teaspoon salt
freshly ground black pepper
   to taste
olive oil
lemon wedges

Preheat oven to 425 degrees. Open clams, discarding top shell and loosening the meat from the bottom shell. Drain well. Arrange clams in their shells on shallow baking pan or cookie sheet. Sprinkle each with a little lemon juice. Combine cheese, bread crumbs, parsley, garlic, oregano, salt and pepper. Cover each clam with one teaspoon of this mixture. Sprinkle a few drops of oil on each clam and bake 15 minutes. Serve with lemon wedges.

WINE: Verdicchio

# Caviar Pie

Must prepare ahead                                                  10-12 servings

6 boiled eggs, chopped
3 tablespoons mayonnaise
1 medium onion, minced
1 8-ounce package cream
   cheese, softened
⅔ cup sour cream
3½ to 4 ounces caviar
lemon wedges
parsley sprigs

Combine eggs with mayonnaise. Spread over the bottom of a well-greased 8-inch springform pan. Sprinkle with minced onion. Blend cream cheese with sour cream until smooth; spread over onion with wet spatula. Cover and chill at least 3 hours or overnight. Before serving, top with caviar, spreading to pan edges. Run knife around pan sides to loosen. Lift off. Garnish with lemon wedges and parsley sprigs.

# Conch Fritters
*A Bahamian favorite*

**May prepare partially ahead**                                        **4 dozen**

1 cup ground conch (about
   10 ounces)
1 medium onion, finely
   chopped
1 stalk celery, finely chopped
3 tablespoons Worcestershire
   sauce
1 tablespoon tomato paste
1 cup flour
1 egg, slightly beaten
1½ teaspoons baking powder
vegetable oil for frying
seafood cocktail sauce

Thoroughly blend conch, onion, celery, Worcestershire sauce, tomato paste, flour, egg and baking powder. Heat oil to 375 degrees. Drop batter by rounded teaspoons into hot oil. Fry until deeply browned, about 4 minutes. Serve with cocktail sauce.

# Clams in a Crock
*Always a hit*

**May prepare ahead**                                        **6 servings**

36 (4 ounces) Ritz crackers
1 6½-ounce can minced clams
   in juice
6 tablespoons butter, melted
1 tablespoon minced onion
2 to 3 drops lemon juice

With a rolling pin or metal blade in food processor, crumble crackers. Put crumbs in a bowl and add clams, butter, onion and lemon juice. Mix well. Pour mixture into a 1-quart crock or casserole. Bake uncovered in a preheated 350 degree oven for 30 minutes. Serve hot or cold with party rye bread.

# Crab Butter

**Must prepare ahead**                          **10 servings**

¾ cup margarine, softened
4 tablespoons mayonnaise
2 tablespoons minced onion
3 to 4 drops lemon juice
1 4-ounce can crabmeat*,
   drained

*May substitute shrimp or
  lobster.

Mix margarine, mayonnaise, onion
and lemon juice; beat until fluffy.
Stir in crabmeat. Refrigerate. Serve
with crackers.

# Crabmeat Yummies

**Must prepare partially ahead**                **4 dozen**

½ cup butter or margarine,
  softened
1 5-ounce jar Old English
  cheese spread, softened
1½ teaspoons mayonnaise
½ teaspoon garlic salt
1 7-ounce can crabmeat, drained
  or 1 6-ounce box frozen
  crabmeat, thawed
6 English muffins, split in half

Mix butter and cheese with mayonnaise and garlic salt. Stir in crabmeat. Spread on muffins. Freeze
at least 10 minutes. Remove from
freezer, cut into quarters and broil
5 to 10 minutes until hot and bubbly. Serve warm.

May be made several weeks ahead
and frozen until ready to cook.

# Seviche (Pickled Fish)
*The lime juice actually "cooks" the fish*

**Must prepare ahead**                                   **6-8 servings**

1 pound fresh red snapper filet*
2 onions, thinly sliced and
   separated into rings
1 tomato, thinly sliced or
   chopped
½ green pepper, thinly sliced
1¼ teaspoons salt
½ teaspoon coarsely ground
   black pepper
juice of 4 or more limes
   or lemons

*May substitute grouper,
   snook or any meaty white fish.

WINE: Chilean Chardonnay

Cut filet into ¾-inch squares and place in large glass bowl. Add onions, tomato, green pepper, salt and pepper. Mix well. Put mixture into glass quart jar and add enough lime juice to completely cover mixture. Cover jar and marinate at room temperature about 4 hours or place in refrigerator overnight. Drain and serve on crisp greens as individual appetizers or serve as an hors d'oeuvre with crackers on the side.

Refrigerate leftovers up to one week. Recipe may be doubled or tripled.

# Shrimp in Mustard Sauce

**Must prepare ahead**                                   **8 servings**

2½ pounds shrimp, peeled
   and deveined

Mustard Sauce:
¼ cup finely chopped parsley
¼ cup finely chopped shallots
¼ cup tarragon vinegar
¼ cup wine vinegar
½ cup olive oil
4 to 5 tablespoons Dijon
   mustard
2 teaspoons crushed red pepper
2 teaspoons salt
freshly ground black pepper

Cook shrimp in boiling salted water until they turn pink. Drain and transfer to a large bowl.

Mix sauce ingredients and pour over warm shrimp, coating well. Cover and refrigerate.

Serve cold with toothpicks.

# Shrimp Wrapped in Bacon
*Always gets "oohs" and "aahs" from guests*

**Must prepare partially ahead**                    **8 servings**

1 pound sliced lean bacon
1½ pounds medium to large
    raw shrimp, peeled and
    deveined
1 18-ounce bottle barbecue
    sauce
½ box toothpicks

Slice bacon strips in half. Wrap a bacon strip around each shrimp and secure with two toothpicks. Place wrapped shrimp in a large bowl. Pour barbecue sauce over shrimp and mix gently with hands to coat. Cover and refrigerate 2 to 24 hours.

When ready to cook, place marinated shrimp in a grid-type basket or on skewers. Grill over medium heat or low coals for about 10 minutes, turning occasionally. Serve immediately.

May be served as an entrée. Serves four.

# Smoked Salmon Pâté

**Must prepare ahead**                    **10-12 servings**

1 1-pound can red salmon
1 8-ounce package cream
    cheese, softened
1 tablespoon lemon juice
2 teaspoons chopped onion
1 teaspoon grated horseradish
¾ teaspoon liquid smoke
1 lemon, thinly sliced

WINE: Gewürztraminer or
    Spanish Sparkling
    Wine

Bone and flake salmon. Mix salmon thoroughly with cream cheese, lemon juice, onion, horseradish and liquid smoke. Place in 3-cup mold or bowl that has been lined with plastic food wrap. Chill 6 hours and unmold onto a plate. Garnish with thinly-sliced lemon. Serve with wheat crackers.

# Terrace Scallops

**May prepare partially ahead**                                    **6-8 servings**

¾ pound bay scallops
½ pound bacon
2 eggs, beaten
½ cup milk
salt to taste
pepper to taste
⅓ cup sesame seeds, toasted
lime wedges

WINE: Alsatian
        Gewürztraminer

Clean and dry scallops. Cut the bacon strips in half. In a small mixing bowl, combine eggs, milk, salt and pepper. Dip scallops in egg mixture; roll in sesame seeds. Wrap each scallop in a piece of bacon and secure with toothpick.

Place scallops on a wire rack in a 9 x 13-inch baking dish. Place under preheated broiler about 4 to 5 inches below heat. Broil approximately 2 minutes on each side, watching closely to prevent burning. Serve at once with fresh lime wedges.

Scallops may be prepared up to 4 hours ahead and kept in refrigerator until time to cook. If they have been refrigerated, allow 2 to 3 minutes extra cooking time.

# Bacon Stuffed Avocado
*Unusual and delicious*

**May prepare partially ahead**                                    **8 servings**

4 small ripe avocados, unpeeled
fresh lemon juice
8 to 12 slices crisply cooked
    bacon
½ cup butter
¼ cup sugar
¼ cup ketchup
¼ cup wine vinegar
1 tablespoon soy sauce
lettuce leaves

Halve avocados lengthwise and remove pits. Brush each half with lemon juice. Crumble bacon and fill avocado cavities. Combine butter, sugar, ketchup, vinegar and soy sauce in a small saucepan. Heat to boiling. Arrange avocados on lettuce leaves on individual plates. Spoon warm sauce over each avocado. Serve immediately. Pass any extra warm sauce.

# Smoked Mullet Log

**Must prepare partially ahead**                    **8-10 servings**

1 pound smoked mullet
1 8-ounce package cream
  cheese, softened
1 tablespoon lemon juice
2 teaspoons grated onion
1 teaspoon prepared
  horseradish
¼ teaspoon salt
½ cup finely chopped pecans
2 tablespoons chopped parsley
whole pimento for garnish

WINE: Dry Sherry or
    Sparkling Wine

Remove skin from mullet; remove fish from bones and flake finely with fork. Combine cream cheese, lemon juice, onion, horseradish, salt and fish, mixing well. Refrigerate 2 to 3 hours, then shape mixture into a "log." Mix chopped pecans and parsley; roll fish log in mixture. Garnish with fish shapes cut from whole pimento.

Serve on bed of fresh parsley with wheat crackers.

# Microwaved Greek Stuffed Mushrooms

**May prepare partially ahead**                    **6-8 servings**

1 10-ounce package frozen
  chopped spinach
½ cup grated Parmesan cheese
4 ounces Feta cheese, rinsed
  and crumbled
½ cup finely chopped
  green onions
½ cup finely chopped parsley
24 large mushrooms, cleaned
  and stemmed

In microwave, cook spinach on high for 3 minutes or until barely defrosted. Drain well, squeezing out moisture. Combine spinach, cheeses, onion and parsley; mix well. Fill mushroom caps with spinach mixture and arrange on microwave-proof plate. Cook on high for 3 to 4 minutes or until hot. Serve immediately. May be reheated in microwave.

# Curry Puffs
*Great filled with chicken, tuna or shrimp salad*

**May prepare ahead**                                    **15 puffs**

¾ cup water
6 tablespoons butter
½ teaspoon curry powder
⅛ teaspoon salt
¾ cup sifted flour
3 eggs

Preheat oven to 400 degrees. Heat water, butter, curry powder and salt in a saucepan until butter melts and water boils. Add flour all at once. Stir over moderate heat until mixture forms a ball. Remove from heat. Beat in eggs, one at a time, beating until smooth after each addition. Spoon 15 mounds onto greased baking sheet about 1½ inches apart. Bake 20 minutes until puffs are high and golden brown. Quickly pierce each at base with sharp knife. Reduce heat to 300 degrees and bake 15 more minutes.

May be kept in freezer for up to one month.

# Hot Spinach Balls

**Must prepare partially ahead**                         **4 dozen**

2 10-ounce packages frozen
   chopped spinach
2 cups herb-seasoned stuffing
   mix
1 large onion, diced
4 eggs
½ cup grated Parmesan
   cheese
¾ cup butter, melted
½ tablespoon thyme
1 garlic clove, minced
salt to taste
pepper to taste

Cook spinach and drain, squeezing out all liquid. Mix all ingredients. Chill 2 hours or more. Roll into 1-inch balls. Freeze or refrigerate until ready to use. Bake in a preheated 300 degree oven 30 minutes or until golden brown.

# Artichoke and Bacon Hors d'Oeuvres
*A favorite hors d'oeuvre*

**Must prepare partially ahead**                    **6 servings**

6 tablespoons vegetable oil
3 tablespoons wine vinegar
½ teaspoon salt
¼ teaspoon ground black
  pepper
1 9-ounce package frozen
  artichoke hearts, cooked
  according to package
  directions or 1 14-ounce
  can artichoke hearts, drained
10 to 12 bacon slices
toothpicks

Combine oil, vinegar, salt and pepper to make marinade. Place cooked artichoke hearts into marinade, making sure all hearts are covered. Let mixture marinate several hours or overnight in the refrigerator.

Cut bacon slices in half; cook until brown, but not so crisp they can't wrap around each heart. Wrap a bacon slice around each heart and fasten with a toothpick. Place hearts on a cookie sheet and bake in a preheated 500 degree oven 5 minutes. Serve warm.

Wrapped hearts can be refrigerated on cookie sheet until just before needed.

# Marinated Broccoli

**Must prepare ahead**                    **8 servings**

3 bunches fresh broccoli

Marinade:
1 cup cider vinegar
1 tablespoon sugar
1 tablespoon dill weed or seed
1 tablespoon Accent
1 teaspoon salt
1 teaspoon pepper
1 teaspoon garlic salt
1½ cups vegetable oil

Wash broccoli. Dry and cut into bite-size florets. Place in plastic container.

Combine ingredients for marinade and mix well. Pour over broccoli. Cover and refrigerate 24 hours, stirring occasionally.

When ready to serve, drain broccoli thoroughly and place in glass dish.

# Artichoke Nibbles

May prepare ahead                                           6-6½ dozen

2 6-ounce jars marinated
   artichoke hearts
1 small onion, finely chopped
1 garlic clove, minced
4 eggs
¼ cup fine dry bread crumbs
¼ teaspoon salt
⅛ teaspoon pepper
¼ teaspoon oregano
⅛ teaspoon hot pepper sauce
8 ounces sharp cheddar cheese,
   shredded
2 tablespoons minced parsley

Drain marinade from one jar artichoke hearts into frying pan. Drain
and discard marinade from second
jar. Chop artichokes and set aside.
Sauté onion and garlic in heated
marinade for 5 minutes.

In a bowl, beat eggs with fork. Add
bread crumbs, salt, pepper, oregano
and hot pepper sauce. Fold in cheese
and parsley. Add artichoke and
onion mixture; blend well. Pour
into greased 7 x 11-inch pan. Bake
uncovered at 325 degrees for 30
minutes. Cool slightly; cut into 1-
inch squares. Serve hot or cold.

# Zucchini Appetizers

May prepare ahead                                             4 dozen

3 cups coarsely chopped
   zucchini (about 4 small ones)
1 cup Bisquick
½ cup finely chopped onion
½ cup grated Parmesan cheese
2 tablespoons snipped parsley
½ teaspoon salt
½ teaspoon seasoned salt
½ teaspoon dried marjoram or
   oregano
dash of pepper
1 garlic clove, minced
½ cup vegetable oil
4 eggs, slightly beaten

Preheat oven to 350 degrees. Grease
a 9 x 13-inch baking pan. Mix all
ingredients and spread in pan. Bake
uncovered 25 minutes or until gold-
en brown. Cut into 1 x 2-inch pieces.

Bake in mini-muffin tins for a more
pleasing appearance. May be frozen
and reheated just before serving.

# Marinated Mushrooms
*Men love these mushrooms*

**Must prepare ahead**                                          **6 servings**

2 pints fresh mushrooms

Marinade:
⅔ cup tarragon vinegar
½ cup vegetable oil
1 garlic clove, minced
1 tablespoon sugar
1 tablespoon water
1 teaspoon salt
1 medium onion, sliced into
   rings
dash hot pepper sauce
dash pepper

Clean mushrooms and remove ends. Set aside.

Mix marinade ingredients, blending well. Pour over mushrooms. Cover and marinate for 24 hours in refrigerator.

# Rolled Mushroom Appetizer
*Easy and very popular*

**Must prepare partially ahead**                    **6½-7½ dozen**

1 pound fresh mushrooms,
   cleaned and chopped
1 to 3 teaspoons chopped onion
1 tablespoon butter
1 3-ounce package cream
   cheese
⅛ teaspoon salt
⅛ teaspoon pepper
2 tablespoons sherry
1 teaspoon Worcestershire
   sauce
16 to 18 slices white bread,
   crusts removed
melted butter

Sauté mushrooms and onion in butter for 3 to 4 minutes. Add cream cheese to hot pan and blend. Remove from heat and add salt, pepper, sherry and Worcestershire sauce, blending well. Flatten bread slices between two sheets of wax paper. Spread 1 tablespoon of mixture on each slice of bread, then roll each slice in jelly roll fashion. Chill or freeze rolls.

When ready to serve, cut each roll into ½-inch slices; place on cookie sheet. Spread with melted butter. Broil about 4 minutes until toasted. Serve warm.

# Polynesian Meatballs

**May prepare ahead**                                    **6 dozen**

**Meatballs:**
**1 pound ground round**
**½ cup milk**
**¼ cup corn meal**
**1 egg, beaten**
**2 tablespoons chopped onion**
**2 tablespoons chopped green pepper**
**1 teaspoon dry mustard**
**1 teaspoon salt**
**1 teaspoon chili powder**
**¼ teaspoon pepper**

**vegetable oil for cooking**

**Sauce:**
**1 10½-ounce can beef broth**
**1 15½-ounce can pineapple chunks, drained**
**½ green pepper, coarsely chopped**
**¼ cup sugar**
**¼ cup red wine vinegar**
**2 tablespoons soy sauce**
**½ teaspoon salt**
**½ cup water**
**3 tablespoons cornstarch**

Combine all ingredients for meatballs, mixing well. Form into 6 dozen 1-inch meatballs.

Heat small amount of oil in heavy skillet and cook meatballs over medium heat 15 to 20 minutes.

In a medium saucepan, combine beef broth, pineapple chunks, green pepper, sugar, vinegar, soy sauce and salt. Simmer 15 minutes, stirring frequently. In a separate bowl, slowly add water to cornstarch, stirring until smooth. Stir into broth mixture. Cook until thick and bubbly.

Pour sauce over meatballs and toss gently. Serve in chafing dish.

Meatballs may be frozen up to two weeks.

Serves 4 to 6 as an entrée. Make larger meatballs and serve over rice.

# Brandy Slush

Must prepare partially ahead                    25-30 servings

7 cups water
2 cups sugar
2 cups boiling water
4 green tea bags
1 12-ounce can frozen orange
   juice, thawed and undiluted
1 12-ounce can frozen
   lemonade, thawed and
   undiluted
2½ cups brandy
Sprite or 7-Up

Bring 7 cups water and sugar to a boil and cool. Make tea with 2 cups boiling water. Cool. Combine sugar mixture, tea, orange juice, lemonade and brandy. Freeze at least 2 days.

For each serving, put a scoop of the slush into a glass and add carbonated beverage.

# Coffee 'N' Cream
*Sensational in front of a glowing fire*

Must prepare partially ahead                    8 servings

Grand Marnier Sauce:
2 eggs
⅔ cup butter, melted
3 cups confectioners' sugar
2 teaspoons vanilla extract
½ teaspoon nutmeg
½ cup Grand Marnier
2 cups heavy cream, whipped

Beat eggs until frothy. Slowly beat in melted butter, confectioners' sugar, vanilla, nutmeg and Grand Marnier. Fold in whipped cream. Chill.

Drink:
8 cups strong hot coffee
Grand Marnier sauce
2 pints French vanilla ice cream
   or coffee ice cream
1 cup heavy cream, whipped
semi-sweet chocolate shavings

For each serving, pour coffee into a very large goblet. Add a scoop of ice cream. Top with a ladle of Grand Marnier sauce and a spoonful of whipped cream. Garnish with chocolate shavings. Serve immediately.

# Champagne Punch
*Wonderfully light and fruity*

**May prepare partially ahead**                    **2½-3 quarts**

2 6-ounce cans frozen orange
   juice, thawed and undiluted
1 6-ounce can frozen lemonade,
   thawed and undiluted
6 cups water
1 750-ml. bottle champagne
1 frozen ice ring
1 cup fresh strawberries

Combine orange juice, lemonade, water and champagne in punch bowl. Place an ice ring in bowl and float fresh strawberries. Makes 15 6-ounce servings.

# Eggnog
*A delicious variation of the traditional holiday beverage*

**Must prepare partially ahead**                    **6 quarts**

12 eggs
3 cups sugar
dash of nutmeg
dash of cinnamon
1 tablespoon vanilla extract
1 gallon milk
2 pints heavy cream, whipped
brandy to taste

Beat eggs until lemon yellow and strain through cheesecloth. Mix in sugar, nutmeg, cinnamon and vanilla. Refrigerate 24 hours.

To make eggnog, combine milk and egg mixture and blend thoroughly. Fold eggnog into whipped cream. Whipped cream should float on top. Add brandy to taste. Serve immediately. Makes 32 6-ounce servings.

# Mimosa

**May not prepare ahead**                    **1½ quarts**

1 750-ml. bottle champagne,
   chilled
3 cups freshly squeezed orange
   juice, chilled
orange slices

Mix chilled champagne and orange juice. Garnish each glass with an orange slice. Serve immediately.

# Hot Buttery Spiced Wine
*Super at holidays*

**May prepare ahead**                                              **1½ quarts**

1 quart dry wine (red, white
   or rosé)
2 cups water
1 cup sugar
2 tablespoons butter
10 whole cloves
10 whole allspice
2 cinnamon sticks
½ lemon, thinly sliced

In 3-quart saucepan combine wine, water, sugar and butter. Over medium heat, stir until sugar is dissolved. Add spices and lemon. Cook 10 to 15 minutes, stirring occasionally. Makes 8 6-ounce servings.

# Sangria

**Must prepare partially ahead**                                  **2 quarts**

2 cups sugar
1 cup water
2 oranges, thinly sliced
2 limes, thinly sliced
1 lemon, thinly sliced
1 1.5-liter bottle red wine

Combine sugar and water in saucepan. Heat, stirring, until sugar is dissolved and mixture comes to a boil. Remove from heat and add sliced fruit. Allow to marinate at least 4 hours. Pour syrup-fruit mixture and wine over block of ice in a punch bowl, or mix in a large pitcher. Serve in glasses over ice, garnishing each glass with slices of the fruit.

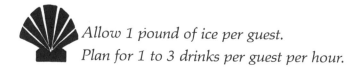

*Allow 1 pound of ice per guest.*
*Plan for 1 to 3 drinks per guest per hour.*

# Rum Punch
*Delicious, but sneaky*

**May not prepare ahead**                    **3 quarts**

2 6-ounce cans frozen limeade,
   thawed and undiluted
2 cups light rum
1 frozen ice ring
3 750-ml. bottles Cold Duck
fresh fruit

Combine limeade and rum. Add an ice ring. Add Cold Duck. Use fresh fruit for garnish. Makes 20 5-ounce servings.

# Whiskey Sour
*So smooth*

**May not prepare ahead**                    **4 servings**

1½ cups crushed ice
1 6-ounce can frozen lemonade
¼ cup rum
½ cup whiskey
7 ounces Sprite or 7-Up

Place all ingredients in blender. Blend for 2 minutes. Serve over ice.

# Fruit Punch Slush

**Must prepare partially ahead**                    **6 quarts**

6 ripe bananas
1 6-ounce can frozen lemonade,
   thawed and undiluted
1 12-ounce can frozen orange
   juice, thawed and undiluted
1 46-ounce can pineapple juice
3 cups water
2 cups sugar
2 2-liter bottles Sprite or
   7-Up, chilled
orange slices

Combine bananas and fruit juice concentrates in blender. Blend until smooth. Combine banana mixture, pineapple juice, water and sugar. Pour into plastic freezer container. Freeze.

To serve, thaw until mushy and add carbonated beverage. Garnish with orange slices. Makes 24 8-ounce servings.

# Hot Punch Deluxe
*Fantastic holiday beverage*

**May prepare ahead**                    **3 quarts**

1 12-ounce bag fresh
  cranberries
2 quarts water
2 tablespoons grated
  orange rind
1 teaspoon cinnamon
12 whole cloves
1 quart freshly squeezed
  orange juice
1 cup freshly squeezed
  lemon juice
1½ cups sugar

Wash cranberries and drain well. Heat cranberries, water, orange rind, cinnamon and cloves in a large pot. Bring to a boil; reduce heat and simmer 5 minutes or until cranberries pop. Strain, discard pulp, and add juices and sugar. Stir constantly over medium heat until sugar is dissolved and punch is thoroughly heated. Serve hot.

# Hot Apple Cider

**May prepare ahead**                    **2 quarts**

2 quarts apple cider
2 teaspoons allspice
2 teaspoons whole cloves
4 cinnamon sticks
lemon slices

Combine cider and spices in a 3-quart pan. Bring to boiling point and immediately reduce to low heat. Cook slowly for 20 minutes. Remove cinnamon sticks and cloves. Serve hot with lemon slices. Makes 16 4-ounce servings.

If made ahead, refrigerate and reheat before serving.

*A crystal or glass punch bowl should never be used for hot punches; it may crack or break.*

# Spiced Mocha Mix

**May prepare ahead**                    **20-30 servings**

1 cup dry non-dairy creamer
1 cup instant hot chocolate mix
2/3 cup powdered instant coffee
  (not crystals)
1/2 cup sugar
1 teaspoon cinnamon
1/2 teaspoon nutmeg

Mix all ingredients. Store in airtight container.

For one serving, combine 2 to 3 heaping teaspoons of mix with 3/4 cup boiling water. Top with ice cream or whipped cream, if desired.

# Hot Chocolate Mix

*Delicious on a chilly winter evening*

**May prepare ahead**                    **36 servings**

2 1-quart packages dry milk
  powder
1/2 cup instant cocoa mix
1/2 cup sifted confectioners'
  sugar
3 tablespoons powdered
  non-dairy creamer

Sift all ingredients. Mix well. Store in airtight container.

For one serving, combine 1/4 cup mix with 3/4 cup boiling water. Top with marshmallows or whipped cream, if desired.

# Spiced Tea Mix

**May prepare ahead**                    **5½ cups mix**

2 cups orange Tang
2½ cups sugar
2 3-ounce packages lemonade
  mix
1/2 cup instant tea
1 teaspoon ground cloves
2 teaspoons cinnamon

Mix all ingredients. Store in airtight container.

For one serving, stir 1 heaping teaspoon mix into 3/4 cup boiling water.

Also great as iced tea.

soups

# Soups

### COLD FRUIT SOUPS

Cream of Mango Soup . . . . . . . . 39
*Strawberry Fruit Soup . . . . . . . 271

### COLD VEGETABLE SOUPS

Chilled Avocado Soup . . . . . . . . 39
Cold Spinach Soup . . . . . . . . . . 40
Gazpacho . . . . . . . . . . . . . . . . . 41

### HOT CHEESE AND VEGETABLE SOUPS

*Black Bean Soup . . . . . . . . . . . . 95
Cauliflower and Cheese Soup . . . . . 44
Chablis Cheddar Soup . . . . . . . . 40
Corn and Cheese Chowder . . . . . . 43
Cream of Artichoke Soup . . . . . . 46
French Onion Soup . . . . . . . . . . 44

Mushroom Bisque . . . . . . . . . . . 47
Soupe au Pistou . . . . . . . . . . . . . 42
Swiss Cheese Soup . . . . . . . . . . . 43
Swiss Onion Soup . . . . . . . . . . . 45
Zucchini Soup . . . . . . . . . . . . . . 41

### HOT FISH AND MEAT SOUPS

Clam Chowder . . . . . . . . . . . . . 50
Fort Myers Gumbo . . . . . . . . . . 51
*Lobster Bisque . . . . . . . . . . . . . 267
Mary's Fish Soup . . . . . . . . . . . 52
Oyster Stew . . . . . . . . . . . . . . . 51
Ricardo's Festa Zuppa . . . . . . . . 48
Seafood Bisque . . . . . . . . . . . . . 50
Seafood Gumbo . . . . . . . . . . . . 49

*Found elsewhere in the book.

## ROSEATE SPOONBILL

*Seen from a distance, this showy and spectacular pink bird is frequently mistaken for the flamingo. On closer view, however, its true nature is given away by the distinctive flat rounded bill, from which it derives its name. The most common place for sighting the spoonbill is in the Ding Darling Sanctuary on Sanibel.*

# Cream of Mango Soup
*Wonderful Florida soup*

**Must prepare ahead**                    **1½ quarts**

2 eggs, well beaten
⅓ cup sugar
1 tablespoon vanilla extract
juice and grated rind of 1 lemon
1 ripe mango, pitted, peeled
  and coarsely chopped
2 cups heavy cream
3 cups milk
blueberries for garnish
strawberries, coarsely chopped,
  for garnish

Purée eggs, sugar, vanilla, lemon juice, lemon rind and mango in a food processor or blender. Whisk cream and milk together in large bowl until frothy. Slowly add mango mixture, whisking constantly. Cover and chill well.

To serve, stir, ladle into chilled bowls and garnish each serving with fresh blueberries and strawberries.

# Chilled Avocado Soup
*Perfect for serving around the pool on a warm evening*

**Must prepare ahead**                    **6 servings**

2 large ripe avocados
2 tablespoons fresh lemon juice
1½ cups chicken broth
½ teaspoon salt
hot pepper sauce to taste
1 teaspoon grated onion
1½ cups half and half cream
chopped chives for garnish
paprika for garnish

Peel avocados; cut a few thin slices, sprinkle with 1 or 2 teaspoons lemon juice and reserve for garnish. Cut remainder of avocado into chunks and place in blender. Add remaining lemon juice, chicken broth, salt, hot pepper sauce and onion. Blend at medium speed until smooth. Pour into a pitcher or bowl; stir in cream. Cover and chill 1 hour or longer.

To serve, pour into chilled wine glasses and garnish with reserved avocado slices. Sprinkle with chives and paprika.

# Cold Spinach Soup

**Must prepare ahead**                                    **8 servings**

3 tablespoons butter
1½ cups chopped scallions
1 10-ounce package frozen
  chopped spinach, thawed
  and drained
2 10¾-ounce cans cream of
  potato soup
2 10¾-ounce cans chicken
  broth
2 tablespoons lemon juice
¼ teaspoon pepper
salt to taste
½ cup half and half cream
1 cup sour cream
chopped parsley for garnish
grated lemon rind for garnish

In a large frying pan, melt butter and sauté scallions. Add spinach, potato soup, chicken broth, lemon juice, pepper and salt. Simmer for a few minutes until warm. Place in blender or food processor and purée. Pour into large bowl and stir in half and half cream and sour cream. Chill at least 8 hours. Garnish with chopped parsley and lemon rind.

# Chablis Cheddar Soup

**May prepare ahead**                                    **4 servings**

2 tablespoons butter
3 green onions with tops,
  thinly sliced
½ cup finely chopped celery
1 10¾-ounce can condensed
  cheddar cheese soup
½ cup water
½ cup half and half cream
1 teaspoon instant chicken
  bouillon
⅛ teaspoon ground nutmeg
¼ cup Chablis
paprika for garnish
croutons for garnish

Melt butter over medium heat. Add onions and celery; stir until onions are tender, about 10 minutes. Remove from heat. Stir soup into onion mixture, mixing until smooth. Return to heat. Stir water, cream, bouillon and nutmeg gradually into soup mixture. Mix until smooth. Cook until thick, about 8 minutes, stirring occasionally. Stir in Chablis.

To serve, pour into soup bowls and sprinkle each serving with paprika. Garnish with croutons.

# Gazpacho
*A Mexican classic*

**Must prepare ahead**

**2 quarts**

1 medium tomato, peeled
    and seeded
1½ teaspoons minced garlic
¼ cup red wine vinegar
½ cup olive oil
1 tablespoon Worcestershire
    sauce
½ teaspoon salt
¼ teaspoon hot pepper sauce
2 beef bouillon cubes
1 cup boiling water
4 cups tomato juice
1 medium onion, finely
    chopped
1½ medium cucumbers,
    finely chopped
2 medium green peppers,
    cleaned and finely chopped
1¼ pounds tomatoes, peeled,
    seeded and finely chopped

Purée in food processor or blender 1 medium tomato, garlic, vinegar, olive oil, Worcestershire sauce, salt and hot pepper sauce. Dissolve bouillon cubes in boiling water. Add to puréed mixture. Stir in tomato juice and remaining vegetables. Combine well. Chill several hours before serving.

# Zucchini Soup
*A cooling treat*

**Must prepare ahead**

**6-8 servings**

4 medium zucchini,
    quartered and sliced
4 cups chicken broth
8 green onions, chopped
1 teaspoon salt
1 teaspoon pepper
dill weed to taste
2 8-ounce packages
    cream cheese
1 cup sour cream
chopped chives or paprika
    for garnish

In a saucepan, combine zucchini, chicken broth, green onions, salt, pepper and dill weed. Cook mixture until soft, about 20 to 30 minutes. Blend the cream cheese and sour cream in a blender until smooth. Add zucchini mixture, a portion at a time, blending until smooth. Chill overnight or until very cold. Garnish with chopped chives or paprika.

41

# Soupe au Pistou

*Provençal vegetable soup with garlic and basil*

**May prepare ahead**                                                   **5 quarts**

**Soupe:**
1 large onion, chopped
4 tablespoons olive oil
1 pound tomatoes, peeled,
   seeded and coarsely chopped
3 quarts water
1½ cups diced carrots
1½ cups diced potatoes
1 cup sliced leeks
1 cup celery leaves
1 tablespoon salt
½ teaspoon pepper
2 cups cooked navy beans
1½ cups green beans, cleaned
   and snapped
1½ cups diced zucchini
½ cup vermicelli, broken
   into pieces

In a 6-quart kettle, sauté onions in oil 3 to 4 minutes. Add tomatoes; cook 3 to 4 minutes. Add water and bring to a boil. Add carrots, potatoes, leeks, celery leaves, salt and pepper. Simmer uncovered 15 minutes. Add navy beans, green beans, zucchini and vermicelli. Simmer 15 minutes or until vegetables are tender. Stir in pistou.

**Pistou:**
2 teaspoons minced garlic
½ cup grated Parmesan cheese
5 tablespoons dried basil
2 tablespoons tomato paste
6 tablespoons olive oil

Combine all ingredients to make a paste. Thin by stirring ½ cup of the soup broth into the paste. Stir into soup kettle.

*To reduce an excessively salty taste in stews, soups or casseroles, add several slices of raw potato and cook for about 10 minutes. Remove potato slices before serving.*

# Corn and Cheese Chowder

**May prepare ahead**                    **8-10 servings**

2 cups water
2 cups diced potatoes
½ cup chopped onion
½ cup diced celery
2 tablespoons margarine
½ teaspoon dried whole basil
1 bay leaf
1 17-ounce can cream-style
  corn
2 cups milk
1 cup canned tomatoes,
  drained and chopped
1½ teaspoons salt
⅛ teaspoon pepper
2 ounces cheddar cheese,
  shredded

Combine water, potatoes, onion, celery, margarine, basil and bay leaf in a Dutch oven; bring to a boil. Reduce heat and simmer 10 minutes or until potatoes are tender. Discard bay leaf. Stir in corn, milk, tomatoes, salt and pepper; heat thoroughly. Add cheese and cook over low heat, stirring constantly, until cheese is melted. Serve immediately.

# Swiss Cheese Soup

**May prepare ahead**                    **4-6 servings**

2 10½-ounce cans beef bouillon
2 10¾-ounce cans chicken
  broth
3 cups water
2 large onions, chopped
2 large potatoes, peeled and
  shredded or diced
1 carrot, chopped
12 mushrooms, sliced
2 tablespoons tomato paste
½ cup butter or margarine
½ cup flour
salt to taste
pepper to taste
10 ounces Swiss cheese,
  shredded

Combine beef bouillon, chicken broth, water, onions, potatoes, carrot, mushrooms and tomato paste in a large pot. Cover; simmer 30 minutes. Melt butter in skillet; add flour and stir until golden brown. Add flour mixture to soup and stir until thickened. Season soup with salt and pepper. Stir ½ of cheese into soup.

To serve, place soup in individual bowls and sprinkle with remaining cheese.

May be prepared ahead of time and reheated in microwave.

# Cauliflower and Cheese Soup

**May prepare partially ahead**      **6 servings**

1 pound cauliflower florets
3 cups vegetable stock or
   chicken stock
¼ cup butter
½ medium onion, chopped
1 garlic clove, minced
¼ cup flour
3 cups half and half cream
¾ teaspoon Worcestershire
   sauce
½ teaspoon salt
½ teaspoon celery salt
⅛ teaspoon nutmeg
⅛ teaspoon pepper
2½ cups shredded cheddar
   cheese
2 tablespoons sherry
chopped fresh parsley for
   garnish

Reserve 6 tiny cauliflower florets for garnish. Simmer remaining cauliflower in stock until just tender. Melt butter and sauté onions and garlic until transparent; blend in flour and cook 3 minutes. Slowly whisk in cream, stirring constantly until thickened. Combine mixture with cooked cauliflower and stock. Add salt, celery salt, nutmeg, pepper and cheddar cheese; simmer 15 minutes. Add sherry just before serving.

Garnish each bowl with chopped parsley and a tiny cauliflower floret.

# French Onion Soup
*A dazzling first course or a special lunch*

**May prepare partially ahead**      **6 servings**

12 onions, finely chopped
9 tablespoons butter
6 tablespoons vegetable oil
¾ teaspoon prepared mustard
3 teaspoons Worcestershire
   sauce
3 teaspoons salt
2½ cups white wine
7½ cups consommé
6 1-inch slices crusty French
   bread
6 1-ounce slices Swiss cheese

Slowly brown onions in butter and oil, about 30 minutes. Add mustard, Worcestershire sauce, salt, wine and consommé; slowly simmer 30 minutes. Pour soup into 6 ovenproof soup bowls. Float 1 slice French bread in each bowl. Place 1 slice Swiss cheese across top of bowls. Place under broiler until cheese is melted.

# Swiss Onion Soup

**May prepare partially ahead**                    **8 servings**

8 cups sliced onions
¼ cup butter, melted
½ cup all-purpose flour
1 teaspoon salt
2 cups beef broth
2 cups water
½ teaspoon white pepper
2 cups half and half cream
2 cups milk

Sauté onions in butter in large pan, about 15 minutes. Stir in flour and salt. Add broth, water and white pepper; bring to boil. Reduce heat, cover and simmer 30 to 40 minutes. Stir in cream and milk. Heat to serving temperature. Do not boil.

Croutons:
½ cup butter, melted
⅛ teaspoon garlic powder
8 slices French bread, cut
  1½ inches thick

Combine butter and garlic powder. Dip both sides bread in butter. Place on cookie sheet and toast in 325 degree oven 10 minutes. Turn and toast 5 minutes or until lightly browned.

2 cups shredded Swiss cheese

To serve, place about 1 cup soup in each of 8 ovenproof bowls. Top each with 1 crouton and ¼ cup Swiss cheese. Bake at 325 degrees 10 minutes or until cheese melts.

# Cream of Artichoke Soup

May prepare ahead 6 servings

3 tablespoons butter
2 tablespoons finely chopped
  onion
½ cup thinly sliced fresh
  mushrooms
2 tablespoons flour
1 14½-ounce can chicken
  broth
2½ cups half and half cream
1 14-ounce can artichoke
  hearts*, drained and chopped
½ teaspoon salt
cayenne pepper to taste
2 teaspoons chopped fresh
  parsley

*May substitute 1½ cups
 cooked, chopped, drained
 spinach, broccoli or asparagus.

In a 2-quart saucepan, melt butter; sauté onions and mushrooms 5 minutes. Stir in flour and cook on medium heat 2 minutes. Slowly stir in broth, then cream, stirring constantly with whisk until smooth. Heat very slowly until thickened. Stir in artichokes, salt, pepper and parsley. Serve hot.

May be cooled and refrigerated up to 48 hours and rewarmed on top of stove or in microwave.

# Mushroom Bisque
*Superb*

**May prepare ahead**                                                    **2½ quarts**

8 tablespoons butter, divided
1 pound fresh mushrooms,
   sliced
2 shallots, minced
1 quart chicken broth
6 tablespoons flour
3 cups whole milk
1 cup heavy cream
2 tablespoons sherry
1½ teaspoons salt
9 to 10 drops hot pepper sauce
pepper to taste
1 7-ounce box wild and long
   grain rice, cooked, optional
parsley for garnish

Melt 2 tablespoons butter in skillet. Add mushrooms and shallots; sauté 5 minutes. Place mushrooms, shallots and chicken broth in blender and blend until smooth. Melt remaining butter in saucepan and add flour. In another saucepan bring milk to a boil and add all at once to butter-flour mixture, stirring vigorously until thick and smooth. Add heavy cream, mushroom mixture, sherry, salt and hot pepper sauce. Season with pepper. If desired, add cooked rice. Garnish with parsley.

May keep in refrigerator up to 1 week. Reheat and serve.

*Celery sticks, a mushroom slice, parsley, a slice of zucchini, a small tomato slice, a green onion or a carrot curl are great garnishes for soups.*

# Ricardo's Festa Zuppa

**Must prepare ahead**                                   **5 quarts**

**Beef Broth:**
4 quarts water
1 pound beef short ribs
1 large onion, peeled
1 tablespoon salt
1 12-ounce can tomato paste

Fill 6-quart soup kettle with 4 quarts water. Add remaining broth ingredients. Bring to boil. Reduce heat and simmer 3 to 4 hours. Remove short ribs and onion. Discard onion. If using meatballs, discard short ribs. If not using meatballs, strip meat from short ribs and return meat to pot.

**Soup:**
2 medium potatoes, peeled
1 10-ounce package frozen
   chopped spinach, thawed
½ cup grated Romano cheese
1 egg, slightly beaten
meatballs, optional

Boil potatoes in broth 10 minutes or until tender. Remove and mash, adding enough broth to make creamy; return to pot. Add spinach and cheese. Bring to boil. Add egg slowly so it shreds into soup. Add meatballs, if using. Reduce heat to medium and cook 1 hour.

**Meatballs, optional:**
1 pound ground chuck
1 egg, beaten
⅔ cup bread crumbs
2 tablespoons grated Romano
   cheese
salt to taste
pepper to taste
onion powder to taste
garlic powder to taste

Mix all meatball ingredients well. Roll into 1-inch balls. Add to soup immediately after adding egg. There is no need to cook meatballs before adding to soup.

# Seafood Gumbo
### *An impressive Creole dish*

**May prepare ahead**                                          **6-8 quarts**

½ cup vegetable oil
1 cup flour
11 cups water, divided
2 cups diced onions
1 cup diced green peppers
3 heaping tablespoons
   tomato paste
1 8-ounce can whole tomatoes,
   chopped
1 teaspoon black pepper
salt to taste
1 16-ounce package frozen
   cut okra, thawed
4 drops hot pepper sauce
2½ pounds shrimp, peeled
   and deveined
1 pound crabmeat
1 to 2 pints oysters
3 tablespoons gumbo filé

In a heavy skillet, make a roux by cooking oil and flour over medium heat, stirring constantly until browned, about 20 to 30 minutes. Regulate heat so as not to brown too fast. The roux will be a milk chocolate color and will begin smoking when ready. Add 3 cups water, stirring constantly, scraping roux from sides and bottom of pan to prevent sticking. Transfer to large pot. Add 8 cups water, onions and green pepper. Slowly bring to low boil, stirring frequently. Add tomato paste, tomatoes, pepper, salt, okra and hot pepper sauce. Simmer, stirring occasionally, until vegetables are tender. Add remaining ingredients. Simmer 1 hour, stirring occasionally. May need to add more water if gumbo gets too thick.

*A lettuce leaf dropped into a pot absorbs grease from the top of soup. Remove lettuce as soon as it has served its purpose and discard.*

# Clam Chowder

**May prepare partially ahead**                    **4 servings**

2 cups diced potatoes
1½ cups chopped onions
1½ cups chopped celery
¼ teaspoon salt
1 cup water
1 10½-ounce can Manhattan
   clam chowder
1 cup milk
1 7½-ounce can minced clams
3 tablespoons dry white wine
½ cup heavy cream, whipped
2 tablespoons chopped parsley
salt to taste
pepper to taste

In a 2-quart saucepan, combine potatoes, onions, celery, salt and water. Cook 30 minutes or until potatoes are done. Add chowder, milk, clams and wine. Heat thoroughly, but do NOT bring to a boil. Approximately 10 to 15 minutes prior to serving, fold in whipped cream and sprinkle with parsley. Season with salt and pepper. Mix and serve.

# Seafood Bisque

**May prepare ahead**                    **6 servings**

¼ cup chopped onion
2 tablespoons butter
2 10¾-ounce cans condensed
   cream of celery or
   mushroom soup
1 soup can milk
1 soup can water
1 7¾-ounce can red salmon*
2 tablespoons chopped parsley
dash of pepper
paprika for garnish

*May substitute crab, tuna
   or shrimp.

Sauté onion in butter until tender. Blend in soup, milk, water, salmon, parsley and pepper. Heat thoroughly. Garnish with paprika.

# Fort Myers Gumbo
*A long-time favorite*

May prepare ahead

6 servings

½ cup butter
1 cup finely chopped celery
½ cup finely chopped green
　pepper
1 cup finely chopped onion
½ cup sliced okra
2 10¾-ounce cans cream of
　chicken soup
1 6-ounce can tomato paste
2 cups water
1½ pounds shrimp, peeled,
　deveined and cooked
1 pint oysters, undrained
1 3 to 4-ounce can minced
　clams, undrained
salt to taste
pepper to taste
hot pepper sauce to taste
rice, optional

In a large pot, melt butter and sauté celery, green pepper, onion and okra. Add soup, tomato paste and water. Cover and cook over low heat 30 minutes. Add shrimp, oysters, clams, salt, pepper and a few drops hot pepper sauce. Cover and simmer 1 hour.

May serve over hot, fluffy rice.

# Oyster Stew

May not prepare ahead

4 servings

¼ cup flour
¼ cup water
1 teaspoon salt
4 teaspoons Worcestershire
　sauce
1 pint fresh oysters
8 cups half and half cream
3 tablespoons butter
2 tablespoons chopped parsley

Blend flour, water, salt and Worcestershire sauce in 4-quart saucepan. Add oysters and their liquid. Cook over medium low heat for 10 to 15 minutes until oysters curl and centers are firm. Add half and half cream and butter. Increase heat to medium and bring to a boil. Remove and let stand 10 minutes. Garnish with parsley.

# Mary's Fish Soup

**May prepare ahead**                                    **4-6 servings**

3 tablespoons butter
2 medium onions, chopped
½ green pepper, chopped
½ cup chopped celery
1 garlic clove, minced
1½ teaspoons flour
1 14½-ounce can stewed
   tomatoes
1 12-ounce can Clamato or
   V-8 juice
1 teaspoon salt
2 teaspoons sugar
4 bay leaves
1 teaspoon dried thyme
½ teaspoon allspice
3 tablespoons Worcestershire
   sauce
¼ teaspoon hot pepper sauce
1 7-ounce can tuna, drained
1 7-ounce can shrimp,
   undrained
1 3-ounce can clams, undrained
1 pound fresh or frozen fish
   filets, cut into chunks
½ cup white wine, optional

Melt butter in heavy skillet; sauté onions, green pepper, celery and garlic until tender. Blend in flour. Add stewed tomatoes, Clamato juice, salt, sugar, bay leaves, thyme, allspice, Worcestershire sauce and hot pepper sauce; simmer 15 minutes. Add remaining ingredients and simmer 15 minutes.

*Always simmer soups, never boil them.*

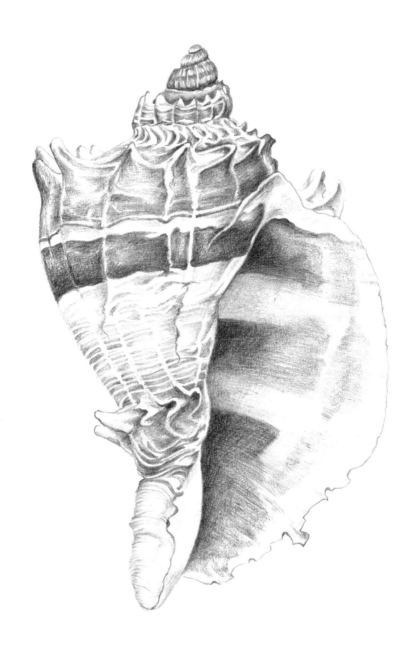

salads

# Salads and Dressings

## SALADS

### FIRST COURSE SALADS
Marina Bay Salad. . . . . . . . . . .  55
*Seviche (Pickled Fish). . . . . . . . .  22

### FRUIT SALADS
Apricot Salad. . . . . . . . . . . . . .  55
Fruit Salad. . . . . . . . . . . . . . .  56
Holiday Salad. . . . . . . . . . . . .  57
Mandarin Surprise. . . . . . . . . . .  59
Noel Salad. . . . . . . . . . . . . . .  59
Orange Salad. . . . . . . . . . . . . .  58
Orange Yogurt Salad. . . . . . . . .  56
Pineapple Cheese Salad. . . . . . .  57
Strawberry Nut Salad. . . . . . . .  58

### GREEN SALADS
Annie Bea's Caesar Salad. . . . . . . 64
Fresh Spinach Salad. . . . . . . . . .  62
Hearts of Palm Salad. . . . . . . . .  61
Mandarin Orange Salad. . . . . . . .  60
Outdoor Cabbage Slaw. . . . . . . .  63
Seven Layer Salad. . . . . . . . . . .  63
Spinach and Melon Salad. . . . . . .  65

### MAIN DISH SALADS
Avocado Surprise. . . . . . . . . . .  67
*Baked Chicken Salad. . . . . . . . . 140
*Conch Salad. . . . . . . . . . . . . . 270
Cranapple Turkey Mold. . . . . . . .  68
Dilled Chicken and Potato
  Salad. . . . . . . . . . . . . . . . . .  69
French Beef Salad. . . . . . . . . . . .  70

Greek Salad. . . . . . . . . . . . . . .  71
Salade Niçoise. . . . . . . . . . . . . .  66
Seafood Salad. . . . . . . . . . . . . .  65
Succulent Shrimp Salad. . . . . . . .  73
Taco Salad. . . . . . . . . . . . . . . .  70
Tropical Chicken Salad. . . . . . . .  72

### VEGETABLE SALADS
German Potato Salad. . . . . . . . . .  75
Mushroom Salad. . . . . . . . . . . .  72
Tomatoes Lutece. . . . . . . . . . . .  74
Virginia's Broccoli Cauliflower
  Salad. . . . . . . . . . . . . . . . . .  74
Zucchini Mushroom Salad. . . . . .  73

### SALAD DRESSINGS
Annie Bea's Caesar Salad
  Dressing. . . . . . . . . . . . . . . .  64
Bleu Cheese Dressing. . . . . . . . .  76
Cooked Potato Salad
  Dressing. . . . . . . . . . . . . . . .  77
*Crème Fraîche. . . . . . . . . . . . .  179
French Vinaigrette Dressing. . . . .  77
Fruit Salad Dressing. . . . . . . . . .  56
Garlic Dressing. . . . . . . . . . . . .  66
Marie's Salad Dressing. . . . . . . . .  75
Onion Dressing. . . . . . . . . . . . .  78
Poppy Seed Dressing. . . . . . . . .  76
*Raw Vegetable Dip. . . . . . . . . . .  18
Spinach Salad Dressing. . . . . . . .  76
Sweet and Sour Dressing. . . . . . .  78
*Found elsewhere in the book.

## KING CROWN CONCH
*The beautiful King Crown Conch with its sculptured shell and attractive short spines inhabits the inner tidal shores of Florida. What a lovely place to relax—on the beaches of the Gulfshore!*

# Marina Bay Salad

Must prepare partially ahead                              6 servings

**Dressing:**
½ cup sugar
1 teaspoon dry mustard
¼ teaspoon curry powder
1 teaspoon salt
3 tablespoons grated onion
⅓ cup vinegar
1 tablespoon lemon juice
2 tablespoons chutney
1 cup vegetable oil

In blender, combine sugar, mustard, curry powder, salt, onion, vinegar, lemon juice and chutney. Mix on high. Slowly add oil. Chill.

**Salad:**
1 pint cherry tomatoes, halved
1 6 to 8-ounce bag frozen
   shrimp, thawed
⅓ cup coconut
1 11-ounce can mandarin
   oranges, drained
romaine or iceberg lettuce

Combine tomatoes, shrimp, coconut and oranges. Pour dressing over mixture and gently toss. Serve immediately over lettuce.

# Apricot Salad
*Good with pork roast or baked ham*

Must prepare ahead                                        8 servings

2 3-ounce packages apricot
   gelatin
1¼ cups hot water
2 17-ounce cans apricots,
   drained
1 cup sour cream
1 20-ounce can crushed
   pineapple, drained

Dissolve gelatin in hot water. Purée apricots in blender. Add gelatin and sour cream; blend. Remove from blender and stir in pineapple. Pour into gelatin mold; chill.

# Fruit Salad

**May prepare partially ahead**                    **10 servings**

**Dressing:**
½ cup sugar
dash of salt
grated rind from 1 orange
¼ cup lemon juice
¼ cup orange juice
¾ cup pineapple juice (from drained pineapple below)
2 tablespoons cornstarch
¼ cup cold water

Mix sugar, salt, rind and juices in a saucepan. Bring to a boil. Mix the cornstarch and cold water; add slowly to sugar-fruit juice mixture. Stir over medium heat until thick. Cool.

**Salad:**
4 bananas, sliced
1 15½-ounce can pineapple chunks or tidbits, drained and juice reserved for dressing
1 cup halved white seedless grapes
2 11-ounce cans mandarin oranges, drained
3 apples, diced

Mix fruit in a large bowl. Pour dressing over fruit and mix.

# Orange Yogurt Salad

**Must prepare ahead**                    **4 servings**

1 cup orange juice
1 3-ounce package orange or apricot gelatin
1 6-ounce carton pineapple yogurt

Heat orange juice just to the boiling point. Pour over gelatin and mix well. Cool slightly and stir in yogurt. Divide among 4 molds and chill until set.

Sliced mangoes may be added.

# Holiday Salad

**Must prepare ahead**                          **10-12 servings**

1 3-ounce package cherry
  gelatin
¾ cup boiling water
1 16-ounce can whole berry
  cranberry sauce
1 8-ounce can crushed
  pineapple, drained
1 cup sour cream
1 3-ounce package raspberry
  gelatin
¾ cup boiling water
1 10-ounce package frozen
  raspberries, partially thawed

Dissolve cherry gelatin in ¾ cup boiling water; add cranberry sauce and crushed pineapple. Pour into an 8 x 12-inch pan. Refrigerate until set. Spread with sour cream and refrigerate 1 hour. Meanwhile, dissolve raspberry gelatin in ¾ cup boiling water. Add raspberries. Refrigerate until thickened; spoon over top of sour cream. Refrigerate until set.

# Pineapple Cheese Salad

**Must prepare ahead**                          **10-12 servings**

½ cup sugar
1 8-ounce can crushed
  pineapple, undrained
juice of 1 lemon
1 ¼-ounce envelope
  unflavored gelatin
1 cup cold water
1 8-ounce package cream
  cheese, softened
1 cup grated cheddar cheese
1 cup chopped pecans

Combine sugar, pineapple and lemon juice in a saucepan. Bring to a boil. Stir gelatin into cold water; add to hot mixture. Cool until it begins to thicken. Beat cream cheese well. Gradually add pineapple-lemon mixture. Add grated cheese and pecans. Pour into a lightly oiled 4-cup mold. Refrigerate until set.

# Strawberry Nut Salad
*Makes you want to forget the main course*

**Must prepare ahead**                                    **12 servings**

2 3-ounce packages
   strawberry gelatin
1 cup boiling water
2 10-ounce packages frozen
   strawberries, thawed
1 20-ounce can crushed
   pineapple, drained
3 medium bananas, mashed
1 cup coarsely chopped nuts
1 pint sour cream

In a large pan, combine gelatin with boiling water, stirring until dissolved. Fold in strawberries with juice, pineapple, bananas and nuts. Turn ½ of mixture into an 8 x 12-inch glass dish. Refrigerate until firm, about 1½ hours. Keep remaining ½ mixture at room temperature. Spread sour cream on top of set gelatin. Gently spoon on remaining strawberry mixture. Refrigerate until firm.

# Orange Salad
*Quick*

**May prepare ahead**                                    **4-6 servings**

1 3-ounce package orange
   gelatin
1 12-ounce container cottage
   cheese
1 8-ounce container frozen
   whipped topping, thawed
1 11-ounce can mandarin
   oranges, drained

Mix dry gelatin with cottage cheese. Fold in whipped topping and oranges. Chill until ready to serve.

*Grease mold with a vegetable spray to ease unmolding of a congealed salad.*

# Noel Salad

**Must prepare ahead**                                 **12 servings**

1 3-ounce package lime
  gelatin
1 3-ounce package lemon
  gelatin
1 cup heavy cream
2 tablespoons sugar
1 8-ounce can crushed
  pineapple, drained
1 3-ounce package cream
  cheese, softened
½ cup chopped nuts
1 3-ounce package strawberry
  or cherry gelatin

Dissolve lime gelatin according to package directions. Pour into an 8 x 12-inch pan; chill until thoroughly set. Dissolve lemon gelatin according to package directions. Add cream, sugar, pineapple, cream cheese and nuts. Pour lemon gelatin mixture over set lime gelatin. Chill until firm. Dissolve strawberry gelatin according to package directions; pour over set lemon gelatin layer. Chill until firm.

# Mandarin Surprise
*A refreshing salad*

**Must prepare ahead**                                 **10 servings**

2 11-ounce cans mandarin
  oranges, drained
2 8-ounce cans crushed
  pineapple, well drained
½ cup miniature marshmallows
1 3½-ounce can shredded
  coconut
1 pint sour cream
1 4-ounce package chopped
  pecans

Mix all ingredients; refrigerate overnight.

# Mandarin Orange Salad
*Wonderful mélange of flavors*

**Must prepare partially ahead**                    **4 servings**

**Dressing:**
1/4 cup vegetable oil
2 tablespoons white vinegar
2 tablespoons sugar
1 tablespoon snipped parsley
1/2 teaspoon salt
dash of pepper
dash of hot pepper sauce

Shake all dressing ingredients in a tightly covered jar. Refrigerate at least 1 hour. Makes 1/2 cup.

**Salad:**
1/4 cup slivered almonds
1 tablespoon + 1 teaspoon sugar
1/2 head Bibb lettuce, torn
1/2 head romaine, torn
1 cup chopped celery
3 green onions, thinly sliced
1 11-ounce can mandarin oranges, drained

Cook and stir almonds and sugar in skillet over low heat until sugar is melted and nuts are coated. Cool on wax paper, break apart and set aside. Place greens, celery and onions in plastic bag. Fasten bag securely and refrigerate. Pour dressing into bag 5 minutes before serving. Add oranges. Fasten bag securely and shake until all is well coated. Add almonds and shake again.

# Hearts of Palm Salad

Must prepare partially ahead                    4 servings

**Dressing:**
1 egg
1 teaspoon salt
1 tablespoon sugar
¼ teaspoon paprika
2 tablespoons spicy brown
   mustard
1 teaspoon Worcestershire
   sauce
1 garlic clove, minced
1 cup wine vinegar
2 cups vegetable oil

Combine all dressing ingredients except oil and mix well. Slowly add oil, beating constantly. Chill. Makes 4 cups.

**Salad:**
Bibb lettuce leaves
3 14-ounce cans hearts of
   palm, drained
½ pound mushrooms, sliced
1 cup chopped walnuts

Arrange lettuce leaves on 4 salad plates. Arrange hearts of palm in spoke formation on lettuce. Sprinkle each salad with mushrooms and nuts. Just before serving, spoon dressing over salads.

*An egg slicer makes a great uniform mushroom slicer.*

# Fresh Spinach Salad
*This dressing is pure magic on spinach*

**May prepare ahead**                    **8-10 servings**

**Salad:**
1½ pounds fresh spinach,
    washed, drained and stems
    removed
½ pound bacon, cooked
    and crumbled
2 hard-boiled eggs, sliced
4 ounces mushrooms, sliced
croutons, optional

Place spinach in paper towel-lined salad bowl. Add bacon, eggs and mushrooms. Cover with plastic wrap and place in refrigerator to crisp.

**Dressing:**
⅔ cup vegetable oil
¼ cup wine vinegar
2 tablespoons red wine
2 teaspoons soy sauce
½ teaspoon garlic salt
½ teaspoon pepper
1 teaspoon sugar
1 teaspoon dry mustard
½ teaspoon salt

Combine all dressing ingredients in a bottle and shake. Place in refrigerator until ready to serve. Dressing may be made ahead and stored in the refrigerator for 2 to 3 weeks.

When ready to serve, remove paper towels from salad. Toss salad with croutons and ½ to ¾ of dressing.

# Outdoor Cabbage Slaw

*No mayonnaise, great for picnics*

**Must prepare ahead**                                   **6-8 servings**

1 large head cabbage, finely
    shredded
2 large white Bermuda onions,
    thinly sliced
1 cup + 2 teaspoons sugar,
    divided
1 teaspoon dry mustard
1 teaspoon celery seed
1 tablespoon salt
1 cup vinegar
¾ cup vegetable oil

Layer cabbage 2 inches thick in a large bowl; then layer onions ¼-inch thick. Repeat layers of cabbage and onions. Sprinkle 1 cup sugar over top of layers.

Heat 2 teaspoons sugar, mustard, celery seed, salt, vinegar and oil in a medium saucepan. Bring to a rolling boil and pour immediately over cabbage mix. Do not stir. Cover and refrigerate 4 hours. Stir mixture before serving.

May be kept in refrigerator 2 to 6 days.

# Seven Layer Salad

*Easy, colorful—a great luncheon salad*

**Must prepare ahead**                                   **4 servings**

½ head lettuce, shredded
1 small onion, thinly sliced
1 cup coarsely chopped green
    pepper
2 stalks celery, chopped
1 cup small green peas, well
    drained
1 to 1½ cups mayonnaise
2 tablespoons sugar
1½ cups grated Parmesan
    cheese
5 strips bacon, cooked and
    crumbled
julienne strips of ham, turkey
    and chicken (about 4
    ounces of each)

Place ½ of lettuce in bottom of glass bowl. In layers, add onion, pepper, celery, peas and remaining lettuce. Mix mayonnaise, sugar and cheese and spread on top. Sprinkle with crumbled bacon. Top with strips of ham, turkey and chicken. Refrigerate at least 4 hours before serving.

May be made the night before.

# Annie Bea's Caesar Salad

**May prepare partially ahead**            **6 servings**

**Dressing:**
4 to 6 anchovy filets, mashed, optional
6 tablespoons olive oil
3 tablespoons tarragon vinegar
1 egg, beaten
½ cup grated Parmesan cheese
1 teaspoon garlic salt

In a mixing bowl, whisk together anchovies, oil, vinegar and egg. Add cheese and garlic salt and whisk again. Set aside.

**Salad:**
1 garlic clove
2 cups bread cubes
2 tablespoons butter, melted
garlic salt to taste
6 cups torn romaine lettuce
2 thick slices bacon, fried and crumbled

Rub salad bowl with garlic clove and discard clove. Mix bread cubes lightly in melted butter; sprinkle with garlic salt. Place in microwave on high for 3½ to 4 minutes, stirring once at 2 minutes. Place lettuce, bacon and croutons in prepared salad bowl. Pour in salad dressing, tossing lightly.

*Always tear lettuce for tossed salads as cutting or slicing gives the lettuce a bitter taste.*

# Spinach and Melon Salad
*Colorful*

**May prepare partially ahead**                    **6 servings**

**Dressing:**
¼ cup vegetable oil
1 tablespoon white wine
  vinegar
¼ teaspoon salt
¼ teaspoon Dijon mustard

Blend dressing ingredients in food processor.

**Salad:**
4 cups washed, torn spinach
  leaves
2 cups cantaloupe balls*
1 cup thinly sliced zucchini
2 tablespoons finely chopped
  scallions

Combine salad ingredients in a large bowl. Pour dressing over salad and toss.

*May substitute orange
  sections.

# Seafood Salad

**May prepare partially ahead**                    **2 servings**

1 cup fresh crabmeat
1 cup cooked, chopped shrimp
1 small onion, chopped
2 or 3 stalks celery, chopped
½ cup mayonnaise
juice of ½ lemon or lime
1 teaspoon prepared mustard
salt to taste
pepper to taste
lettuce leaves
1 tomato, sliced, for garnish

In a large bowl, mix crabmeat, shrimp, onion and celery. Combine mayonnaise, lemon juice and mustard. Mix thoroughly with crabmeat-shrimp mixture. Season with salt and pepper. Serve on lettuce leaves and garnish with tomato slices.

# Salade Niçoise
*A Mediterranean favorite*

**Must prepare partially ahead**                    **6 servings**

**Garlic Dressing:**
1 tablespoon dry mustard
1 teaspoon sugar
1 tablespoon salt
freshly ground pepper
2 garlic cloves, crushed
½ cup tarragon vinegar
¼ cup fresh lemon juice
2 cups olive oil

Combine mustard, sugar, salt and a generous amount of pepper. Mix in remaining dressing ingredients. Stir or shake vigorously before using. Makes 3 cups.

**Salade Niçoise:**
2 pounds red potatoes, boiled and sliced
2 cups cooked cut green beans
1 cup cooked artichoke hearts
1 large onion, thinly sliced
3 cups Garlic Dressing
salad greens
3 7-ounce cans tuna, drained and broken into pieces
1 pint cherry tomatoes
1 cup pitted black olives
6 hard-boiled eggs, quartered
1 large green pepper, cut into strips
½ small red pepper, cut into strips
2 2-ounce cans rolled anchovies with capers
¼ cup chopped parsley

Combine potatoes, beans, artichoke hearts and onions with dressing. Refrigerate 2 hours, stirring occasionally.

To serve, line a salad bowl with greens. Drain vegetables, reserving dressing. Spoon vegetables into lined bowl. Place tuna in center of bowl and arrange tomatoes, olives, eggs, peppers and anchovies around it. Sprinkle with parsley. Pass dressing.

# Avocado Surprise
*Super lunch for two*

**May prepare partially ahead**                    **2 servings**

**Filling:**
2 cups cooked, cubed chicken
½ cup orange sections
½ cup halved green grapes
¼ cup chopped walnuts
¼ cup chopped onion

Combine filling ingredients and chill 1 hour.

Filling may be made the day before serving.

**Dressing:**
5 tablespoons olive oil
2 tablespoons fresh lemon juice
2 tablespoons chopped fresh parsley
1 tablespoon chopped fresh basil or 1 teaspoon dried basil
seasoned salt to taste
pepper to taste

Mix dressing ingredients in a covered jar. Chill.

1 large ripe avocado
lemon juice
crisp lettuce leaves

Cut avocado in half lengthwise; remove pit and brush with lemon juice to prevent discoloring. Shake dressing and mix with filling. Heap mixture onto avocado halves. Arrange on a bed of crisp lettuce leaves. Serve immediately.

*The usual proportion in salad dressing is 1 part acid, either lemon juice or vinegar, to 2 or 3 parts oil.*

# Cranapple Turkey Mold
*Refreshing and attractive luncheon dish*

**Must prepare ahead**　　　　　　　　　　　**6 servings**

**Cranapple Mold:**
5 cups cranapple juice,
　　divided
4 ¼-ounce envelopes
　　unflavored gelatin
¼ cup sugar
1½ cups rosé wine

**Salad:**
1¼ cups mayonnaise
4 cups diced, cooked turkey
1 red unpeeled apple, diced
1 cup halved seedless grapes
½ cup diced celery
½ cup chopped walnuts
salt to taste
pepper to taste

Heat 2 cups cranapple juice to boiling. Meanwhile, in a large bowl combine gelatin and sugar. Add hot juice and stir about 3 minutes until gelatin is completely dissolved. Add wine and remaining juice. Pour into a 6½-cup ring mold. Refrigerate until set, about 3 hours.

In large bowl, combine salad ingredients. Cover and refrigerate until serving time.

To serve, dip base of gelatin mold into warm water for 30 seconds to loosen. Invert onto serving platter. Fill center with turkey salad. Pass remaining salad in a separate bowl.

# Dilled Chicken and Potato Salad

*Perfect for summer entertaining*

**May prepare partially ahead**                    **6 servings**

**Dressing:**
**⅓ cup red wine vinegar**
**1 teaspoon sugar**
**2 to 3 tablespoons Dijon**
   **mustard**
**salt to taste**
**pepper to taste**
**1 cup olive oil**

Combine vinegar, sugar, mustard, salt and pepper in food processor. With motor running add oil in a steady stream through the feed tube. Refrigerate.

**Salad:**
**2 whole skinless, boneless**
   **chicken breasts, cooked**
**1½ pounds small new potatoes,**
   **cooked in chicken broth**
**1 large red pepper, chopped**
**4 to 5 scallions, sliced**
**¼ cup chopped fresh dill**
**¼ cup capers**

Cut chicken into large bite-size pieces. Mix with potatoes, pepper, scallions, dill and capers. Refrigerate. Just before serving, add dressing to taste.

**Optional Garnishes:**
**tomatoes**
**black olives**
**melon balls or other**
   **fresh fruit**

Garnish as desired.

*Wrap rinsed salad greens in paper towels and refrigerate for an hour or more. Excess moisture will be absorbed.*

# Taco Salad
## *Olé*

**May prepare partially ahead**                    **4 servings**

1 pound ground beef
1 1¼-ounce envelope taco
  seasoning mix
¾ cup water
1 head iceberg lettuce, shredded
2 ripe tomatoes, chopped
1 cup grated cheddar cheese
⅓ cup ripe olives, halved
¾ cup sour cream
1 or 2 green chilies, chopped
tortilla chips

Brown beef in skillet; drain. Stir in taco seasoning mix and water; simmer until dry.

Layer lettuce, tomatoes, beef mixture, cheese and olives in salad bowl. Dollop sour cream mixed with green chilies in center and arrange chips around edge. Mix before serving.

# French Beef Salad
## *This hearty salad makes an excellent luncheon dish*

**Must prepare ahead**                    **8-10 servings**

2 pounds small boiling
  potatoes, sliced ¼-inch thick
2 pounds sirloin
1 pound green beans, cleaned
  and snapped
1 beef bouillon cube
¼ cup boiling water
1 teaspoon minced garlic
4 tablespoons minced shallots
2 tablespoons Dijon mustard
2 teaspoons salt
1 teaspoon black pepper
⅓ cup red wine vinegar
1 cup olive oil
1 large red onion, thinly sliced
1 pint cherry tomatoes

Boil potatoes just until tender; drain and place in a large bowl. Meanwhile, broil sirloin until just rare. Cook green beans until just tender, about 7 minutes; plunge into ice water. Drain. Dissolve bouillon cube in boiling water. Combine garlic, shallots, beef bouillon, mustard, salt, pepper, vinegar and olive oil to make a vinaigrette. Pour vinaigrette over potatoes and toss. Slice sirloin into ½-inch cubes. Add sirloin, green beans, onions and tomatoes to bowl. Toss gently, but thoroughly. Allow to marinate in refrigerator 1 to 3 days. Remove from refrigerator and bring to room temperature before serving.

# Greek Salad

**May prepare ahead**                                    **12 servings**

**Potato Salad:**
**10 boiling potatoes**
**4 green onions, finely diced**
**½ cup thinly sliced**
**green pepper**
**salt to taste**
**⅔ cup mayonnaise**

Boil potatoes in jackets about 30 minutes until tender. Drain, cool and peel. Slice into bowl. Fold in onions and pepper. Sprinkle with salt. Add mayonnaise and blend well.

**Platter:**
**1 large head lettuce**
**4 cups potato salad**
**5 tomatoes, cut in wedges**
**3 peeled cucumbers, cut in**
**wedges**
**2 avocados, sliced**
**1 1-pound jar Feta cheese**
**2 green peppers, sliced in rings**
**1 16-ounce can cooked beet**
**slices**
**1 large onion, thinly sliced**
**1 5-ounce jar Greek olives**
**1 cup white vinegar**
**½ cup vegetable oil**
**½ cup olive oil**
**oregano**

Line a large platter with lettuce leaves; mound potato salad in center. Shred remaining lettuce over potato salad. Place tomatoes around outer edge of potato salad, placing a few on the top. Place cucumbers between tomato wedges. Decorate outside edge of platter with avocado slices. Crumble sliced Feta cheese over vegetables. Arrange green pepper slices, beet slices and onion slices on platter. Place olives on top. Sprinkle entire salad with vinegar. Blend oils and sprinkle on salad. Sprinkle with oregano.

# Tropical Chicken Salad

**May prepare partially ahead**                                    **8 servings**

**Curry Dressing:**
1¼ cups mayonnaise
2 teaspoons curry powder
½ teaspoon salt
juice of ½ lemon

Mix all dressing ingredients.

**Chicken Salad:**
8 skinless, boneless chicken*
  breast halves, cooked and
  cut into chunks
1 8-ounce can water chestnuts,
  drained and sliced
1 20-ounce can pineapple
  chunks, drained, or fresh
  pineapple
1 cup halved seedless grapes,
  optional
¾ cup slivered almonds,
  toasted
3 stalks celery, chopped

Mix all chicken salad ingredients.
Pour dressing over salad; mix well.
Chill until served.

Serve in pineapple boats or on lettuce leaves with croissant.

*May substitute 4 6½-ounce
  cans white tuna.

# Mushroom Salad

**May prepare partially ahead**                                    **4 servings**

9 tablespoons olive oil
3 tablespoons wine vinegar
2 heaping tablespoons Dijon
  mustard
1½ pounds mushrooms,
  thinly sliced
1 tablespoon finely chopped
  parsley
Bibb lettuce

Combine olive oil, vinegar and mustard. Mix well with a wire whisk until smooth and creamy. Just before serving, pour dressing over mushrooms; add parsley and toss. Serve on a bed of Bibb lettuce.

# Succulent Shrimp Salad
*Simple and delightful*

May prepare ahead                                    6 servings

2 cups large shrimp, peeled,
  deveined and cooked
1 tablespoon lemon juice
1 cup finely chopped celery
1 tablespoon finely chopped
  onion
1 cup mayonnaise
salt to taste
pepper to taste
lettuce leaves, optional
6 avocado halves, optional
paprika for garnish

Cut shrimp into bite-size pieces. Add lemon juice, celery, onion, mayonnaise, salt and pepper; mix well. Serve on lettuce leaves or stuff in avocado halves. Sprinkle with paprika.

# Zucchini Mushroom Salad
*A wonderful combination*

May prepare partially ahead                          6-8 servings

Dressing:
1 tablespoon Dijon mustard
1 teaspoon salt
½ teaspoon pepper
¼ cup wine vinegar
¾ cup olive oil

Whisk all dressing ingredients together. May be kept in refrigerator for 2 weeks.

Salad:
½ pound mushrooms,
  quartered or sliced
1 pound zucchini, shredded
1 pint cherry tomatoes, halved
  or quartered
2 cups shredded endive,
  optional

Combine all ingredients, mixing well. Just before serving, add the dressing to the salad. Serve immediately.

# Virginia's Broccoli Cauliflower Salad

*Nice change from tossed salads*

May prepare ahead                                                        8 servings

**Salad:**
1 bunch broccoli, cut into florets
1 medium cauliflower, cut into florets
1 firm tomato, diced
1 small onion, chopped

Mix salad ingredients.

**Dressing:**
1 cup mayonnaise
2 teaspoons prepared mustard
2 teaspoons cider vinegar
2 tablespoons sugar
dash of Worcestershire sauce

Combine dressing ingredients; add to salad and toss lightly. Chill.

May be prepared 1 day in advance, except for tomato. Dice and add tomato just before serving.

# Tomatoes Lutece

Must prepare ahead                                                      6-8 servings

8 ripe tomatoes
¼ cup chopped parsley
1 garlic clove, minced
1 teaspoon salt
1 teaspoon sugar
¼ cup olive oil
2 tablespoons red wine vinegar
2 teaspoons prepared yellow mustard

Dip whole tomatoes briefly in boiling water. Remove and slip off skins. Slice and arrange in a glass serving bowl. Sprinkle with parsley. Mix remaining ingredients with a wire whisk and pour over tomatoes. Refrigerate 30 minutes before serving.

# German Potato Salad
*Terrific with hamburgers and hotdogs*

**Must prepare ahead**　　　　　　　　**8 servings**

3 pounds new potatoes
6 to 8 slices bacon, cut into
　pieces
salt to taste
pepper to taste
2 tablespoons sugar
3 tablespoons cider vinegar
2 onions, sliced

Scrub potatoes and cook in boiling water until tender, about 15 to 20 minutes; drain and peel while warm. Meanwhile, fry bacon pieces until crisp. Save drippings. Slice potatoes thinly. Mix bacon, salt, pepper, sugar, vinegar, onions and bacon drippings; pour over potatoes. Mix well. Keep covered in a warm place several hours to develop flavor.

# Marie's Salad Dressing
*A winner on any tossed salad*

**May prepare ahead**　　　　　　　　**⅔ cup**

6 tablespoons olive oil or
　vegetable oil
2 tablespoons white wine
　vinegar
1 garlic clove, minced
¾ teaspoon salt
freshly ground black pepper
　to taste
¼ teaspoon dried thyme
　(not powdered)
2 tablespoons grated Parmesan
　cheese

Place all ingredients in food processor or blender and blend well.

Delicious on fresh spinach, Bibb or romaine lettuce salads.

# Bleu Cheese Dressing

**Must prepare ahead**                              **3½ cups**

2 cups mayonnaise
1 cup buttermilk
½ teaspoon garlic salt
½ teaspoon garlic powder
1 teaspoon Worcestershire
   sauce
6 ounces bleu or Roquefort
   cheese, crumbled

Blend mayonnaise, buttermilk, garlic salt, garlic powder and Worcestershire sauce until smooth. Fold in bleu cheese. Refrigerate at least 2 hours, but preferably overnight, before serving.

# Poppy Seed Salad Dressing

**May prepare ahead**                              **3 cups**

⅔ cup white vinegar
1 medium onion, quartered
2 teaspoons salt
2 teaspoons dry mustard
1¼ cups sugar or 1 cup
   honey
1 cup vegetable oil
2½ tablespoons poppy seeds

Put vinegar, onion, salt, mustard and sugar in blender or food processor and blend 1 minute. With blender running, add oil slowly. Blend at low speed 30 seconds. Pour into a jar and add poppy seeds. Keep well-covered in refrigerator. Shake well before serving.

# Spinach Salad Dressing

**May prepare ahead**                              **½ cup**

3 heaping tablespoons
   mayonnaise
1 tablespoon honey
1 teaspoon spicy brown
   mustard
½ teaspoon Salad Supreme
½ teaspoon minced onion
1 tablespoon wine vinegar

Mix all ingredients and refrigerate until ready to use.

# Cooked Potato Salad Dressing

**May prepare ahead**                                           2-2½ cups

6 egg yolks or 3 eggs
1 cup sugar
½ teaspoon dry mustard
¼ teaspoon paprika
½ cup water
½ cup cider vinegar
salt to taste
¼ cup butter

Mix eggs, sugar, mustard, paprika, water, vinegar and salt in the top of a double boiler. Cook, stirring occasionally, over simmering water until thickened, about 30 minutes. Add butter, cool and refrigerate or make potato salad, using your favorite recipe.

This is also very good on cole slaw or as a sandwich spread instead of mayonnaise.

# French Vinaigrette Dressing
*Lovely to have on hand*

**Must prepare ahead**                                          2½ cups

1 cup vegetable oil
½ cup olive oil
¼ cup dry white wine
½ cup red wine vinegar
2 teaspoons salt
½ teaspoon pepper
½ teaspoon dry mustard
½ teaspoon dried basil
½ cup chopped parsley
1 garlic clove, minced

Combine all ingredients in food processor or blender and blend well. Pour into jar with tight-fitting lid. Refrigerate covered at least 2 hours, preferably 1 day. Shake well before serving.

*Use salad dressings sparingly; a thin coating is all that is needed.*

# Onion Dressing

**May prepare ahead**                                    1¾ cups

1 medium onion, cut into
   chunks
1 cup vegetable oil
¼ cup cider vinegar
¼ cup sugar
1 teaspoon salt
1 teaspoon dry mustard
1 teaspoon celery seed

Place all ingredients in blender or food processor. Blend on high 10 to 15 seconds. Refrigerate until ready to use.

# Sweet and Sour Dressing

**May prepare ahead**                                    1½ cups

1 cup vegetable oil
½ cup cider vinegar
1 teaspoon poppy seed or
   celery seed
½ cup sugar
1 teaspoon salt
1 teaspoon dry mustard
1 teaspoon grated onion

Mix all ingredients in blender or food processor. Use immediately or store in refrigerator and mix again before serving.

# cheese and eggs

# Cheese and Eggs

## SHELLING ON THE ISLANDS

*Sanibel and Captiva beaches offer some of the world's finest shelling—yielding more than 400 species. After high tide, waves of shellers equipped with pails and plastic bags stalk the shoreline, each courting lumbar problems with the familiar "Sanibel-Captiva stoop."*

# Cheese Strata
*A Christmas morning favorite*

**Must prepare ahead**                    **6-8 servings**

8 slices buttered white bread, crusts removed
¼ cup butter or margarine, softened
4 eggs, slightly beaten
2½ cups milk
1 teaspoon salt
¼ teaspoon dry mustard
3 cups shredded cheddar cheese

Cut bread slices into quarters. Alternate layers of bread and cheese in greased 7 x 11-inch baking dish, ending with cheese. Mix eggs, milk, salt and mustard. Pour over cheese and bread layers. Cover. Chill 6 hours or overnight.

Bake uncovered in a preheated 325 degree oven 45 minutes or until firm. Let stand a few minutes and cut into squares.

May be frozen after baking. Defrost before reheating.

# Chili Cheese Eggs
*Great brunch dish*

**May prepare ahead**                    **8 servings**

3 4-ounce cans peeled green chilies, seeded and diced
8 ounces Monterey Jack cheese, grated
16 ounces cheddar cheese, grated
4 eggs
1 13-ounce can evaporated milk
2 tablespoons flour
dash of salt
1 6-ounce can tomato paste, optional

Preheat oven to 350 degrees. Grease a 9 x 13-inch baking dish and line with diced chilies. Sprinkle grated cheeses evenly over chilies. Beat eggs, milk, flour and salt with wire whisk. Pour egg mixture over cheeses and chilies. Bake uncovered for 30 minutes. Top with tomato paste if desired. Cool 15 minutes before cutting. Serve within 30 minutes.

# Never-Fail Cheese Shrimp Soufflé
*Marvelous breakfast for houseguests*

**Must prepare partially ahead**                    **8-10 servings**

10 slices buttered white bread, crusts removed

12 ounces sharp cheddar cheese, shredded

12 ounces mozzarella cheese, shredded

1 pound shrimp*, peeled, deveined and cooked

8 eggs, slightly beaten

3½ cups half and half cream

¼ teaspoon paprika

1 teaspoon minced onion

½ teaspoon curry powder

⅛ teaspoon cayenne pepper

1 teaspoon Worcestershire sauce

1 teaspoon dry mustard

*May substitute ham.

WINE: Red Burgundy
      or Bordeaux

Butter sides and bottom of a 9 x 13-inch baking dish. Cut bread into cubes. Place ½ the buttered cubes in baking dish and sprinkle with ½ of the cheeses. Spread shrimp on top of cheeses. Add remaining bread; top with remaining cheeses. Combine remaining ingredients; pour over bread and cheese layers. Cover and refrigerate overnight.

Bake uncovered in a preheated 325 degree oven 1 hour or until knife inserted in center comes out clean and top is lightly browned.

*Stale eggs float; fresh eggs sink. Cooked eggs spin evenly; raw eggs wobble.*

# Shrimp, Tomato and Cheese Pie

May prepare ahead                                    **2 pies**

¾ cup mayonnaise
1 egg
2 egg yolks
4 ounces Monterey Jack
   cheese, grated
12 ounces Swiss cheese,
   grated
1½ pounds shrimp, peeled,
   deveined and cooked
4 medium tomatoes, cut into
   small chunks
1 small onion, chopped
2 small green peppers, chopped
6 tablespoons butter
salt to taste
pepper to taste
3 garlic cloves, minced
1 tablespoon basil leaves
½ cup chopped fresh parsley
2 tablespoons chopped chives
   or scallions
2 9-inch unbaked pie shells

Topping:
4 tablespoons butter, melted
¼ cup bread crumbs
¼ teaspoon paprika

WINE: Pouilly-Fumé or
      Muscadet

Beat mayonnaise, egg, egg yolks and cheeses. Cut shrimp into large chunks. Add shrimp and tomatoes to cheese mixture.

Sauté onion and peppers in butter. Add salt, pepper, garlic, basil, parsley and chives. Add to cheese-shrimp mixture. Divide between 2 unbaked pie shells.

Blend topping ingredients; sprinkle on top of pies.

Bake in a preheated 450 degree oven 10 minutes; reduce heat to 350 degrees and continue baking 40 to 45 minutes.

May be frozen after baking. Thaw. Reheat in a 350 degree oven.

# Crab Quiche
*An elegant and easy luncheon dish*

May prepare ahead                                    6-8 servings

½ cup mayonnaise
2 tablespoons flour
2 eggs, beaten
½ cup milk
1 6-ounce can crabmeat,
   drained and flaked
½ pound Swiss cheese, cut
   in ¼-inch cubes or shredded
⅓ cup chopped scallions
1 9-inch unbaked pie shell

WINE: German Qualitätswein

Preheat oven to 350 degrees. Combine mayonnaise, flour, eggs and milk; beat. Stir in crabmeat, cheese and scallions. Pour into unbaked pie shell. Bake 30 to 40 minutes or until golden brown on top.

May be frozen after baking.

# Chili Relleno Casserole
*Zippy*

May prepare partially ahead                          6 servings

2 8-ounce cans whole green
   chilies, rinsed, seeded
   and chopped
8 ounces Monterey Jack cheese,
   grated
8 ounces cheddar cheese,
   grated
1 10-ounce can tomatoes with
   green chilies
5 eggs
1 cup flour
3½ cups milk
½ teaspoon salt

Preheat oven to 350 degrees. Butter a 3-quart casserole dish. Arrange ½ of the chilies on bottom; sprinkle with ½ of the grated cheeses. Repeat with remaining chilies and cheeses. Pour can of tomatoes with chilies on top. Beat eggs, flour, milk and salt. Pour over layers in casserole. Bake uncovered for 1 hour. Let casserole rest about 15 minutes before cutting into squares.

# Salmon Quiche
*If you like salmon, you'll love this*

**May prepare ahead**                    **6 servings**

**Crust:**
1 cup whole wheat flour
⅔ cup shredded sharp cheddar cheese
¼ cup chopped almonds
½ teaspoon salt
¼ teaspoon paprika
6 tablespoons vegetable oil

**Filling:**
1 15½-ounce can red salmon
3 eggs, beaten
1 cup sour cream
¼ cup mayonnaise
½ cup shredded sharp cheddar cheese
1 tablespoon grated onion
¼ teaspoon dried dill weed
3 drops hot pepper sauce

**WINE: White Bordeaux or White Zinfandel**

Preheat oven to 400 degrees. Combine flour, cheese, almonds, salt and paprika in a bowl. Stir in oil. Set aside ½ cup of the crust mixture. Press remaining mixture in the bottom and up the sides of a 10-inch pie plate. Bake 10 minutes. Remove from oven.

Reduce oven temperature to 325 degrees. Drain salmon, reserving liquid. Add water to reserved liquid, if necessary, to make ½ cup of liquid. Flake salmon, removing bones and skin; set aside.

Blend eggs, sour cream, mayonnaise and reserved salmon liquid. Stir in salmon, cheese, onion, dill weed and hot pepper sauce. Spoon filling into crust. Sprinkle with reserved crust mixture if desired. Bake 45 minutes or until firm in center.

May be frozen after baking.

*When replacing dried herbs with fresh herbs, use twice the amount.*

# Ham and Swiss Quiche
### *Superb Sunday supper*

**May prepare ahead**                                    **6 servings**

½ cup mayonnaise
½ cup milk
2 eggs, beaten
1 tablespoon cornstarch
6 ounces ham, ¼-inch thick,
   diced
8 ounces Swiss cheese,
   shredded
⅓ cup sliced scallions
½ teaspoon white pepper
1 10-inch unbaked pie shell

WINE: Riesling Kabinett

Preheat oven to 400 degrees. Blend mayonnaise, milk, eggs and corn-starch until smooth. Add ham, cheese, scallions and pepper. Mix to distribute ingredients evenly. Pour mixture into unbaked pie shell. Bake 10 to 15 minutes until filling has begun to set. Reduce heat to 350 degrees and bake another 25 min-utes or until knife inserted in center comes out clean. Allow quiche to set for a few minutes before cutting. Serve warm.

May also be served as an hors d'oeuvre.

# German Pancake

**May prepare ahead**                                    **4 servings**

2 eggs
½ cup flour
½ cup milk
¼ cup butter
juice of 1 lemon
orange marmalade*
confectioners' sugar
nutmeg, optional

*May use any flavor
  marmalade, frozen or fresh
  fruit, or syrup.

Preheat oven to 400 degrees. Blend eggs, flour and milk with wire whisk. Mixture will be lumpy. Melt butter in an 8 x 8-inch glass pan and pour in egg mixture. Bake 15 minutes. The egg mixture will puff up. Re-move from oven. Sprinkle lemon juice over pancake. Pancake will shrink. Spread with orange marma-lade and sprinkle with confection-ers' sugar. Sprinkle with nutmeg, if desired. Cut and serve.

You may reheat in the microwave within an hour or so.

# Crêpes

**Must prepare partially ahead**                    **20 crêpes**

2 eggs
2 tablespoons vegetable oil
1 cup milk
1 cup flour

Place all ingredients in blender. Blend on high speed 2 to 3 minutes. Let batter rest in refrigerator several hours or overnight.

When ready to use, pour into a glass pie plate. Dip heated crêpe griddle into batter briefly. Cook crêpes on 1 side only. Crêpes may be frozen.

Fill with ratatouille, chicken and spinach filling or your favorite filling.

# Crêpes Marquis

**May prepare partially ahead**                    **4 servings**

8 slices bacon
2 tablespoons bacon drippings
½ cup chopped onion
½ cup chopped green pepper
1 cup sliced mushrooms
2 cups grated cheddar cheese
1 8-ounce can tomato sauce
12 crêpes*
grated cheddar cheese for
    topping

*See preceding recipe.

Cook bacon, reserving 2 tablespoons of drippings. Let drain; crumble and set aside. Sauté onion and green peppers in reserved drippings. Add crumbled bacon, mushrooms and cheese. Mix.

Fill each crêpe with ¼ cup cheese mixture. Put crêpes into a lightly greased 9 x 13-inch baking dish and top with tomato sauce. Bake immediately or refrigerate until needed.

Bake in a preheated 350 degree oven for 15 minutes. Remove and sprinkle with cheese; bake until cheese melts.

# Grandma Pearl's Egg Noodles

May prepare partially ahead                              6 servings

3 egg yolks
½ teaspoon salt
1½ tablespoons evaporated
  milk
1 cup flour
1½ to 2 quarts chicken broth

Mix egg yolks, salt and milk. Set aside. Pour flour into a shallow bowl and hollow out center. Pour egg mixture into the center. Stir slowly and gently with a fork, adding flour from the edges until a non-stick dough forms. (You won't use all of the flour.)

Roll out the dough on a floured surface until paper thin. Sprinkle with remaining flour. Slice in half, then slice crosswise into 1-inch strips. Stack strips and slice crosswise through all layers every ¼ inch. Finished noodles will be ¼ x 1 inch.

Bring chicken broth to a boil; drop noodles into broth making sure the slices are separated. Boil for approximately 15 to 20 minutes.

You may freeze the dough for up to 1 month. Thaw and then prepare for cooking.

*The best egg white and yolk separator is your hand. Crack egg into cleanly washed hand; let egg white run through fingers into bowl. Extra benefit—great for your hands.*

# French Toast Fondue

**Must prepare partially ahead**                    **4-6 servings**

**Orange Sour Cream Dip:**
**1 6-ounce can frozen orange**
  **juice, thawed**
**1¼ cups cold milk**
**1 3-ounce box instant vanilla**
  **pudding**
**¼ cup sour cream**

Combine orange juice and milk in blender. Add pudding and blend on low speed 2 minutes. Stir in sour cream. Chill 2 hours.

**Maple butter:**
**1½ cups sifted confectioners'**
  **sugar**
**½ cup butter**
**½ cup maple-flavored syrup**
**1 egg yolk**
**1 egg white, stiffly beaten**

Thoroughly cream confectioners' sugar, butter, syrup and egg yolk. Fold in beaten egg white. Makes 2 cups.

**French Toast:**
**1 loaf French bread**
**2 eggs, well beaten**
**½ cup milk**
**1¼ teaspoons salt, divided**
**vegetable oil**

Cut bread into about 50 bite-sized cubes, leaving crust on each cube. Combine eggs, milk and ¼ teaspoon salt. Set aside.

**fresh assorted fruit for dipping**

Fill fondue pot ½ full with oil. Heat on range to 375 degrees. Add 1 teaspoon salt to oil. Place fondue pot over lighted sterno. Spear a bread cube, dip in egg mixture, letting excess drip off. Cook in hot oil until golden brown, about 1 to 2 minutes. Dip in maple butter.

Serve with fresh fruit and Orange Sour Cream Dip.

# Apple Pancakes with Apple Syrup

May prepare ahead                                    18 pancakes

**Apple Syrup:**
¾ cup sugar
3 tablespoons cornstarch
¼ teaspoon cinnamon
¼ teaspoon nutmeg
1½ cups apple juice
2 tablespoons lemon juice
2 tablespoons butter

In saucepan, mix sugar, cornstarch and spices. Stir in juices. Cook, stirring constantly, until mixture thickens and boils. Boil and stir 1 minute. Remove from heat and stir in butter. Keep warm until pancakes are prepared.

**Pancakes:**
2 cups Bisquick
½ teaspoon cinnamon
1 egg
1⅓ cups milk
1 cup applesauce

Beat Bisquick, cinnamon, egg and milk until smooth. Stir in applesauce. Grease griddle if necessary. Pour ¼ cup batter onto hot griddle. Cook until bubbles appear. Turn; cook until golden.

sour cream

Serve pancakes with a dollop of sour cream and with apple syrup on the side.

# Sausage and Egg Casserole
*Terrific company breakfast*

May prepare partially ahead                          6-8 servings

1 pound hot bulk sausage,
   crumbled
8 to 10 slices bread, cubed
1 cup grated sharp cheddar
   cheese
6 eggs
1 teaspoon salt
1 teaspoon dry mustard
2 cups milk

Brown sausage and drain. In a greased 9 x 13-inch pan, layer ½ bread cubes, ½ sausage and ½ cheese. Repeat. Beat eggs, salt, mustard and milk. Pour over bread, sausage and cheese layers. Bake in a preheated 350 degree oven 45 minutes.

May be assembled the day before and refrigerated until ready to bake.

vegetables

# Vegetables

## ROYAL PALM

*These stately palms planted throughout the city but most notably along McGregor Boulevard have given Fort Myers the title "City of Palms." The tall, arrow-straight, silver trunks topped by glossy green fronds mark these trees as the true "royalty" of the palm family. Thomas A. Edison is credited with planting the first of the royal palms lining McGregor Boulevard.*

# Asparagus with Maltaise Sauce

*A tasty orange Hollandaise sauce makes this dish unique*

**May prepare ahead**                           **4-5 servings**

**1 pound fresh asparagus***

**Maltaise Sauce:**
**2 egg yolks**
**3 tablespoons butter or**
   **margarine, softened**
   **and divided**
**¼ cup orange marmalade**
**¼ cup sour cream**
**dash of salt**
**dash of white pepper**

*****May substitute broccoli.**

Cook asparagus as desired. Drain well.

Meanwhile, in small saucepan, combine egg yolks and 1 tablespoon butter. Cook and stir with wire whisk over low heat until butter melts. Add another tablespoon of butter and continue stirring. As mixture thickens and butter melts, add remaining butter, stirring constantly with whisk. When butter is melted, remove from heat. Stir in orange marmalade. Return to heat. Cook and stir until heated through, about 2 to 3 minutes. Remove saucepan from heat. Blend small amount of hot mixture into sour cream; fold sour cream mixture into orange sauce. Add salt and white pepper. Pour over cooked asparagus.

May prepare sauce 2 to 3 days in advance and reheat in double boiler. If too thick, add a little orange juice.

May also be used as a filling for crêpes. Pour additional Maltaise sauce over the crêpes.

# Hilton's Calico Beans
*Great for covered dish dinners*

**May prepare ahead**                                **12 servings**

¼ pound bacon, diced
1 pound ground beef
½ cup chopped onion
½ cup brown sugar
½ cup ketchup
2 tablespoons vinegar
1 tablespoon prepared mustard
1 teaspoon salt
1 20-ounce can Lima beans
1 16-ounce can kidney beans
1 27-ounce can pork and beans

Brown bacon, beef and onions. Drain off grease. Drain a little juice from each can of beans; discard. Mix all ingredients. Bake uncovered in a 9 x 13-inch baking dish at 300 degrees for 1½ to 2 hours.

May also be served as an entrée. Serves 6 to 8.

# Beans, Beans, Beans
*A hearty, delicious dish that will be the hit of any barbecue*

**May prepare ahead**                                **15 servings**

1 15-ounce can pinto beans
1 16-ounce can pork and beans
1 16-ounce can French-style
    green beans
1 15½-ounce can kidney beans
3 strips bacon, diced
1 medium onion, chopped
1 green pepper, chopped
¾ cup packed brown sugar
1 cup chili sauce

Drain all beans. Brown bacon in skillet; remove with slotted spoon. Sauté onion in bacon drippings. Combine all ingredients in 2-quart casserole. Bake uncovered at 350 degrees for 1 hour.

# Black Beans
## *Authentic "Conch" cooking*

**May prepare ahead**                                    **6 servings**

1 pound dried black beans
1 green pepper, finely chopped
2 medium onions, finely
    chopped
3 garlic cloves, finely chopped
¼ cup olive oil
salt to taste
pepper to taste
2 teaspoons oregano
3 bay leaves
1 tablespoon wine vinegar
1 2-ounce jar diced pimento,
    drained

Rinse beans and soak overnight. Drain. Place beans in 2 quarts of water and simmer uncovered until almost tender, about 1 hour. Sauté green pepper, onions and garlic in olive oil until tender. Add to beans along with salt, pepper, oregano, bay leaves and vinegar. Cook uncovered over LOW heat about 4 hours until thick and creamy, mashing beans if necessary. Be careful not to burn beans! Remove bay leaves. Garnish with diced pimento before serving.

For an authentic "Conch" meal, serve over yellow or white rice with picadillo and bowls of chopped onion and diced avocado.

BLACK BEAN SOUP: Purée beans after cooking. Let stand for 30 minutes to 1 hour, then reheat. Serve with lime slices, diced avocado, chopped onions or croutons.

# Herbed Green Beans
## *Flavor and bouquet are delightful*

**May prepare partially ahead**                          **4 servings**

1 pound fresh green beans, cut
    in 1-inch lengths
2 to 3 tablespoons butter
½ cup chopped onion
¼ cup chopped celery
1 garlic clove, minced
¼ teaspoon basil
¼ teaspoon rosemary

Cook beans, covered, in very small amount of boiling salted water until almost tender, about 10 minutes; drain. Stir in remaining ingredients. Cover and cook 10 minutes longer or until beans are tender.

# Broccoli Casserole
*Delicious side dish for poultry or broiled fish*

**May prepare partially ahead**                    **6 servings**

1 bunch fresh broccoli or
  2 10-ounce packages frozen
  broccoli spears or florets
1 cup mayonnaise
½ cup grated sharp cheddar
  cheese
1 10¾-ounce can cream of
  mushroom soup
2 tablespoons grated onion
1 2-ounce package sliced
  almonds

Cut fresh broccoli stalks into small pieces and separate florets. Cook in boiling salted water 4 minutes or until tender; drain well. (Cook frozen broccoli according to package directions.) Add mayonnaise, cheese, soup and onion; mix well. Pour into buttered 1½-quart casserole and sprinkle almonds on top. Bake uncovered at 375 degrees for 20 minutes.

# Brussels Sprouts and Egg Casserole

**May prepare ahead**                    **6-8 servings**

4 cups fresh Brussels sprouts or
  2 10-ounce packages frozen
  Brussels sprouts
3 hard-boiled eggs, sliced
1 cup shredded sharp cheddar
  cheese
¼ cup milk
1 10¾-ounce can cream of
  mushroom soup*
½ cup cornflake crumbs
2 tablespoons butter, melted

*May substitute cream of
 celery or cream of
 chicken soup.

Cook the sprouts just until tender. Do NOT overcook. Drain well. Cut large sprouts in half. Place sprouts in a buttered 6 x 10-inch baking dish. Arrange egg slices over the sprouts and sprinkle with cheese. Blend milk and soup; pour over casserole. Combine crumbs and butter and sprinkle on top. Bake uncovered in a 350 degree oven for 25 to 30 minutes.

May be frozen for about a month.

# Cabbage Scramble
*Good low-calorie vegetable combination*

**May prepare partially ahead**                    **4 servings**

3 cups coarsely chopped
   cabbage
1 cup thinly sliced celery
1 cup thinly sliced onion
½ cup chopped green or
   red pepper
2 ripe tomatoes, diced
1 teaspoon salt
pepper to taste

Place all the vegetables in a heavy pan without water. Cover and cook over medium-low heat 20 minutes or until vegetables are done. Add salt and pepper.

# Carrots Braised in Butter
*Colorful and outstanding*

**May prepare ahead**                    **4-6 servings**

8 to 12 slender carrots
4 tablespoons butter or
   margarine
1 medium onion, chopped
2 tablespoons cognac or
   brandy, optional
¼ cup minced parsley
salt to taste
pepper to taste

In a large frying pan, lay carrots flat and add water to cover. Bring to boiling on high heat; cover, reduce heat to simmer. Cook until carrots are tender when pierced, about 15 to 20 minutes; drain. Add butter, onion and brandy. Cook over medium-high heat, shaking pan, until carrots are lightly browned on all sides. Mix in parsley and season with salt and pepper.

To reheat, toss with additional butter.

*A 1-pound head of cabbage yields approximately 4 cups shredded cabbage.*

# Marinated Copper Carrots

**Must prepare ahead**                                          **8 servings**

2 pounds carrots, pared and
  sliced into 1-inch lengths
1 teaspoon salt
¼ teaspoon pepper
1 teaspoon prepared mustard
½ cup vegetable oil
¾ cup sugar
¾ cup cider vinegar
1 10¾-ounce can condensed
  tomato soup
1 large onion, chopped
1 large green pepper, finely
  chopped

Boil carrots for 5 minutes. Drain and cool.

In a separate bowl, mix salt, pepper and mustard with a small amount of oil. Add remaining oil, sugar, vinegar and soup; beat to blend. Stir in onion and green pepper. Pour mixture over cooled carrots. Cover tightly and chill overnight. Can be refrigerated several days if sealed tightly.

May also be served as an appetizer.

# Sunshine Carrots

**May prepare partially ahead**                                **4 servings**

5 medium carrots
2 tablespoons water
1 tablespoon sugar
1 teaspoon cornstarch
¼ teaspoon salt
¼ teaspoon ginger
¼ cup orange juice
2 tablespoons butter

Slice carrots diagonally, about 1 inch thick. Place in covered 1½-quart glass casserole with water. Cook on high in microwave for 8 minutes. Stir halfway through cooking time. Drain.

Meanwhile, combine sugar, cornstarch, salt and ginger in a small saucepan. Add orange juice; cook, stirring constantly, until mixture thickens and bubbles. Boil 1 minute. Stir in butter. Pour over hot carrots, tossing to coat evenly.

If you do not have a microwave, cook carrots covered in a small amount of boiling salted water until just tender, about 20 minutes. Drain.

# Celery Casserole
*A winner every time*

**May prepare partially ahead**                    **6 servings**

3 cups diced celery
1 4-ounce can sliced
  mushrooms, drained
¼ cup slivered almonds
6 tablespoons butter, divided
3 tablespoons flour
1 10¾-ounce can cream of
  chicken soup
¾ cup half and half cream
½ cup grated Parmesan cheese
½ cup bread crumbs

Cook celery in pan with a small amount of water until slightly soft. Drain. Add mushrooms and almonds. Put in greased 8 x 12-inch baking dish.

Melt 3 tablespoons butter in medium saucepan. Add flour, soup and cream; stir until smooth. Pour over celery. Combine cheese and bread crumbs; crumble over casserole. Melt remaining butter and drizzle over top. Bake uncovered at 350 degrees for approximately 25 minutes.

# Fresh Mushroom Casserole
*Fabulous with steaks*

**May prepare partially ahead**                    **6 servings**

1 pound fresh mushrooms
¼ cup butter or margarine
2 beef bouillon cubes
½ cup hot water
2 tablespoons flour
½ cup half and half cream
dash of salt
dash of pepper
½ to 1 cup grated Parmesan
  cheese
½ cup bread crumbs

Clean mushrooms and slice off ends. Place in buttered 1-quart casserole. Set aside.

Melt butter and bouillon cubes in hot water. Blend in flour, cream, salt and pepper. Pour over mushrooms. Mix cheese and bread crumbs; add to mushrooms and toss gently. Bake uncovered at 350 degrees for approximately 30 minutes.

# Cauliflower au Gratin

*This beautiful vegetable can make a meal special*

**May prepare ahead**                                    **6 servings**

1 large head fresh cauliflower
¾ teaspoon salt, divided
3 tablespoons butter, melted
3 tablespoons flour
1½ cups milk
¾ cup grated sharp
    cheddar cheese
½ cup Italian seasoned
    bread crumbs
2 tablespoons butter

Pull the outside leaves off the cauliflower and cut the stem off close under the head. Wash and drain. Place cauliflower in pan and add water to cover and ½ teaspoon salt. Cover and simmer 15 to 20 minutes. Remove from heat; drain and place in buttered 2-quart casserole.

In a small saucepan, combine melted butter and flour over medium-low heat; gradually stir in milk and bring to boil, stirring constantly. Add ¼ teaspoon salt and cook 1 minute longer while stirring. Add cheese, stir and cook until melted and smooth. Pour over cauliflower and sprinkle bread crumbs on top. Dot with butter. Bake uncovered at 325 degrees for 25 to 30 minutes until hot and bubbly.

# Eggplant Royale

**May prepare ahead**                                    **4-6 servings**

1½ cups peeled, cooked and
    mashed eggplant
3 eggs, beaten
½ cup cottage cheese
½ cup grated mozzarella cheese
½ cup chopped onion
2 tablespoons butter, melted
½ teaspoon nutmeg
¼ cup finely chopped pecans

Mix all ingredients and pour into a greased 1½-quart baking dish. Bake uncovered at 400 degrees for 30 minutes.

If doubling recipe, increase baking time to 45 minutes.

# Ratatouille

**May prepare ahead**                                 **8-10 servings**

1 large eggplant, cut into
  1-inch squares
4 medium zucchini, cut into
  1-inch chunks
4 teaspoons salt, divided
½ cup olive oil, divided
2 large green peppers, cleaned
  and cut into chunks
3 medium onions, peeled and
  cut into chunks
5 medium tomatoes, peeled,
  seeded and cut into chunks
2 bay leaves
¼ to ½ teaspoon pepper
2 teaspoons minced garlic
1 teaspoon thyme

Toss eggplant and zucchini in colander with 3 teaspoons salt and let drain in sink 30 minutes. Rinse thoroughly and squeeze dry with hands.

Heat ¼ cup olive oil in large skillet and sauté eggplant and zucchini briefly. Remove from skillet and reserve. In same skillet, brown green peppers and onions, adding a bit more oil if necessary. Remove and reserve. Add remaining oil to skillet. Sauté tomatoes and bay leaves. Season with pepper and remaining salt. Return all reserved vegetables to skillet. Simmer, covered, for 30 minutes, stirring frequently. Add garlic and thyme. Remove cover and simmer 30 more minutes or until thick. Remove bay leaves.

Serve hot or cold as an appetizer, first course or side dish. It is delicious as a crêpe filling.

*When peeling fresh tomatoes, dip the whole tomato into boiling water for one minute, then plunge into cold water. The skin will slip right off.*

🐚 🐚 🐚 🐚 🐚 🐚 🐚 🐚 🐚 🐚 🐚

# Creamy Potato Puff

May prepare partially ahead

6 servings

7 to 8 medium potatoes, pared
   and cut into 1-inch slices
¼ cup butter
¼ cup hot milk
1 8-ounce package cream
   cheese, softened
1 egg, beaten
½ cup finely chopped onion
¼ cup chopped pimento
dash of white pepper
salt to taste
paprika for garnish

In large pot, cover potatoes with water. Bring to boil; reduce heat and cook until tender, about 30 minutes. Drain well. Mash. Add butter. Gradually add hot milk; beat until light and fluffy. Set aside.

Beat cream cheese and blend in egg, onion, pimento, pepper and salt. Gradually add mashed potatoes and beat well with electric mixer. Place in a buttered 2-quart casserole or soufflé dish. Bake uncovered at 350 degrees for 45 minutes. Potatoes will rise above dish and brown lightly. Sprinkle with paprika and serve immediately.

# Tarragon Potato and Zucchini Casserole

May prepare partially ahead

8-10 servings

8 to 10 medium potatoes
butter
salt to taste
pepper to taste
tarragon to taste
5 to 7 medium zucchini,
   sliced

Peel potatoes, if desired. In large pot, cover potatoes with water. Place over medium-high heat and cook 15 minutes. Slice and layer ½ of potatoes in a greased 9 x 13-inch casserole. Dot with butter; sprinkle with salt, pepper and tarragon. Layer zucchini on top of potatoes. Dot with butter; sprinkle with salt, pepper and tarragon. Layer remaining potatoes on top of zucchini. Dot with butter; sprinkle with salt, pepper and tarragon. Bake uncovered at 350 degrees for 45 minutes.

# Crispy Oven Potatoes
*Nice change from baked or mashed potatoes*

May prepare partially ahead                              6 servings

¼ cup butter, melted
1 tablespoon grated onion
1 tablespoon chopped fresh
   parsley
½ teaspoon dried whole thyme
½ teaspoon salt
⅛ teaspoon pepper
4 large unpeeled potatoes,
   scrubbed and thinly sliced
1½ cups shredded cheddar
   cheese

Combine butter, onion, parsley, thyme, salt and pepper. Layer potatoes in a lightly greased 9 x 13-inch baking dish, brushing each layer with butter mixture. Bake at 425 degrees for 40 minutes or until potatoes are tender. Sprinkle with cheese and bake 5 more minutes or until cheese melts.

# Sour Cream Potato Pancakes

May prepare partially ahead                              2½ dozen

3 large potatoes (about
   2 pounds)
2 eggs
1 small onion, grated
1 cup sour cream
½ cup sifted flour
¼ teaspoon baking powder
1 teaspoon salt
¼ teaspoon white pepper
vegetable oil for frying

Pare potatoes and shred coarsely into a large bowl of cold water. Drain, then rinse in cold running water. Squeeze firmly in clean toweling to remove as much water as possible. Beat eggs in a large bowl until frothy. Add potatoes, onion, sour cream, flour, baking powder, salt and pepper. Stir.

Heat ¼-inch depth of oil in a large skillet. Drop potato mixture by tablespoonfuls into hot oil, adding more oil as needed. Flatten with pancake turner to make an even thickness. Brown on one side, about 5 to 6 minutes, then turn and brown on other side. Drain on paper toweling and serve warm.

These are delicious served with cranberry or cranapple sauce.

# Apricot-Glazed Sweet Potatoes
### *Dandy for the holidays*

May prepare ahead                                                6 servings

3 pounds sweet potatoes
1 cup firmly packed brown
   sugar
4½ teaspoons cornstarch
¼ teaspoon salt
⅛ teaspoon cinnamon
½ teaspoon vanilla extract
1 cup apricot nectar
½ cup hot water
2 tablespoons butter
½ cup chopped pecans

Cook sweet potatoes in boiling salted water until tender. Cool to touch. Peel and cut into ½-inch slices. Arrange slices in buttered 2-quart casserole.

Combine brown sugar, cornstarch, salt and cinnamon in a saucepan; stir well. Add vanilla, nectar and water. Cook over medium heat, stirring constantly, until thick and bubbly. Stir in butter and pecans. Pour sauce over sweet potato slices. Bake covered at 350 degrees for 25 minutes.

# Sweet Potato Supreme

May prepare ahead                                                8 servings

1 40-ounce can sweet potatoes,
   mashed and drained
1 cup sugar
½ cup milk
½ cup butter or margarine,
   melted
1 teaspoon vanilla extract
2 eggs, beaten
1 cup coconut

Topping:
½ cup butter or margarine,
   melted
1 cup brown sugar
½ cup flour
1 cup chopped nuts

Mix all ingredients in a large saucepan. Bring mixture to a boil and pour into a greased 2-quart casserole.

Mix all topping ingredients and spread over sweet potato mixture. Bake uncovered at 350 degrees for 20 to 25 minutes.

May be made the day before serving.

# Sweet Potato Bake

**May prepare partially ahead**                                    **6 servings**

1 22-ounce can sweet potatoes,
   cut up, reserving ½ cup juice
1 8-ounce can unsweetened
   pineapple chunks, reserving
   ½ cup juice
1 11-ounce can mandarin
   oranges, drained
cinnamon
butter
½ cup dark corn syrup
½ cup brown sugar

Combine potatoes, pineapple and oranges in a greased 7 x 11-inch baking dish. Sprinkle with cinnamon and dot with butter. Combine reserved juices, corn syrup and brown sugar in a saucepan. Heat to boiling. Boil 2 to 3 minutes. Cool slightly. Pour over potato mixture. Bake uncovered at 350 degrees for 45 minutes.

# Spinach Rice Casserole

**May prepare ahead**                                              **8 servings**

1 10-ounce package frozen
   chopped spinach
4 eggs
1 cup milk
1 tablespoon onion juice
   or flakes
1 tablespoon Worcestershire
   sauce
2 teaspoons salt
¼ teaspoon thyme
¼ teaspoon rosemary
1 pound cheddar cheese,
   shredded
3 cups cooked rice
   (¾ cup raw)
¼ cup butter, melted

Cook and drain spinach. Beat eggs in large bowl. Stir in milk, onion juice, Worcestershire, salt and seasonings. Add cheese. Fold in spinach, cooked rice and butter. Turn into greased 2-quart casserole. Bake uncovered at 350 degrees for 35 minutes.

# Spinach Casserole

May prepare ahead

8-10 servings

½ pound sliced bacon
2 10-ounce packages frozen
  chopped spinach
2 eggs
1¾ cups milk
1 teaspoon salt
⅔ cup soft bread crumbs
1½ cups shredded Provolone
  cheese*
paprika

*May substitute any favorite
  cheese.

Dice bacon and pan broil until crisp; drain. Cook spinach according to package directions; drain. Beat eggs slightly; add milk and salt. Stir in bacon, spinach, bread crumbs and ½ of the cheese. Pour into greased 1½-quart baking dish. Sprinkle remaining cheese around outside edge. Sprinkle paprika in middle. Bake uncovered at 375 degrees for 30 to 35 minutes.

# Heavenly Spinach
*A good covered dish for a picnic*

May prepare ahead

8-10 servings

3 10-ounce packages frozen
  chopped spinach
2 cups herb-seasoned stuffing
  mix
½ cup butter
1 1.375-ounce package onion
  soup mix
2 cups sour cream

Cook and drain spinach. Brown stuffing mix in butter and reserve ½ cup. Mix spinach, stuffing, soup mix and sour cream. Place in a greased 2-quart casserole. Sprinkle with reserved stuffing. Bake uncovered at 350 degrees for 20 to 30 minutes.

# Squash Casserole

May prepare ahead                                                8 servings

1 pound yellow summer squash
1/4 cup finely grated onion
3 tablespoons margarine, melted
1 cup grated sharp cheddar
  cheese
1 tablespoon sugar
3 eggs, well-beaten
1 cup milk
salt to taste
pepper to taste
1½ cups cracker crumbs

Wash squash and cut into chunks. Cook in boiling water until tender, approximately 15 minutes. Drain. Add onion, margarine, cheese, sugar, eggs, milk, salt and pepper. Mix well and pour into a greased 1½-quart casserole. Top with crumbs. Bake uncovered at 375 degrees for 40 minutes.

Freezes well.

# Squash-Cheese Soufflé

May prepare ahead                                                6-8 servings

1 cup milk
1 cup bread crumbs
3 eggs, beaten
3/4 teaspoon pepper
3 tablespoons butter or
  margarine
1 tablespoon grated onion
4 to 5 medium yellow summer
  squash, sliced and cooked
1 cup shredded cheddar cheese

Warm milk and pour over bread crumbs. Add eggs, pepper, butter and onion; mix well. Stir in squash and cheese. Pour into a greased 2-quart casserole or soufflé dish. Bake uncovered at 350 degrees for 25 to 30 minutes or until firm. Serve immediately.

 *For quick, accurate and handy seasoning while cooking, keep on hand a large shaker containing 6 parts salt and 1 part pepper.*

# Summer Squash Patties

**May not prepare ahead**                    **24 patties**

1¼ cups self-rising flour
½ teaspoon sugar
¾ teaspoon salt
½ cup sour cream
1 egg, beaten
1 tablespoon vegetable oil
3 cups coarsely grated yellow
    summer squash
1 medium onion, coarsely
    grated
pepper to taste

Combine flour, sugar, salt, sour cream, egg and oil, blending until smooth. Stir in squash and onion, then pepper. Drop by tablespoons into hot, greased skillet. Cook until golden brown, turning once. Drain on paper towels.

# Squash with Walnuts
*A colorful tasty dish*

**May prepare partially ahead**                    **6 servings**

¾ pound zucchini squash
¾ pound yellow summer
    squash
½ cup diced onions
½ cup vegetable oil
½ cup dry white wine or
    vermouth
2 tablespoons fresh lemon
    juice
½ teaspoon salt
½ cup coarsely chopped
    walnuts

Wash squash and cut crosswise into ½-inch slices. Sauté squash and onion in hot oil for 5 minutes. Add wine, lemon juice and salt; simmer for 5 minutes. Add walnuts. Serve hot. Do not freeze.

# Broiled Stuffed Tomatoes

**May prepare partially ahead**                    **4 servings**

4 large ripe tomatoes
salt to taste
pepper to taste
⅓ cup grated Parmesan cheese
1½ tablespoons butter, melted
3 slices stale bread, torn into
   small pieces
2 strips uncooked bacon, diced

Slice the top off each tomato, including the core, to make a flat surface. Discard tops. Sprinkle cut surfaces of tomatoes liberally with salt and pepper, then with Parmesan cheese. Mix bread with melted butter and mound on top of each tomato. Top with diced bacon. Put tomatoes in a pan and bake at 350 degrees for 30 minutes.

# Buffet Tomatoes

**May prepare partially ahead**                    **12 servings**

12 tomatoes
2 10-ounce packages frozen
   chopped spinach
2 large onions, chopped
¼ cup chopped parsley
6 celery stalks, chopped
1 large green pepper, chopped
4 carrots, chopped
6 tablespoons butter, melted
1½ cups seasoned bread
   crumbs
⅔ cup milk
2 eggs, beaten
salt to taste
pepper to taste
grated Parmesan cheese

Cut tops from tomatoes and scoop out seeds and pulp. Salt shells and invert to drain.

Cook spinach according to package directions; drain very well. Sauté onions, parsley, celery, green pepper and carrots in butter until just tender. Add spinach. Stir in bread crumbs, milk, eggs, salt and pepper; mix well. Pack into tomatoes and sprinkle with cheese. Place in buttered baking dish and bake uncovered at 400 degrees for 20 minutes.

# Vegetables, Dilled and Chilled
*Excellent for buffets and picnics*

**Must prepare ahead**                                 **10 servings**

1 1-pound can French-style
  green beans, drained and
  rinsed
1 1-pound can white corn,
  drained and rinsed
1 1-pound can small early peas,
  drained and rinsed
1 4-ounce can sliced
  mushrooms, drained
1 2-ounce jar pimentos,
  chopped and drained
¼ cup chopped green pepper
½ cup chopped onion
1½ cups raw cauliflower,
  broken into bite-size pieces

Place all canned and fresh vegetables in a 1½-quart serving bowl.

**Dressing:**
1 cup sugar
½ cup vegetable oil
½ teaspoon pepper
½ teaspoon dill weed
¾ cup white vinegar
1 teaspoon salt
1 tablespoon water

Combine all dressing ingredients and pour over vegetables. Cover dish tightly with plastic wrap and refrigerate until thoroughly chilled.

Use slotted spoon for serving.

# Zucchini and Tomato Casserole

**May prepare ahead**  **6-8 servings**

1 medium onion, chopped
¼ cup butter
4 cups sliced zucchini
1 carrot, thinly sliced
½ teaspoon oregano
¼ teaspoon garlic powder
1 15-ounce can tomato sauce
¾ cup grated Parmesan cheese
½ to 1 cup shredded cheddar or
mozzarella cheese

Sauté onion in butter; add zucchini, carrot and spices. Add tomato sauce and Parmesan cheese, mixing well. Pour into a 1½ to 2-quart casserole and top with remaining cheese. Bake at 350 degrees until heated through, about 20 minutes.

Does not freeze well.

# Prize-Winning Zucchini Casserole
*This recipe won a cooking contest*

**May prepare partially ahead**  **6 servings**

6 cups sliced zucchini
¼ cup chopped onion
½ cup condensed cream of
chicken soup
½ cup condensed cream of
mushroom soup
1 cup sour cream
1 8-ounce package
herb-seasoned stuffing mix
½ cup butter or margarine,
melted
grated Parmesan cheese,
optional

Cook zucchini and onion in salted water until tender. Drain well. Combine soups and sour cream and fold into zucchini. Combine stuffing mix with melted butter. Spread a thick layer of stuffing in an 8 x 12-inch covered baking dish. Spoon zucchini mixture on top of stuffing. Top with remaining stuffing. Sprinkle generously with Parmesan cheese, if desired. Bake covered at 350 degrees for approximately 30 minutes.

# Zucchini with Pesto

**May prepare partially ahead**                    **4-6 servings**

**Pesto Sauce:**
¼ cup freshly grated Parmesan
    cheese
¼ cup olive oil
3 tablespoons coarsely
    chopped fresh basil or
    1 tablespoon dried,
    crumbled basil
1 garlic clove, minced

Combine all ingredients for pesto in food processor or blender and mix well.

**Saltato:**
2 tablespoons olive oil
3 medium zucchini, cubed
1 medium onion, minced
3 medium tomatoes, cubed
1 teaspoon salt
pesto sauce

Place large skillet over high heat until very hot, about 30 seconds. Add oil, coating bottom evenly. Add zucchini and stir-fry 3 minutes. Add onion and continue stirring 3 more minutes. Add tomatoes and salt; stir-fry 1 more minute. Remove from heat; add pesto sauce, stirring until thoroughly mixed. Serve hot.

May also be used as a topping for spaghetti.

Do not freeze.

*Ripen green tomatoes by placing in a paper bag and storing in a cool, dark place.*

pasta and grains

# Pasta and Grains

## THE PELICAN

*"A marvelous bird is the pelican, his beak can hold more than his belly can," goes the old saying. Whether soaring gracefully through the air, diving into the water after fish with a tremendous splash or sunning himself on an old piling, the pelican is loved by everyone. While numbers may be reduced elsewhere, Southwest Florida is blessed with an abundance of pelicans.*

# White Lasagne
*Rich and heavenly*

**May prepare ahead**                    **8 servings**

**Béchamel Sauce:**
1 onion, coarsely chopped
3 tablespoons butter, melted
3 tablespoons flour
1 teaspoon salt
½ teaspoon nutmeg
¼ teaspoon white pepper
1 cup milk
2 cups light cream, divided
2 egg yolks

Sauté onion in butter until transparent. Stir in flour and cook 3 minutes, stirring constantly; do not brown. Stir in salt, nutmeg and pepper. Gradually add milk and 1 cup cream. Stir constantly until sauce thickens. Beat remaining cream with egg yolks, stir into sauce and continue stirring until mixture almost boils. Do not boil.

**Lasagne:**
1½ pounds sweet Italian
    sausage
1 garlic clove, minced
½ teaspoon salt
8 ounces lasagne noodles
1 pint ricotta cheese
2 eggs
béchamel sauce
1 cup freshly grated Parmesan
    cheese
½ pound mozzarella cheese,
    chopped
½ pound fresh mushrooms,
    sliced and sautéed in butter
paprika
minced parsley

Remove casing from sausage; crumble and cook sausage until done. Cool. Grind in food processor. Mix with garlic and salt. Cook lasagne noodles according to package directions; drain. Combine ricotta cheese with eggs. Arrange ⅓ noodles in buttered 9 x 13-inch pan. Spoon ⅓ béchamel sauce over noodles, sprinkle with ⅓ sausage, then ⅓ Parmesan and mozzarella cheese, and then ⅓ ricotta cheese mixture. Repeat twice. Top with mushrooms, sprinkle with paprika and parsley. Bake at 375 degrees for 20 minutes. Allow to stand 10 minutes before serving.

**WINE: Frascati or Zinfandel**

# Pasta Primavera

**May prepare partially ahead**                    **4 servings**

½ cup unsalted butter
1 medium onion, finely
  chopped
1 large garlic clove, minced
1 pound asparagus, tough ends
  trimmed, sliced in ¼-inch
  slices
½ pound mushrooms, thinly
  sliced
1 medium zucchini,
  ¼-inch slices
1 small carrot, ⅛-inch slices
1 cup heavy cream
½ cup chicken stock
2 tablespoons chopped fresh
  basil or 2 teaspoons dried
  basil
1 cup frozen tiny peas, thawed
2 ounces prosciutto or cooked
  ham, chopped
5 green onions, chopped
salt to taste
pepper to taste
1 pound linguine, cooked and
  drained
1 cup grated Parmesan cheese
1 pound shrimp, peeled,
  deveined and cooked,
  optional

WINE: Frascati or Alsatian
  Gewürztraminer

Heat wok or large deep skillet to medium high. Add butter, onion and garlic; sauté until onion is softened. Add asparagus, mushrooms, zucchini and carrot to skillet; stir-fry about 2 minutes. Reserve some vegetables for garnish. Increase heat to high. Add cream, stock and basil; allow mixture to boil until liquid is slightly reduced, about 3 minutes. Add peas, ham (shrimp, if desired) and green onions; cook 1 minute. Salt and pepper to taste. Add pasta and cheese; toss thoroughly. Turn onto platter and garnish with reserved vegetables.

May be used as a side dish, serving 8.

# Beef and Cheese Pasta

May prepare ahead                                    **4-6 servings**

1 pound ground beef
½ cup chopped onion
2 8-ounce cans tomato sauce
1 teaspoon sugar
¾ teaspoon salt
¼ teaspoon garlic salt
¼ teaspoon pepper
4 cups uncooked egg noodles
1 8-ounce package cream
  cheese, softened
1 cup cream style cottage
  cheese
¼ cup sour cream
⅓ cup chopped green onion
¼ cup chopped green pepper
2 tablespoons grated Parmesan
  cheese
1 cup grated mozzarella cheese

**WINE: Chianti Classico
  or Zinfandel**

Brown meat and onion. Drain off grease. Stir in tomato sauce, sugar, salt, garlic salt and pepper. Simmer 25 to 30 minutes. Remove from heat. Cook noodles according to package directions; drain. Combine cream cheese, cottage cheese, sour cream, onion and green pepper. In a greased 9 x 13-inch pan, layer ½ noodles, ½ meat mixture and ½ cheese mixture. Repeat layers. Top with Parmesan and mozzarella cheeses. Bake at 350 degrees for 45 minutes. Let stand 10 minutes before serving.

May be frozen.

*To keep noodles from boiling over, add 1 tablespoon butter to the cooking water.*

# Spaghetti Carbonara
*Super for a casual dinner with friends*

**May prepare partially ahead**                    **4 servings**

4 egg yolks
½ cup heavy cream
1 cup grated Parmesan cheese
½ pound bacon, diced
2 tablespoons olive oil
1 bunch scallions, trimmed
    and sliced
1 cup cooked peas
½ cup finely chopped parsley
1 cup chopped prosciutto or
    smoked ham
1 ripe tomato, diced
1 pound uncooked spaghetti
Parmesan cheese, grated

**WINE: Charbono or Chianti
    Classico Riserva**

In a small bowl, beat egg yolks with cream until smooth. Stir in cheese.

In a skillet, fry bacon until golden brown and crisp; remove bacon and drain bacon drippings. Add oil to skillet and heat. Stir in scallions, peas, parsley, prosciutto, tomato and bacon. Stir a few minutes until mixture is hot.

Cook spaghetti according to package directions; drain and place in large serving bowl. Add egg yolk mixture and bacon mixture. Toss quickly and gently until all spaghetti strands are coated. The heat from the spaghetti cooks the egg yolks forming a sauce. Serve at once sprinkled with extra Parmesan cheese.

*Small amounts of salt and oil added to water when cooking pasta shorten cooking time and lessen sticking.*

# Linguine with Sausage and Eggplant
*Delightful to look at, delicious to eat*

**May prepare partially ahead**                    **6 servings**

1½ pounds sweet Italian
  sausage
1 large eggplant, unpeeled
2 tablespoons olive oil
2 tablespoons butter
3 bacon slices, diced
2 medium onions, diced
2 large garlic cloves, minced
⅓ cup minced parsley
1 teaspoon salt
½ teaspoon freshly ground
  black pepper
1 green pepper, thinly sliced
1 red pepper, thinly sliced
1 1-pound can plum tomatoes,
  finely chopped
3 large ripe tomatoes, peeled
  and finely chopped
1 pound linguine
Parmesan cheese, grated

WINE: Côtes-du-Rhône or
    Red Rioja

Remove casing from sausage; cut meat into small pieces. Cut eggplant into 8 crosswise slices and then into ¼-inch cubes.

Brown sausage in Dutch oven, about 10 minutes; drain and set aside. Combine olive oil, butter and bacon in Dutch oven. Add onions and sauté until transparent. Add garlic, parsley, salt, pepper and sausage. Cook 10 minutes over medium heat. Add peppers and eggplant; cook 5 minutes, stirring frequently. Add canned and fresh tomatoes; simmer 30 minutes, stirring occasionally.

Cook linguine according to package directions; drain well. Place linguine in a large bowl; pour sausage and eggplant sauce over linguine, mixing well. Serve and pass Parmesan cheese.

# Spaghetti with Meat Sauce
*Everybody loves it*

**May prepare ahead**                                    **12 servings**

½ cup olive oil
1½ cups minced onion
3 garlic cloves, minced
1½ pounds ground beef
4 16-ounce cans whole
   tomatoes, cut up
5 teaspoons salt
½ teaspoon pepper
½ teaspoon basil
1 6-ounce can sliced
   mushrooms
1 12-ounce can tomato paste
¼ cup minced parsley
3 pounds uncooked spaghetti
1½ cups grated Parmesan
   cheese

WINE: Barbera, Rubesco
   or Zinfandel

Heat oil in large saucepan. Cook onions and garlic until transparent but not brown. Add beef; cook until brown. Add tomatoes, spices, mushrooms, tomato paste and parsley. Mix well. Bring to a boil. Lower heat; simmer uncovered 30 minutes, stirring frequently.

Cook spaghetti according to package directions; drain. Serve sauce over spaghetti. Sprinkle with cheese.

# Cheese Grits
*A Southern favorite*

**May prepare partially ahead**                          **6 servings**

1 teaspoon salt
3 cups water
1 cup quick grits
1 6-ounce tube garlic cheese,
   sliced
6 tablespoons butter
¼ cup milk
2 egg yolks, beaten

Add salt to water, bring to a boil. Stir in grits and cook until thick, about 2½ to 5 minutes. Add remaining ingredients and stir until all cheese is melted. Pour into a greased 2-quart baking dish. Bake uncovered at 350 degrees for 1 hour. If not served immediately, cover and hold in warm oven.

# Oven Rice

**May prepare ahead**                                    **6 servings**

½ cup butter, melted
1 10¾-ounce can onion soup
1 10¾-ounce can beef broth
1 cup raw rice*
1 4½-ounce jar sliced
   mushrooms, drained,
   optional

Put all ingredients in a 1½-quart casserole. Cover and bake at 375 degrees for 1 hour.

*May substitute brown rice. Increase cooking time by 15 to 30 minutes.

# Rice Pilaf
*Goes with almost any entrée*

**May prepare partially ahead**                          **4 servings**

4 tablespoons butter or
   margarine
1 medium onion, chopped
2 to 3 garlic cloves, minced
1 cup long-grain rice,
   uncooked
1 14-ounce can chicken or
   beef broth, undiluted
salt to taste

In a 2-quart saucepan over medium heat, melt butter. Add onion and garlic. Cook, stirring, until onion is soft and lightly browned, about 5 minutes. Add rice and continue cooking and stirring until rice is lightly browned, about 7 minutes. Pour in broth. Bring to a boil; cover, reduce heat, and simmer until rice is tender and liquid is absorbed, about 20 minutes. Before serving stir once or twice to fluff rice. Season with salt.

*One cup of raw rice yields about 3 cups of cooked rice.*

# Daddy's Wild Rice Casserole
*Elegant*

May prepare ahead                                        10 servings

1 cup chopped onion
1 cup chopped celery
2 tablespoons margarine
1 cup uncooked wild rice*
2 10¾-ounce cans cream of
mushroom soup
1 4½-ounce jar sliced
mushrooms, drained
1 2-ounce jar sliced pimento,
drained
12 ounces Swiss cheese, grated
3 tablespoons sherry
¾ cup chopped walnuts

Sauté onion and celery in margarine. Wash rice in cold water, drain and add to vegetables. Stir in remaining ingredients. Turn into a lightly buttered 2-quart casserole. Cover and bake at 325 degrees for 1 hour and 15 minutes.

*May substitute wild rice mix.

# Rice Casserole
*Almonds add a nice touch*

May prepare partially ahead                                4 servings

½ cup butter, melted
2 tablespoons chopped green
pepper, optional
2 tablespoons chopped onion
1 cup raw rice
2 ounces sliced almonds
1 4-ounce can mushrooms,
undrained
1 10¾-ounce can chicken
broth

Melt butter in large skillet. Add pepper, onion, rice and almonds; brown lightly. Add mushrooms and chicken broth. Pour into a 2-quart casserole. Bake covered at 325 degrees for 1 hour.

entrées

# Entrées

## EDISON HOME

*"There is only one Fort Myers and 90 million people are going to find it out."— Thomas Alva Edison, 1914*

*America's greatest inventor was one of the first to discover the beauty of Fort Myers, building his winter home and laboratory here in 1886. Now owned by the City of Fort Myers, the Edison Home and grounds have been visited by millions of awe-struck admirers.*

# Beef Curry with Seven Boys
*Excellent for "cook-ahead" entertainment*

**May prepare ahead**                    **12 servings**

⅔ cup finely chopped onion
4 tablespoons butter, divided
2½ tablespoons curry powder
2 cups beef bouillon or broth
1 cup coconut milk*
⅛ teaspoon pepper
3 tablespoons preserved ginger,
   chopped or crystallized
dash of cloves
1 chopped mint leaf
2½ pounds beef chuck or
   round, cut into 1-inch cubes

Sauté onion in 2 tablespoons butter. Add curry, broth and coconut milk. Stir in pepper, ginger, cloves and mint; remove from heat. Brown beef in remaining 2 tablespoons butter. Place meat and curry mixture in crock pot or slow cooker and cook on medium heat for 6 hours.

cooked rice

**Seven Boys:**
1 small green pepper, chopped
¾ cup chopped salted
   peanuts
¾ cup grated coconut
3 boiled eggs, chopped
¾ cup chutney
¾ cup grated olives
¾ cup cooked and crumbled
   bacon

Serve over cooked white rice. Pass seven "boys," or garnishes, in separate bowls to add zest and flavor.

*May find canned coconut
  milk on gourmet food shelves.

**WINE: Gewürztraminer**

# Beef Strips in Red Wine with Thyme

May prepare partially ahead

2 servings

1 pound beef sirloin, cut into ¼-inch strips
2 tablespoons butter
1 small onion, chopped
½ pound fresh mushrooms, sliced
1 teaspoon tomato paste
1 tablespoon flour
½ cup beef stock
½ cup red wine
juice of ½ lemon
¼ teaspoon thyme
salt to taste
pepper to taste
parsley

WINE: California Cabernet or Merlot

Sauté strips of steak in foaming butter over high heat. Add onion and mushrooms; cook until onion has softened, stirring constantly to prevent burning. Lower heat, add tomato paste and flour; cook 1 minute. Stir with a wire whisk until flour has absorbed pan juices. Slowly add beef stock and wine, stirring to form a smooth sauce. Flavor sauce with lemon juice, thyme, salt and pepper. Continue cooking another 5 minutes until beef is tender. Garnish with parsley.

Serve on bed of noodles.

# Beef Teriyaki

Must prepare partially ahead

4 servings

Marinade:
½ cup packed brown sugar
½ cup pineapple juice
½ cup vegetable oil
1 10-ounce bottle soy sauce
3 garlic cloves, minced

1½ to 2 pounds flank steak

WINE: Rubesco or Australian Cabernet

Mix all marinade ingredients.

Pour marinade over steak and refrigerate 24 hours. Remove steak; broil 20 minutes, turning at least once. Cut into very thin diagonal slices.

May also cook on grill, turning frequently.

# Beef Wellington
*Exquisite*

**May prepare partially ahead**                    **6-8 servings**

1 3 to 3½-pound beef
  tenderloin, trimmed
2 tablespoons brandy
1 4-ounce can liver pâté*
1 box of 6 frozen puff pastry
  patty shells, thawed
1 egg
1 teaspoon water

Rub tenderloin with brandy and bake at 325 degrees 10 minutes per pound. Remove from oven; cool to room temperature. Spread liver pâté or mushroom pâté all over roast. Roll out thawed pastry to form a rectangle large enough to completely wrap roast. Place roast on pastry and wrap as you would a package, pinching seams. Beat egg with water; brush pastry seams. Place meat, seam side down, on a greased baking sheet. Any leftover pastry can be used to create a design on top. Bake at 425 degrees for 20 to 25 minutes until crust is golden brown. Serve within 30 minutes.

The beef may be prepared up to the last baking time and refrigerated. Remove from refrigerator and bring to room temperature before final baking.

*May substitute Mushroom
  Pâté:
1 pound fresh mushrooms,
  finely chopped
½ cup chopped scallions
¼ cup butter
¼ cup chopped parsley

In a medium skillet, cook and stir all ingredients until scallions are tender and all liquid is absorbed.

**WINE: Mature Fine Bordeaux
  or Burgundy**

# Braised Beef

**Must prepare partially ahead** **6 servings**

**Marinade:**
1 teaspoon salt
½ teaspoon freshly
   ground pepper
1 large onion, chopped
2 carrots, sliced
2 whole cloves
2 bay leaves
3 garlic cloves, sliced
10 peppercorns
3 sprigs parsley, chopped
1½ cups dry red wine
½ cup olive oil
¼ cup white vinegar

1 4-pound round of beef

**Braised Beef:**
½ pound salt pork
larding needle
3 tablespoons shortening
1 onion, diced
4 tablespoons brandy or
   cognac, warmed
2 teaspoons tomato paste
4 tablespoons flour
½ cup beef stock
marinade
salt to taste
pepper to taste

**WINE: Australian Shiraz or
      California Pinot Noir**

Combine all marinade ingredients. Place meat in glass bowl and pour marinade over meat. Refrigerate 24 hours, basting occasionally. Remove meat and dry thoroughly. Strain marinade and reserve.

Cut salt pork into long strips. Thread larding needle with pork. Inserting needle against the grain of the meat, sew pork strips into the inside of beef round. Pork strips should be flush with outside of meat.

In Dutch oven, melt shortening and brown meat on all sides. Add onion and brown. Ignite brandy and pour over meat. Remove meat from pan.

In same Dutch oven, add tomato paste and flour. Stir in stock and marinade. Season with salt and pepper. Bring mixture to a boil. Add meat. Cover; reduce heat and simmer 2½ hours.

For serving, slice meat, place on a hot platter and serve with the gravy.

# Chuletas
### Mexican hamburgers

**Must prepare partially ahead**                     **4 servings**

**Salsa Fria:**
1 10-ounce can tomatoes with
   green chilies, chopped
1 tablespoon olive oil
1 tablespoon wine vinegar

Mix all salsa fria ingredients; chill well.

**Chuletas:**
2 cups finely crushed saltine
   crackers
2 tablespoons finely chopped
   parsley
1 cup finely chopped onions
1 pound lean ground chuck
1 egg
1 teaspoon salt
1 teaspoon chili powder

Spread cracker crumbs on a plate or a sheet of wax paper. Mix parsley, onions, ground chuck, egg, salt and chili powder; blend well. Make 4 patties and coat each with crumbs. Chill at least 1 hour.

1 cup vegetable oil or
   shortening for frying

Cook patties in heated oil until browned on the outside. If the patties are to be well-done, do not get oil too hot or crumb coating will burn.

sliced avocado

Serve with sliced avocado and cold salsa fria.

*Sprinkle a frying pan with salt before adding meat to prevent fat from splattering.*

# Filet with Wine Sauce

**May prepare partially ahead**               **4 servings**

**Wine Sauce:**
**5 tablespoons butter or**
    **margarine**
**1 medium onion, finely**
    **chopped**
**6 green onions (white part**
    **only), minced**
**1 large garlic clove, minced**
**3 ounces cooked ham, minced**
**2 large mushrooms, minced**
**2 tablespoons flour**
**dash of cayenne pepper**
**⅛ teaspoon black pepper**
**¾ cup beef broth**
**½ cup dry red wine**
**¼ teaspoon salt**

In heavy 8-inch skillet, melt butter over medium heat. Add onion, green onions, garlic, ham and mushrooms. Cook, stirring occasionally, until onion is golden brown and tender, about 5 minutes. Stir in flour and peppers. Increase heat to medium-high and stir mixture until well browned, about 5 minutes. Do not burn. Gradually blend in broth and wine. Stir until thickened and smooth. Reduce heat and simmer, stirring occasionally, until sauce is thick, smooth, shiny and reduced to 1¼ cups, about 10 minutes. Add salt.

**Filet:**
**1 tablespoon butter or**
    **margarine**
**4 6-ounce slices filet mignon**
**wine sauce**
**minced parsley**
**cherry tomatoes, optional**
**parsley sprigs, optional**

**WINE: Nuits-St.-Georges or**
    **other Red Burgundy**

Heat heavy skillet. Melt butter; add beef slices and quickly pan-broil both sides over high heat until browned and inside is done as desired. Transfer to hot serving platter or plates; spoon on sauce. Sprinkle with minced parsley. Garnish with tomatoes and parsley sprigs, if desired.

# Flank Steak with Fresh Vegetables

May prepare partially ahead                    4-6 servings

1¼ to 1½ pounds flank steak
1 cup chopped onion
1 cup finely chopped parsley
2 thick slices uncooked bacon, chopped
2 tablespoons vegetable oil
2 14½-ounce cans beef broth
1 teaspoon salt
1 bay leaf
¼ cup celery leaves
8 to 12 small new potatoes, scrubbed
8 to 10 small white boiling onions
3 to 4 carrots, cut in long strips
½ pound small whole green beans, ends removed

Lay steak on cutting board. Mix onion, parsley and bacon. Spread over steak. Roll steak lengthwise in jellyroll fashion; fasten securely with toothpicks. Cut in half. Brown rolls in oil in Dutch oven. Add broth, salt, bay leaf and celery leaves. Cover and simmer 45 minutes or until tender. Skim off fat. Meanwhile, cook vegetables in boiling salted water until barely tender; drain. Remove beef from broth and cut into ¾-inch slices. Arrange beef pinwheels with vegetables on deep platter. Pour hot broth over steak and vegetables.

WINE: Red Bordeaux

# Jim Sherfey's Tenderloin
*A gourmet cookout*

May not prepare ahead                    6-8 servings

1 5 to 7-pound whole beef tenderloin
4 ounces bleu cheese
1 tablespoon Worcestershire sauce
1 tablespoon chopped chives

WINE: Barbaresco or Santenay

Preheat gas or electric grill to hot. Sear meat about 2½ minutes on each side to seal in juices. Turn grill to medium-low and cook about 35 minutes; turn at least once. Combine cheese, Worcestershire sauce and chives. Cover tenderloin with cheese mixture. Grill 5 to 8 minutes. The meat will be medium-rare. Grill a little longer if desired, but never overcook.

# Jan's Beef Tenderloin
*Wonderful for rare beef lovers*

**Must prepare partially ahead**                    **8-10 servings**

½ cup dark rum
½ cup soy sauce
5 to 6 pounds beef tenderloin

WINE: Hermitage or Barolo

Combine rum and soy sauce to make marinade. Pour over tenderloin; marinate in refrigerator 12 hours.

Drain marinade and reserve. Preheat oven to 425 degrees. Bake tenderloin 20 minutes. Reduce heat to 300 degrees and bake 15 minutes longer. Refrigerate in marinade another 12 to 24 hours.

Drain marinade and reserve. Cook tenderloin on grill 15 minutes. Heat reserved marinade. Pour over tenderloin before serving.

# London Broil
*Tender and juicy*

**May not prepare ahead**                    **4-6 servings**

2 pounds London broil
2 tablespoons vegetable oil
garlic or garlic powder to taste
onion or onion powder to taste
salt to taste
pepper to taste
1 cup herb-seasoned
   stuffing mix

aluminum foil
heavy brown paper grocery
   bag

WINE: Red Burgundy or Rioja
   Reserva

Pierce London broil with a fork on both sides. Rub oil on each side of meat. Put garlic, onion, salt and pepper on top of meat. Press stuffing mix on top of meat. Place meat in pan made of aluminum foil; place in the grocery bag. Staple or use paper clips to close bag. Bake, in the bag, at 350 degrees for 45 minutes.

# Hamburger Noodle Stroganoff
*Great informal dinner*

May prepare ahead                                                6 servings

4 to 6 ounces uncooked egg
   noodles
¼ cup butter
½ cup chopped onion
1 garlic clove, minced
1 8-ounce can sliced
   mushrooms, drained
1½ pounds ground chuck
3 tablespoons flour
1 8-ounce can tomato sauce
¼ cup Burgundy
1 10½-ounce can condensed
   beef broth
1 teaspoon salt
¼ teaspoon pepper
1 cup sour cream
½ cup grated Parmesan cheese

WINE: Amarone or Zinfandel

Preheat oven to 375 degrees. Cook noodles according to package directions; drain. Melt butter in large skillet; sauté onion, garlic and mushrooms until onion is golden, about 5 minutes. Add beef and cook until browned. Remove from heat; stir in flour, tomato sauce, wine, beef broth, salt and pepper. Return to medium heat and simmer 10 minutes, stirring occasionally. Blend in sour cream; do not boil. Layer meat mixture with noodles in lightly greased 2-quart casserole. Top with cheese. Bake uncovered 25 minutes.

May be frozen.

*Never prick meat when cooking. Pricking allows juices to escape.*

# Million Dollar Chili

**Must prepare ahead**                    **10 servings**

¼ cup chopped beef suet
3 garlic cloves, minced
4 medium onions, chopped
1 medium green pepper,
    chopped
4 pounds ground chuck
salt to taste
pepper to taste
2 28-ounce cans peeled
    Italian tomatoes
3 15-ounce cans red beans
    in chili gravy
3 tablespoons chili powder
2 tablespoons ground cumin
1 tablespoon oregano
1 tablespoon Hungarian hot
    paprika
¾ cup dry red wine

Suggested Toppings:
chopped onions
grated cheese
sour cream
sliced black olives
taco chips

Melt suet in Dutch oven. Add garlic and onions; cook until golden. Add green pepper and ground chuck; cook just until meat loses color. Drain off grease. Mix in salt, pepper and tomatoes. Add beans, chili powder, cumin, oregano, paprika and wine, mixing after each addition. Simmer 1½ hours. Cool. Refrigerate, preferably for 2 days. Skim fat off top; reheat slowly. Serve with favorite toppings.

# Oriental Beef with Broccoli
*A nice, quick family meal*

**May not prepare ahead**                    **4 servings**

2 pounds flank steak, trimmed*
2 tablespoons vegetable oil
1 large bunch fresh broccoli,
   separated into florets
salt to taste
pepper to taste
½ cup soy sauce
2 tablespoons cornstarch
1 garlic clove, minced
¼ cup beef broth

*May substitute 4 deboned
 chicken breasts; substitute
 chicken broth for beef broth.

WINE: Chinon or Côtes-
      du-Rhône-Villages

Before cutting the steak, freeze it for 30 minutes to make it easier to slice. Slice across the grain into thin slices 1½ to 2 inches long and ¼ inch thick. Heat oil in heavy skillet or wok until very hot. Add beef and stir-fry for 3 minutes. Remove with a slotted spoon and set aside. Place broccoli in wok and stir-fry for 3 to 5 minutes. Return beef to wok. Combine remaining ingredients; pour over beef and broccoli. Combine well. Bring to a boil and simmer 1 minute, stirring constantly. Serve with rice.

*To keep cooked rice warm, place rice in colander over simmering water and cover with cloth or paper towels.*

# Texas Chili

**Must prepare partially ahead**                                      **8 servings**

**Chili:**
2 tablespoons vegetable oil
6 tablespoons flour
1 6-ounce can tomato paste
2 to 3 tablespoons chili powder
1 teaspoon cumin seed
1 teaspoon oregano
1 teaspoon salt
1 10½-ounce can condensed
   beef broth
1 or 2 garlic cloves, minced
3 pounds round steak, trimmed
   and cubed

Mix oil, flour, tomato paste, chili powder, spices and beef broth in a large crock pot. Stir meat into the mixture. Cook, covered, on high until it bubbles; turn to low and cook about 10 hours. Serve over rice with garnishes.

2 cups raw rice

Cook rice according to package directions.

**Garnishes:**
¼ head lettuce, shredded
1 medium onion, chopped
1 medium tomato, chopped
10 ounces cheddar cheese,
   shredded

**BEVERAGE: Ice Cold Beer**

# Picadillo

*Easy, attractive and colorful*

**May prepare ahead**                                    **4 servings**

2 medium onions, chopped
1 medium green pepper, chopped
2 large garlic cloves, finely chopped
¼ cup olive oil
1 pound ground chuck
1 tablespoon oregano
2 bay leaves
salt to taste
pepper to taste
1 8-ounce can tomato sauce
¼ cup ketchup
¼ cup stuffed green olives
1 tablespoon wine vinegar
2 tablespoons capers, optional
½ cup raisins, optional

**WINE: Barbera**

Sauté onions, green pepper and garlic in olive oil until tender. Add meat and stir with a fork to break up the pieces. Add oregano, bay leaves, salt and pepper; cook until meat is brown and tender. Add tomato sauce, ketchup, olives and vinegar, mixing well. Stir in capers and raisins, if desired. Simmer uncovered 30 minutes. Remove bay leaves.

Serve with black beans and yellow rice.

# Sausage Stuffed Meat Loaf
*A delicious microwave recipe*

**May prepare ahead**                    **8-10 servings**

1½ pounds ground beef
12 ounces bulk sausage
1 small onion, finely chopped
1 cup uncooked quick-cooking
   oats
2 eggs
1 teaspoon salt
¾ cup milk
1½ cups herb-seasoned
   stuffing mix
1 4-ounce can sliced
   mushrooms

WINE: Chianti or
      Bulgarian Merlot

Mix beef and sausage. Add onion and oats. Beat eggs slightly with salt; add to milk. Add milk-egg mixture to meats, mixing well. Prepare stuffing mix according to package directions; add mushrooms and set aside. Place ½ meat mixture in microwave-proof tube pan. Make a small indented area all the way around pan in center of meat mixture. Put stuffing into indentation; top with remaining meat mixture. Bake in microwave on high 17 to 20 minutes. Rotate dish after 10 minutes. Let stand 10 minutes before serving.

*Never freeze meat in the store wrapper; rewrap in freezer bags or paper to keep out air.*

# Steak au Poivre
*If you like steaks and pepper, you'll love this*

**May prepare partially ahead**                     **4 servings**

4 1¼-inch thick filets,
   6 to 8 ounces each
salt to taste
1 tablespoon peppercorns
3 tablespoons vegetable oil
2 tablespoons butter, divided
3 tablespoons finely chopped
   shallots
½ cup white wine or vermouth
½ cup heavy cream or
   sour cream

WINE: Cabernet Sauvignon
   or Côte Rôtie

Salt steaks. Crush peppercorns in plastic bag with mallet or rolling pin. Press the crushed peppercorns into both sides of steaks. Cover with wax paper. Let stand at least 10 minutes, preferably 2 to 3 hours. Heat oil over medium-high heat, in heavy skillet. Cook steaks 3 minutes, then turn. Cook 1½ to 3 minutes and remove steaks to heated serving platter. Keep warm while preparing sauce.

Pour fat from skillet. Add 1 tablespoon butter and shallots; cook until wilted. Add wine; cook on high until reduced by half. Add cream and cook 1 minute. Swirl in remaining butter; pour over steaks. Serve immediately.

# Steak Marinade
*Wonderful*

**May prepare ahead**                     **3 cups**

1½ cups vegetable oil
½ cup soy sauce
¼ cup Worcestershire sauce
2 tablespoons dry mustard
2¼ teaspoons salt
1 tablespoon freshly ground
   pepper
½ cup wine vinegar
1½ teaspoons dried parsley
   flakes
2 garlic cloves, crushed
⅓ cup lemon juice

Combine all ingredients. Marinate choice of meat in refrigerator 24 hours making sure meat is completely covered.

If marinade is drained immediately, it may be frozen and used one more time.

# Baked Chicken Salad

**May prepare partially ahead**                                     **6 servings**

2 cups diced, cooked chicken*
2 cups diced celery
1-1¹/2 cups mayonnaise
1 cup grated American
  cheese
¹/2 cup slivered almonds
1¹/2 teaspoons lemon juice
1 teaspoon grated onion
crushed potato chips

*May substitute shrimp or
turkey.

Mix chicken, celery, mayonnaise, cheese, almonds, lemon juice and onion. Put a layer of potato chips in bottom of a 2-quart casserole. Spoon on chicken mixture, then top with another layer of potato chips. Bake uncovered at 350 degrees for 45 minutes. Serve immediately.

# Chicken Cordon Bleu
*So easy, it can be a gourmet treat for a weekday meal*

**May prepare partially ahead**                                     **6 servings**

6 skinless, boneless chicken
  breast halves, 5 to 6 ounces
  each
6 1-ounce slices boiled ham
6 1-ounce slices Swiss cheese
1 cup flour
1 teaspoon salt
freshly ground pepper to taste
3 eggs, slightly beaten
1½ cups bread crumbs
2 tablespoons butter
2 tablespoons vegetable oil

WINE: Pomerol or Merlot

Pound chicken to ¹/2-inch thickness. Place a ham slice and a cheese slice on each chicken breast. Roll up each breast lengthwise; trim excess ham and cheese.

Mix flour, salt and pepper. Dip rolled breasts into seasoned flour, then beaten egg, then bread crumbs. Heat oil and butter in a large skillet. Sauté breasts 3 minutes per side, a total of 12 minutes. Chicken is done when it springs back when pressed with fingertip.

# Breast of Chicken Charente

*Enjoyed by everyone*

**May not prepare ahead**                    **4 servings**

¼ cup all-purpose flour
1 tablespoon dried tarragon
1½ teaspoons salt
½ teaspoon freshly ground
    pepper
4 skinless, boneless chicken
    breast halves, 5 to 6 ounces
    each
4 tablespoons unsalted butter
1 tablespoon vegetable oil
½ cup brandy
1 cup chicken broth
3 tablespoons Dijon mustard
2 tablespoons fresh lemon juice
¼ cup capers, drained

**WINE: Côte Rôtie or Barolo**

On a sheet of wax paper, combine flour, tarragon, salt and pepper. Lightly dredge chicken breasts in the mixture, shaking off excess.

In a large skillet, heat butter and oil over moderate heat. When the foam begins to subside, add chicken and sauté 3 minutes on each side or until lightly browned. Remove skillet from heat.

In a small saucepan, warm the brandy over moderate heat. Pour over chicken and return skillet to heat. Light brandy with a match. Shake the pan constantly until flames subside. Mix chicken broth, mustard and lemon juice. Add to chicken. Bring to a boil, cover and reduce heat to low. Simmer 7 to 10 minutes, turning once.

Arrange chicken breasts on a warm platter. Boil sauce over high heat for 1 to 2 minutes or until the sauce is reduced to a coating consistency slightly thicker than heavy cream. Pour sauce over chicken and sprinkle with capers.

# Chicken and Artichokes

**May prepare ahead**                    **8 servings**

1 to 2 sprigs parsley
1 celery top
1 carrot, quartered
1 bay leaf
2 teaspoons thyme, divided
1 tablespoon salt
¹/₄ tablespoon ground pepper
2 3-pound chickens
water or dry white wine
2 14-ounce cans marinated
   artichoke hearts, drained
¹/₄ cup butter
¹/₄ cup flour
3 cups shredded cheddar
   cheese
¹/₂ teaspoon nutmeg
¹/₂ cup fine dry bread crumbs
1 teaspoon savory
2 tablespoons butter
**WINE: Mâcon-Villages**

Place parsley, celery, carrot, bay leaf, 1 teaspoon thyme, salt, pepper, and chickens into large pot. Cover chickens with water or wine and simmer uncovered for 1 hour. Cool chicken and reserve 2 cups stock. Cut chicken into bitesize pieces. Arrange in a greased 3-quart casserole. Place marinated artichoke hearts on top of chicken. Set aside.

Melt ¹/₄ cup butter and blend in flour until smooth. Gradually add reserved chicken stock. Cook, stirring constantly, until thick and smooth. Stir in cheese and nutmeg. Pour over chicken and artichoke hearts. Mix bread crumbs, savory and 1 teaspoon thyme. Sprinkle mixture on top of cheese sauce. Dot crumbs with butter. Bake uncovered at 350 degrees for 30 minutes.

*Microwave a lemon, lime or orange 30 seconds before squeezing to get more juice.*

# Lemon Chicken
*Simplified chicken piccata — easy but fit for a candlelight dinner*

**May prepare partially ahead**

**6 servings**

6 skinless, boneless chicken
   breast halves, about 5 to 6
   ounces each
½ cup flour
4 tablespoons butter
juice of 1½ lemons
lemon slices for garnish

**WINE: California Riesling**

Pound chicken breast halves until thin; lightly flour. Melt butter in a large skillet on medium-high heat. Place breasts in skillet and add lemon juice. Sauté breasts until golden brown, about 3 minutes on each side.

Place breasts on a platter, garnish with lemon slices and spoon remaining lemon butter mixture over the breasts.

# Chicken and Broccoli Bake

**May prepare ahead**

**8 servings**

1 3-pound chicken, roasted and
   meat removed from bones
2 10-ounce packages frozen
   broccoli spears, cooked
   and drained
1 10¾-ounce can cream of
   mushroom soup
1 10¾-ounce can cream of
   chicken soup
¾ cup mayonnaise
1 tablespoon lemon juice
1 tablespoon prepared mustard
½ cup grated cheddar cheese
⅔ cup dry bread crumbs
1 tablespoon butter, melted

Preheat oven to 350 degrees. Alternate layers of cooked chicken and broccoli in 2-quart casserole. Combine soups, mayonnaise, lemon juice, mustard and cheese. Pour mixture over chicken and broccoli. Toss crumbs in butter and sprinkle over top of casserole. Bake 35 to 40 minutes until hot and bubbly.

# Chicken and Spinach Filling
*A great favorite*

**May prepare ahead**                              **6-8 servings**

4 tablespoons butter, divided
2 tablespoons dry vermouth,
    divided
2 cups chopped fresh spinach
1½ pounds skinless, boneless
    chicken breasts, cooked
    and cubed
2 ounces cream cheese, cubed
    and softened
2 tablespoons flour
¾ cup rich chicken stock
salt to taste
pepper to taste

Melt 2 tablespoons butter in large skillet. Add 1 tablespoon vermouth. Add spinach and toss until it begins to soften. Add chicken. Toss. Remove from heat, add cream cheese and cover until cheese is soft, about 3 to 5 minutes. Toss until even consistency is obtained. Set aside.

In saucepan, melt remaining 2 tablespoons butter. Add flour and cook, making a roux. Add remaining tablespoon of vermouth and chicken stock. Bring to a boil. Pour over chicken-spinach mixture. Combine well. Season with salt and pepper.

Use as a filling for crêpes or serve over noodles.

# Chicken and Wild Rice Casserole

*Delicious, good company entrée*

**May prepare ahead**                                    **6-8 servings**

1 cup water
1 cup white wine
1 medium onion, chopped
½ cup diced celery
½ teaspoon salt
½ teaspoon curry powder or
   to taste
2 3-pound chickens, cut up
2 6-ounce packages long grain
   and wild rice
¼ cup margarine
⅓ cup sliced fresh mushrooms
1 10¾-ounce can cream of
   mushroom soup
1 cup sour cream

**WINE: White Châteauneuf-
   du-Pape or White
   Zinfandel**

In a Dutch oven, combine water, wine, onion, celery, salt, curry powder and chicken. Cover and cook over medium heat for 1 hour or until chicken is tender. Remove chicken with slotted spoon, reserving vegetable-liquid mixture. Debone and skin chicken and cut into bite-size pieces.

Cook rice according to package directions, using reserved liquid and vegetables. Add water, if needed, to complete the amount required for the rice.

Melt margarine in small frying pan. Sauté mushrooms until tender. Combine chicken, rice, mushrooms, soup and sour cream. Place in a 9 x 13-inch baking dish; bake uncovered in preheated 350 degree oven for 1 hour.

Serve with glazed carrots and spinach salad. Casserole freezes well up to 1 month.

*Stock may be frozen, but because freezing causes ingredients to separate it should be brought to a boil before using.*

# Chicken Enchilada Casserole

May prepare ahead                                           8 servings

4 to 5 whole chicken breasts,
   ¾ to 1-pound each
1 10¾-ounce can cream of
   chicken soup
1 10¾-ounce can cream of
   mushroom soup
1 4-ounce can chopped chilies,
   drained
½ to 1 teaspoon chili powder
4 teaspoons minced onion
¼ teaspoon black pepper
¼ teaspoon hot pepper sauce
⅛ teaspoon garlic powder
1 cup chicken broth
1 10-ounce package frozen peas
   and carrots, thawed
8 ounces cheddar or Monterey
   Jack cheese, grated
4 cups corn chips
1 2.8-ounce can onion rings

Steam or simmer chicken breasts until tender, about 30 minutes; do NOT overcook. Remove from pan and cool. Bone and skin breasts; cut meat into large chunks.

Preheat oven to 350 degrees. Blend soups, chilies, chili powder, onion, pepper, hot pepper sauce, garlic powder, chicken broth and peas and carrots. In a greased 9 x 13-inch baking dish, layer 2 cups corn chips, ½ of chicken chunks and 4 ounces of grated cheese. Repeat. Top with soup mixture. Cover with canned onion rings. Bake uncovered 40 minutes.

May be made ahead and frozen. Thaw and bake.

# Chicken Lo Mein
*Low calorie and eye appealing*

**May prepare partially ahead**                    **6 servings**

6 to 8 large skinless, boneless
  chicken breast halves
3 tablespoons soy sauce
1 tablespoon dry sherry
2 teaspoons cornstarch
1 8-ounce package linguine
1 chicken bouillon cube
½ cup hot water
¼ cup olive oil
½ pound mushrooms, sliced
¼ pound snow peas
2 green onions, cut in 2-inch
  pieces
1 large red pepper, thinly
  sliced in strips

**WINE: California Chablis**

Slice breasts on slant into ⅛ to ¼-inch slices. Mix soy sauce, sherry and cornstarch in medium bowl. Blend until smooth. Add chicken slices and set aside.

Cook linguine according to package directions; drain. Set aside. Dissolve bouillon cube in hot water; set aside.

Meanwhile, heat oil in wok or skillet over medium-high heat. Add mushrooms, snow peas, green onions and red pepper. Stir-fry until tender-crisp, approximately 3 to 5 minutes. Do NOT overcook. Remove with slotted spoon to a bowl.

Increase heat to high. Add chicken mixture to skillet and stir-fry until chicken is tender, approximately 2 to 3 minutes. Add bouillon. Heat to boiling, stirring to loosen brown bits from bottom of skillet. Return vegetables to skillet; a gravy will form quickly. Add linguine and heat mixture thoroughly, being sure NOT to overcook vegetables. Toss gently and well.

# Chicken Marengo

**May prepare partially ahead**                    **4 servings**

1 2½ to 3-pound chicken,
  cut up
2 tablespoons butter
2 tablespoons olive oil
2 medium onions, thinly sliced
1½ tablespoons flour
1 14½-ounce can tomatoes,
  drained and cut in chunks
2 tablespoons tomato paste
1 cup chicken broth
½ cup dry white wine
1 to 2 garlic cloves, finely
  minced
1 teaspoon crushed oregano
½ pound mushrooms, thickly
  sliced
½ cup pitted black olives
herb salt to taste
pepper to taste
3 tablespoons chopped fresh
  parsley for garnish
1 teaspoon grated lemon rind
  for garnish

**WINE: Rubesco or Tignanello**

In Dutch oven, sauté chicken in butter and oil until lightly browned. Remove chicken from pan. In same pan, sauté onions until golden. Drain off excess oil. Sprinkle onions with flour. Add tomatoes, tomato paste, broth, wine, garlic, oregano and chicken; mix well. Cover and simmer 30 minutes. Stir in mushrooms and olives. Cover and simmer 15 minutes. Season with herb salt and pepper.

Transfer to a heated platter and sprinkle with parsley and lemon rind. Serve with rice or buttered noodles.

*Freeze citrus rinds for easier grating.*

# Chicken Tetrazzini
*Well worth the time and effort*

**May prepare ahead**                                    **10 servings**

1 4½-pound chicken
4 cups water
1 garlic clove, sliced
3 teaspoons salt, divided
1 medium onion, chopped
4 celery stalks and leaves,
   chopped
½ pound spaghetti
6 tablespoons butter, divided
½ pound mushrooms, sliced
2 tablespoons lemon juice
1 8-ounce can water chestnuts,
   sliced
2 tablespoons flour
¼ teaspoon paprika
½ teaspoon pepper
¼ teaspoon nutmeg
1 cup heavy cream
⅔ cup grated Parmesan
   cheese
paprika for garnish

**WINE: California Chardonnay
   or Champagne**

Cook chicken over medium heat in water, garlic, salt, onion and celery. Simmer covered 1 to 1½ hours, adding water if needed. Remove chicken to a bowl, reserving 2½ cups of broth. Remove meat from chicken and cut into chunks.

Cook spaghetti according to package directions; drain. Place in a greased 9 x 13-inch baking dish.

Heat 3 tablespoons butter. Add mushrooms, lemon juice, water chestnuts and ½ teaspoon salt. Sauté until tender but not brown. Toss sautéed ingredients with spaghetti.

Preheat oven to 400 degrees. In sauté pan, melt remaining butter. Stir in flour, paprika, ½ teaspoon salt, pepper and nutmeg. Slowly stir in the 2½ cups reserved broth. Cook, stirring constantly, until thickened. Add cream; mix well. Pour over chicken. Add chicken mixture to spaghetti and toss well. Top entire casserole with Parmesan cheese and sprinkle with paprika as desired. Bake uncovered for 25 minutes. Serve immediately.

May be frozen before or after baking.

# Chicken with Dill Sauce

**May prepare ahead**          **4 servings**

1 carrot, chopped
1 medium onion, chopped
1 stalk celery, chopped
3 cups water
4 chicken breast halves,
   unboned and unskinned

In a large heavy pan, bring vegetables and water to a boil. Add breasts; return liquid to a boil. Immediately reduce heat to simmer. Do NOT let liquid boil. Cook 12 to 15 minutes until juices of chicken run yellow when pierced. Cool chicken in the stock. When cool, debone and skin chicken breasts; place meat in a 7 x 11-inch baking dish. Strain vegetables from liquid and reserve ½ cup stock for dill sauce. Pour dill sauce over chicken. Bake in a 350 degree oven 20 minutes or refrigerate and serve later, baking in a 350 degree oven 45 minutes until bubbly.

**Dill Sauce:**
½ cup cold reserved chicken
   stock
2 tablespoons butter
1 tablespoon cornstarch
2 tablespoons fresh lemon
   juice
1 teaspoon dill weed
3 to 4 drops hot pepper sauce
½ teaspoon salt
½ teaspoon sugar

Mix all ingredients in a saucepan. Heat to boiling, stirring constantly. Reduce heat and cook, stirring, until slightly thickened.

# Chicken with Watercress
*Cooked in Florida orange juice*

**May prepare partially ahead**                    **4 servings**

1 pound skinless, boneless
   chicken breasts
2 tablespoons butter or
   margarine
4 green onions, trimmed and
   sliced
1¼ cups chicken broth
1 tablespoon brown sugar
3 teaspoons finely shredded
   orange rind, divided
1½ cups orange juice, divided
6 medium carrots, cut
   diagonally into ¼-inch slices
4 teaspoons cornstarch
salt to taste
1 medium-size bunch
   watercress, washed, dried
   and stems cut to 2 inches

**WINE: French Chablis**

Slice chicken into ½-inch strips. Heat butter in a wok or skillet. Add chicken and green onions; stir-fry 5 minutes. Stir in chicken broth, brown sugar, 2 teaspoons orange rind, 1 cup orange juice and carrots. Heat to boiling. Cover and simmer 8 minutes until carrots are tender-crisp.

In a cup, stir remaining orange juice and cornstarch until mixture is smooth. Stir into wok. Cook, stirring constantly, until mixture thickens and boils 1 minute. Add salt, if needed. Place watercress in a ring over chicken and cover. Steam 1 minute. Sprinkle remaining rind over chicken. Serve immediately.

*Partially freeze raw meats before slicing thinly.*

# Chicken with Zucchini
*Terrific company dish*

**Must prepare partially ahead**                    **4 servings**

4 skinless, boneless chicken
    breast halves, about 5 to 6
    ounces each
5 tablespoons olive oil
4 tablespoons lemon juice
pepper to taste
1 bay leaf
4 tablespoons butter or
    margarine
1 pound small zucchini
½ cup finely chopped onion
1 6-ounce can tomato paste
1 teaspoon salt
1 cup grated Parmesan cheese,
    divided
2 eggs

**WINE: Light Zinfandel
    or Barbera**

Place chicken breasts in shallow glass dish. Combine olive oil, lemon juice, pepper and bay leaf. Pour over chicken; marinate 1 hour.

Melt butter in skillet; sauté marinated breasts until golden brown, about 3 minutes on each side. Do not overcook. Remove to 2-quart dish. Wash zucchini, dry and slice into rounds ¼-inch thick. Add onion to skillet in which chicken was sautéed. Cook 5 minutes, stirring, until pale yellow. Add zucchini, sauté about 3 minutes. Add tomato paste and salt. Cook uncovered on low heat 10 minutes. Pour sauce over chicken in baking dish. Sprinkle with ½ of the cheese. Beat eggs with remaining cheese and pour over chicken. Bake in preheated 375 degree oven 15 to 20 minutes until cheese crust is golden brown and sauce is bubbly.

# Crab and Mushroom Chicken Breasts

May prepare partially ahead                    **4-6 servings**

½ cup butter or margarine
8 skinless, boneless chicken
    breast halves, 5 to 6 ounces
    each
2 medium carrots, cut in
    2 x ¼-inch strips
1 cup sliced fresh mushrooms
1 8-ounce package frozen
    crab, thawed, drained and
    cut into chunks (do not use
    canned crab)
¼ cup chopped fresh parsley
¼ cup white wine or apple
    juice
1 teaspoon salt
½ teaspoon tarragon leaves
paprika for garnish

**WINE: California Riesling**

In heavy skillet melt butter over medium heat. Add chicken breasts and carrots. Cook until chicken is lightly browned on both sides. Add mushrooms, crab, parsley, wine, salt and tarragon; stir to blend. Continue cooking over medium heat, stirring occasionally, until fork tender. Remove to platter and sprinkle each breast with paprika.

# Marinated Sliced Chicken Breasts
*A perfect light meal*

**Must prepare partially ahead**                           **4 servings**

1 lemon
4 to 6 skinless, boneless
    chicken breast halves, about
    5 to 6 ounces each
1 teaspoon salt
⅛ teaspoon pepper
½ teaspoon rosemary or thyme
1 to 2 garlic cloves, minced
½ cup olive oil or clarified
    butter, divided
½ cup fresh bread crumbs
¼ cup grated Parmesan cheese

WINE: Beaujolais or California
    Chenin Blanc

Remove the lemon zest and mince. Place the minced zest over the chicken breasts along with 1 tablespoon lemon juice. Combine salt, pepper, rosemary or thyme, garlic and ¼ cup olive oil or clarified butter; add to the chicken. Mix well and let chicken marinate 30 minutes.

Scrape off marinade and dry chicken on paper towels. Cut into slices about 2 inches long and ⅜-inch wide. Combine bread crumbs and Parmesan cheese. Coat chicken slices in the bread crumb mixture. Heat skillet on high with remaining ¼ cup oil or butter. Sauté chicken, tossing frequently until done, about 2 to 3 minutes.

*To clarify butter, place butter in saucepan over low heat. When butter has melted, a milky substance will rise in small bubbles to the surface. Skim this off as it foams. Remove clarified butter from heat and refrigerate. The foam can be used for seasoning vegetables.*

# Savory Southern Chicken Pie

May prepare ahead                                    **6 servings**

**Filling:**
8 ounces bulk pork sausage
4 tablespoons butter or
    margarine
⅓ cup flour
¼ teaspoon salt
⅛ teaspoon pepper
1 cup chicken broth
⅔ cup milk
2 cups cooked, cubed chicken
    or turkey
1 8-ounce can small early peas

Brown sausage and drain. Set aside. Using same pan, blend butter, flour, salt and pepper. Stir over low heat until mixture is a smooth paste. Stir in chicken broth and milk; cook until thickened and bubbly. Add chicken, sausage and peas. Mix thoroughly and remove from heat. Pour into a 10-inch deep dish pie plate.

**Pastry:**
1 cup flour
½ teaspoon salt
½ teaspoon pepper
¼ to ½ teaspoon celery seed
⅓ cup shortening
2 teaspoons cold water

**WINE: Beaujolais Villages
    or Napa Gamay**

Combine flour, salt, pepper and celery seed. Cut in shortening until mixture is well blended. Sprinkle in water and blend with a fork. Roll out dough ⅛-inch thick. Place on top of pie, trimming where necessary. Bake in a preheated 425 degree oven for 25 minutes.

# Chicken Rosé

**May prepare ahead**                                                    **6-8 servings**

2 3-pound chickens, cut up
¼ cup flour
salt to taste
pepper to taste
5 tablespoons butter, divided
3 garlic cloves, minced
4 tablespoons minced fresh
   onion or scallions
1 cup rosé wine
2 teaspoons instant chicken
   bouillon
1 tablespoon tomato paste
¼ teaspoon poultry seasoning
½ teaspoon thyme leaves
1 1-pound jar pearl onions,
   drained

**WINE: California Grenache
   Rosé**

Preheat oven to 350 degrees. Dust chicken lightly in flour. Sprinkle with salt and pepper. Melt 3 tablespoons butter in an 11 x 14-inch roasting pan. Coat chicken with the butter and arrange in 1 layer. Bake 20 minutes.

Sauté garlic and onion in remaining 2 tablespoons butter. Add wine, bouillon, tomato paste, poultry seasoning, thyme, salt and pepper; stir to blend. Pour over chicken. Loosely cover pan with foil and bake 1 hour. Remove cover and add pearl onions, coating them with sauce. Bake uncovered 15 minutes. Remove chicken pieces to a heated platter and pour sauce over chicken.

Can be made day before and reheated.

*When frying, broiling or grilling meats, turn only once to insure maximum juiciness.*

# Chicken Neapolitan

May prepare ahead                                        **4 servings**

4 skinless, boneless chicken
   breasts
2 teaspoons salt
½ teaspoon pepper
4 tablespoons olive oil
10 small white onions
½ pound mushrooms,
   quartered
1 garlic clove, chopped
1 10¾-ounce can tomato
   bisque soup
¾ cup dry red wine
¾ teaspoon oregano
¾ teaspoon basil
2 tablespoons minced parsley
10 pitted ripe olives, sliced

Sprinkle chicken breasts with salt and pepper; let stand 5 minutes. In a large skillet, sauté chicken in hot oil for 5 minutes; turn. Add onions, mushrooms and garlic; cook 5 minutes. Combine soup, wine, oregano and basil; pour over chicken. Bring to boiling, lower heat and cover. Cook 15 minutes or until chicken is tender. Stir in parsley and olives. Serve over rice.

**WINE: Barolo or Red
      Burgundy**

# Spicy Barbecue Sauce
*Great on ribs, pork and chicken*

May prepare ahead                                        **2½ cups**

½ cup minced onion
½ cup minced celery
1 garlic clove, minced
3 tablespoons butter
3 tablespoons brown sugar
2 tablespoons cider vinegar
1 cup ketchup
1 cup beef broth
2 teaspoons Worcestershire
   sauce
1½ teaspoons Dijon mustard
salt to taste
pepper to taste
cayenne pepper to taste
1 tablespoon lemon juice

Sauté onion, celery and garlic in butter until soft. Add brown sugar and vinegar. Cook over medium heat until sugar is dissolved. Add ketchup, beef broth, Worcestershire sauce, mustard and seasonings. Bring to a boil over moderate heat, stirring. Reduce heat. Simmer for 25 minutes, stirring occasionally. Stir in lemon juice.

May be kept in refrigerator for 3 to 4 weeks.

# Roast Stuffed Duckling with Cranberry Orange Sauce

**May prepare partially ahead**                          **4 servings**

1 4½ to 5-pound duckling
¾ teaspoon salt, divided
1½ cups thinly sliced celery
¼ cup chopped onion
2 tablespoons butter or
   margarine
2½ cups ½-inch bread cubes
½ cup chopped pecans
2 tablespoons orange juice
1 teaspoon sugar
1 teaspoon grated orange rind

Sauce:
1 cup water
½ cup sugar
2 cups cranberries
¼ cup orange juice
2 teaspoons cornstarch
2 teaspoons grated orange rind
½ cup orange sections

WINE: Alsatian or Australian
   Gewürztraminer

Wash and drain duckling; dry skin gently with paper towels. Sprinkle body and neck cavities with ½ teaspoon salt. Cook celery and onion in butter until onion is soft. Add bread cubes, pecans, orange juice, sugar, orange rind and remaining ¼ teaspoon salt; toss lightly. Fill neck and body cavities loosely with stuffing. Skewer neck skin to back. Cover opening of body cavity with foil and tie legs together loosely. Place on rack in shallow roasting pan. Bake at 325 degrees until drumstick meat is tender, about 3 hours. Serve duckling with sauce.

Combine water and sugar and bring to a boil; boil 5 minutes. Add cranberries; cook until they pop, about 5 minutes. Combine orange juice and cornstarch; stir until smooth. Add to cranberries; cook until clear and thick. Stir in orange rind and sections.

# Fruited Game Hens

**May prepare partially ahead**           **6 servings**

6 Cornish game hens, 1 to 1¼
  pounds each
2 tablespoons orange juice
2 tablespoons sugar
4 tablespoons butter or
  margarine, melted
2 tablespoons lemon juice
½ teaspoon salt

Preheat oven to 425 degrees. Truss the hens and place them on a rack in a foil-lined roasting pan. Combine orange juice, sugar, butter, lemon juice and salt. Spoon over the hens. Roast 45 minutes to 1 hour or until tender and golden brown. Baste once during roasting with pan drippings. Reserve pan drippings for use in Wine Fruit Sauce.

**Optional Garnishes:**
sweet pickled orange wedges
sweet pickled watermelon
sweet pickled kumquats

Serve with Wine Fruit Sauce and optional garnishes.

**Wine Fruit Sauce:**
½ cup sugar
1 cup orange juice
½ cup dry white wine
pan drippings
2 tablespoons cornstarch
½ teaspoon grated lemon peel
½ teaspoon grated orange peel
½ teaspoon salt
½ teaspoon whole cloves
¼ cup lemon juice

**WINE: Moselle Riesling
      Spätlese**

Caramelize sugar in a large heavy pan by heating over low heat and stirring occasionally until sugar is a medium brown but not burned. Heat orange juice to boiling; pour over caramel; heat and stir until well blended. Mix wine, pan drippings, cornstarch, lemon and orange peels, salt and cloves; stir into hot syrup mixture. Cook and stir over medium heat until mixture is thick and clear. Add lemon juice and heat through. Remove cloves. Serve hot.

# Braised Quail

May prepare partially ahead

4 servings

⅓ cup flour
½ teaspoon salt
¼ teaspoon pepper
8 quail
¾ cup butter, divided
3 to 4 garlic cloves, split
1 lemon, sliced
¼ to ½ cup sherry or
 white wine
1 cup water

Blend flour, salt and pepper. Flour quail. In Dutch oven, melt ¼ cup butter; brown quail. Set aside quail and discard butter. Melt remaining butter in Dutch oven. Add quail, garlic, lemon and sherry or white wine. Add water to cover quail midway. Simmer covered about 1 hour or until quail are tender.

WINE: Moselle Spätlese or
 Saint-Emilion

# Lamb Leg Roast
*The gravy makes this special*

Must prepare partially ahead

8-10 servings

1 6 to 8-pound leg of lamb
1 garlic clove, cut into slivers
juice of 1 lemon
1 cup water
1 cup dark brown sugar
1 teaspoon salt
½ teaspoon freshly ground
 black pepper
1 teaspoon nutmeg
1 teaspoon dry mustard
pinch of cayenne pepper
½ cup wine vinegar

Make small slits in lamb; insert slivers of garlic and rub with lemon juice. Let stand 1 hour. Preheat oven to 500 degrees. Mix remaining ingredients to make gravy. Bake lamb uncovered 20 minutes. Reduce temperature to 325 degrees; add gravy. Bake uncovered 2 to 3 hours, basting every 20 minutes.

Serve with wild rice, gravy and mint jelly.

WINE: Red Bordeaux

# Barbecued Leg of Lamb
*Delicious*

**Must prepare partially ahead**                    8 servings

**Marinade:**
**1 tablespoon paprika**
**2 teaspoons sugar**
**1 teaspoon salt**
**dash of cayenne pepper**
**⅓ cup red wine vinegar**
**1 egg**
**1 cup vegetable oil**
**2 tablespoons dry mustard**
**1 teaspoon onion salt**
**1 teaspoon Accent**
**1 teaspoon soy sauce**
**1 teaspoon ginger**
**2 teaspoons brown sugar**
**2 teaspoons bacon drippings**

**1 8-pound leg of lamb, boned
and butterflied**

**WINE: Zinfandel or
Côtes-du-Rhône**

Mix paprika, sugar, salt and pepper; add vinegar and egg. Beat with electric mixer, adding oil in slow stream. Mix in remaining marinade ingredients. Marinate meat 3 hours or more at room temperature, turning often.

Grill lamb 1 hour, 30 minutes on each side, basting with marinade frequently. Lamb is best cooked until slightly pink.

# Roast Pork, Cuban Style

**May not prepare ahead**                                    **4 servings**

1 3-pound pork roast
3 to 5 garlic cloves, cut in
   small pieces
salt to taste
pepper to taste
oregano to taste
lime juice or sour orange juice
   (oranges from a sour orange
   tree)

Make slits all over the roast and insert garlic. Salt and pepper; sprinkle with oregano. Roast in a 325 degree oven 40 minutes per pound, basting frequently with lime or sour orange juice.

WINE: California Merlot or
    Cabernet Sauvignon

# Fileto Saltedo

*A wonderful authentic Spanish dish from Tampa*

**May prepare partially ahead**                              **4 servings**

2 medium potatoes, peeled
½ cup olive oil
1 small onion, chopped
1 green pepper, chopped
1 garlic clove, minced
1 medium ripe tomato, diced
¼ pound cooked ham, diced
3 1½-ounce chorizos, sliced
   (Spanish sausage)
2 pounds cubed beef
salt to taste
3 tablespoons tomato sauce
¼ cup small peas, cooked
1 pimento, sliced in thin strips
¼ cup sherry

Cut potatoes into small cubes; fry in hot oil in large skillet. Remove potatoes from oil and set aside. In same skillet, sauté onion, green pepper and garlic until onion is transparent. Add tomato and sauté until vegetables are soft. Remove vegetables from skillet; set aside. Sauté ham and chorizos 5 minutes. Add beef; sear quickly. Add potatoes, salt and green pepper mixture. Stir in tomato sauce. Cook according to preferred doneness of beef. When meat is done, arrange peas and pimento on top and pour in sherry. Serve with yellow rice.

WINE: Côtes-du-Rhône

# Roast Pork with Herbs
*A savory entrée*

**May not prepare ahead**                                    **6 servings**

1 2½-pound boned, rolled and
   tied pork loin roast
2 to 3 garlic cloves, cut
   into slivers
½ teaspoon thyme leaves
¼ teaspoon sage
salt to taste
1 medium onion, finely
   chopped
1½ cups chicken broth
1 tablespoon cornstarch
1 tablespoon water

**WINE: White or Red Rioja**

Place meat in small roasting pan. Make slits all over roast and insert garlic. Rub thyme and sage onto meat. Sprinkle lightly with salt. Distribute chopped onion around meat and add ¼ cup broth. Bake, uncovered, at 325 degrees 2 hours or until meat thermometer inserted in center of roast registers 170 degrees. After 1 hour, pour remaining 1¼ cups broth into pan; stir to free any browned particles. Baste meat once or twice. When meat is done, transfer to serving platter. Place roasting pan over high heat and stir as juices come to a boil. Combine cornstarch and water, making a smooth paste. Add to pan a little at a time, stirring constantly, until sauce is of desired consistency. Pour sauce into a bowl and pass with meat.

*For easier carving, let roasts stand for 15 minutes after removing from oven.*

# Sweet and Sour Pork
*Very flavorful*

**May prepare partially ahead**                    **4 servings**

1 to 1½ pounds lean pork,
   thinly sliced

Marinade:
1 teaspoon salt
2 teaspoons soy sauce
2 teaspoons cornstarch

Mix marinade ingredients in a medium-sized bowl. Add pork and mix well; let stand 20 minutes.

Sweet and Sour Sauce:
½ cup water
⅓ cup sugar
⅓ cup white vinegar
1 tablespoon cornstarch
1 tablespoon soy sauce

Combine ingredients for sweet and sour sauce in a small saucepan. Cook over high heat, stirring constantly, until clear and thick. Set aside.

Sweet and Sour Pork:
2 tablespoons vegetable oil
marinated pork (above)
½ cup thinly sliced carrots
2 tablespoons water
1 8-ounce can pineapple
   chunks, drained
sweet and sour sauce (above)
3 green onions, sliced in
   1-inch lengths
1 small green pepper, cubed

Heat wok to high. Add oil and heat until very hot. Remove pork from marinade and stir-fry until white. Add carrots and water; cover and cook 2 minutes. Add pineapple and sweet and sour sauce; bring to a boil. Add onion and pepper. Cook 30 seconds or until bubbly. Serve immediately.

WINE: Dry Chenin Blanc

# Shashlik of Pork

*A savory skewered pork dish*

**May prepare partially ahead**                    **2 servings**

1 pound pork tenderloin
12 small pitted prunes
12 pineapple chunks
1 cup chicken broth
4 wooden skewers

Preheat oven to 325 degrees. Bake pork 45 minutes or until it reaches an internal temperature of 175 degrees. Cool; cut into 1-inch cubes. Alternate pork cubes, prunes and pineapple on skewers. Lay prepared skewers in 7 x 11-inch baking dish. Add chicken broth; cover and refrigerate until 45 minutes before serving. Bake at 350 degrees for 45 minutes. Serve with hot apricot sauce.

**Hot Apricot Sauce:**
1 cup Burgundy
6 tablespoons brown sugar
2 tablespoons wine vinegar
1½ ounces dried apricots, chopped
1 teaspoon dry mustard
1 tablespoon cornstarch
1 tablespoon pork drippings or butter

Combine Burgundy, sugar and vinegar in a saucepan. Bring to a boil, then lower heat and simmer 10 to 15 minutes. Mix apricots, mustard and cornstarch in a bowl. Add to wine mixture and simmer, stirring until sauce is clear and thick, about 5 minutes. Stir in drippings or butter.

**WINE: Chilled Beaujolais Villages**

165

# Ham Steak with Pineapple Glaze
*Great cold for picnics*

**May prepare ahead**                    **4 servings**

1 1-inch thick ham slice,
   about 2 pounds

Preheat oven to 325 degrees. Bake ham steak in a shallow baking pan until heated through. When ham is heated, pour on pineapple glaze. Bake 20 minutes.

**Pineapple Glaze:**
1 cup packed light brown sugar
1 tablespoon cornstarch
¼ teaspoon salt
1 8½-ounce can crushed
   pineapple, undrained
2 tablespoons lemon juice
1 tablespoon prepared mustard

Combine brown sugar, cornstarch and salt in a small saucepan. Stir in pineapple, lemon juice and mustard. Cook over medium heat, stirring constantly, until mixture thickens and boils. Boil and stir 1 minute. Makes 1¾ cups.

WINE: German or Washington
   State Spätlese

# Hot Mustard Sauce

**May prepare ahead**                    **1½ cups**

¼ cup sugar
¼ cup dry mustard
3 eggs, well beaten
½ cup cider vinegar
½ cup heavy cream
salt to taste

Combine sugar and mustard. Add remaining ingredients and mix well. Cook in top of double boiler until thick. It will thicken some as it cools.

Good on ham, egg rolls, sandwiches or in deviled eggs.

# Veal Scallops Italienne
### *Well worth the effort*

**May prepare partially ahead**                    **6-8 servings**

4 medium zucchini
10 to 12 tablespoons butter,
   divided
½ teaspoon salt
pepper to taste
5 medium tomatoes, peeled
   and thickly sliced
2 teaspoons chopped garlic
8 large scallops of veal*,
   pounded very thin
flour for dredging
½ pound Swiss cheese,
   thickly sliced
3 tablespoons brandy
2 tablespoons flour
1 cup chicken broth
2 tablespoons sherry
⅓ cup freshly grated Parmesan
   cheese

*May substitute 8 to 10 large
  chicken breast halves, skinned,
  deboned and pounded very
  thin.

**WINE: Pinot Grigio
      or Bardolino**

Wash and trim zucchini; cut in half lengthwise and then slice ½ inch thick. Melt 2 tablespoons butter in skillet. Add zucchini, salt and pepper. Cover tightly and cook over low heat for 15 minutes, shaking pan occasionally. Place zucchini into a greased 8 x 12-inch baking dish. In same skillet, melt 4 tablespoons butter. Sauté ½ the tomatoes for 2 minutes; turn slices and sprinkle with ½ the garlic; sauté 2 minutes longer. Arrange tomato slices on top of zucchini. Repeat with remaining tomatoes and garlic. Pour all juices remaining in skillet over tomatoes.

Coat veal with flour; season with salt and pepper. In same skillet, heat 2 tablespoons butter and sauté 2 or 3 slices of veal at a time for 2 minutes on each side or until lightly browned, adding more butter to skillet if needed.

Arrange meat and Swiss cheese on top of vegetables. Add brandy to the skillet; ignite brandy and let flame die out. Add remaining 2 tablespoons butter, and when melted add 2 tablespoons flour. Gradually stir in chicken broth. Cook, stirring, until slightly thickened. Stir in sherry. Spoon sauce over meat and cheese and sprinkle with Parmesan cheese. Bake at 350 degrees for 30 minutes.

May cover loosely with foil and refrigerate until ready to bake. If chilled, bake approximately 40 minutes or until top bubbles.

# Veal Scallops with Mushrooms and Tomatoes
*Elegant and impressive*

**May prepare partially ahead**                          **6 servings**

1½ teaspoons salt
¼ teaspoon freshly ground
  pepper
½ cup flour
2 pounds veal scallops,
  ¼-inch thick
5 tablespoons butter, divided
2 tablespoons olive oil
1½ pounds mushrooms, sliced
2 tablespoons finely chopped
  shallots or onions
¾ cup beef broth
¾ cup dry white wine
1 large tomato, peeled, seeded
  and diced
1 teaspoon tarragon
½ teaspoon savory
½ teaspoon dry mustard
2 tablespoons chopped fresh
  parsley

WINE: California or
      Australian Cabernet
      Sauvignon

Mix salt and pepper with flour; spread mixture on wax paper and dip veal, coating lightly. Using a large skillet with cover, melt 3 tablespoons butter with olive oil. When it begins to bubble, add veal so that the pieces do not touch. Cook over moderate heat 3 minutes on each side or until golden brown. Add more butter to skillet as needed. Place cooked veal in a bowl. Add remaining 2 tablespoons butter to skillet. Add mushrooms; sauté until barely golden but still firm. Remove and put into bowl with the veal. Put shallots, broth and wine in skillet; bring to a boil, lower heat and whisk to loosen the particles at the bottom of the pan. Add tomato, tarragon, savory and mustard. Return veal, mushrooms and accumulated juices to skillet. Cook, covered, over low heat 30 minutes, turning occasionally. Serve on warm platter; sprinkle with chopped parsley.

# Veal with Seafood
*Heavenly*

**May not prepare ahead**                    **6 servings**

1½ pounds veal cutlets
1 teaspoon salt
1 teaspoon white pepper
3 tablespoons flour
6 tablespoons butter, divided
1 tablespoon olive oil
2 tablespoons chopped green
  onion
½ cup dry white wine
1 cup heavy cream
½ pound mushrooms, sliced
1 tablespoon lemon juice
2 tablespoons chopped parsley
¼ pound shrimp, peeled,
  deveined and cooked
½ pound crabmeat

WINE: Rhine Spätlese
     or Auslese

Pat cutlets dry with paper towels. Combine salt, pepper and flour. Dredge cutlets, shaking off excess flour. In a large heavy skillet, melt 3 tablespoons butter with oil. When hot, sauté cutlets 2 minutes on each side. Remove to heated platter and keep warm. Reduce heat and sauté onion 1 minute; remove from pan. Add wine and deglaze pan over high heat until liquid is reduced by half, about 2 minutes. Reduce to low heat. Add cream and simmer 4 minutes. Add mushrooms and cook 3 minutes. Add lemon juice and 1 tablespoon parsley; cook 1 minute. Pour sauce over veal.

In a separate pan, melt 3 tablespoons butter and toss shrimp and crabmeat until warm, about 2 minutes. Spoon on top of veal and sprinkle with remaining parsley.

*When coating meat or chicken with flour or breading mix, chill the meat for an hour or two. The coating will adhere better.*

# Veal with Lemon and Brandy
*Quick and elegant*

**May not prepare ahead**                    **2 servings**

¾ to 1 pound veal scaloppine
2 tablespoons butter
½ cup flour
1 tablespoon lemon juice
2 tablespoons brandy
1 tablespoon chopped fresh
    parsley
lemon slices for garnish

WINE: Saint-Véran or
       Pouilly-Fuissé

Dry veal on paper towels. In large skillet, heat butter until very hot but not brown. Dip veal in flour and pat off excess. Brown veal in heated butter 3 minutes on each side. Remove veal; place on warmed serving dish. Add lemon juice and brandy to butter in skillet. Simmer 2 minutes and pour sauce over veal. Garnish with parsley and lemon.

# Veal Scaloppine

**May not prepare ahead**                    **4 servings**

1 pound veal cutlets
salt to taste
pepper to taste
flour for dredging
1 cup thinly sliced mushrooms
½ cup butter, divided
½ cup lemon juice
½ cup Sauterne

WINE: Alsatian Riesling
      or White Rioja

Sprinkle veal with salt and pepper. Dredge in flour. Sauté mushrooms in 2 tablespoons butter in a large heavy skillet until tender. Remove and keep warm. Add remaining butter. When hot, put in several pieces of veal and brown on medium-high, approximately 3 minutes per side. When all meat is browned, return mushrooms and meat to pan. Add lemon juice and Sauterne; cook on high 2 to 3 minutes. Remove meat and mushrooms to platter. Scrape bottom of pan, stirring to mix with Sauterne. Pour over veal.

If more sauce is desired to serve over pasta, increase butter, Sauterne and lemon juice proportionately.

# Broiled Flounder Filets with Mustard Sauce

*A simple but delicious main course for a busy evening*

May not prepare ahead 4 servings

4 small skinless flounder* filets,
   about 1 pound
salt to taste
freshly ground pepper to taste
1 tablespoon oil
2 tablespoons mayonnaise
1 tablespoon Dijon mustard
2 teaspoons finely chopped
   parsley
4 lemon or lime wedges

*May substitute bluefish,
   pompano, halibut or sea trout.

WINE: Vernaccia or Muscadet

Preheat oven to 500 degrees. Arrange filets on a greased baking sheet or dish. Sprinkle with salt and pepper. Brush with oil. Blend mayonnaise, mustard and parsley in a small cup. Spread mixture evenly over fish. Bake 5 minutes or until fish flakes easily. Brown 1 minute under broiler. Serve with lemon or lime wedges.

# Gourmet Grouper

May not prepare ahead 6 servings

3 pounds grouper filets*
juice of 1 lime or lemon
1 cup mayonnaise
1 cup crabmeat
1 cup grated Parmesan cheese
½ cup sliced almonds, toasted

*May substitute red snapper,
   halibut, flounder or haddock.

WINE: White Graves or
         California Sauvignon
         Blanc

Preheat oven to 350 degrees. Wash fish and lay on bottom of foil-covered broiler pan. Sprinkle lime or lemon juice over fish. Bake for 20 to 25 minutes until fish is white and flakes easily. Drain off juice.

Combine mayonnaise, crabmeat and cheese. Spread over fish. Place under broiler until just starting to brown. Sprinkle with almonds and serve immediately.

# Baked Grouper

**May not prepare ahead**                              **4-6 servings**

2 pounds grouper*
½ cup butter
1 lemon or lime
salt to taste
pepper to taste
¼ cup fresh parsley
6 slices stale bread
3 tablespoons cold butter
paprika

*May substitute red snapper,
  haddock, halibut or flounder.

WINE: Alsatian Riesling or
      White Bordeaux

Preheat oven to 350 degrees. Melt ½ cup butter in a glass baking dish. Place the fish in baking dish and turn over to coat with butter. Squeeze lemon or lime over the fish. Season with salt and pepper.

Chop parsley in food processor. Add bread broken into pieces. Add cold butter. Process until bread is in crumbs. Arrange crumbs in a thick layer over fish and sprinkle with paprika. Bake for 45 minutes.

# Broiled Grouper

**May prepare partially ahead**                        **4 servings**

2 pounds grouper filets*
1 teaspoon Salad Supreme
1 teaspoon dill weed
1 teaspoon seasoned salt
1 teaspoon seasoned pepper
3 tablespoons butter
1 cup white wine
1 green pepper, cut in rings
  and quartered
5 to 6 scallions, thinly sliced

*May substitute red snapper,
  halibut, haddock or flounder.

WINE: Pinot Grigio or White
      Zinfandel

Preheat broiler. Cut filets into serving-size pieces. Place filets in well-buttered shallow baking dish. Mix seasonings and sprinkle on both sides of filets. Dot with butter. Pour wine into baking dish. Broil for 5 minutes; turn filets over; broil 5 more minutes. Add green pepper and scallions. Broil 5 more minutes or until flaky.

# Dolphin Gourmet
*Delicious and easy to prepare*

**May not prepare ahead**                    **4 servings**

4 dolphin filets, 6 ounces each
1 tablespoon butter
1 tablespoon vegetable oil
¼ teaspoon salt
¼ teaspoon pepper
¼ teaspoon garlic powder
½ teaspoon paprika
¾ cup herb-seasoned stuffing
  mix
½ cup dry sherry

Brown both sides of filets in butter and oil. Season with salt, pepper, garlic powder and paprika. Add stuffing mix and turn filets a few times, making sure to scrape bottom of pan. Lower the heat, add sherry and cover pan. Simmer about 5 minutes or until fish flakes. Add water if needed to keep moist. Serve immediately.

WINE: German Spätlese

# Baked Sea Trout with Key Limes
*Baking limes smell heavenly*

**May prepare partially ahead**                    **4 servings**

2 pounds sea trout filets,
  skinned
pepper to taste
paprika for garnish
4 tablespoons butter
2 fresh key limes, sliced
1 to 2 key limes, quartered

WINE: Washington or Oregon
  Riesling

Preheat oven to 350 degrees. Place filets in a greased shallow baking dish. Sprinkle filets with pepper and garnish with paprika. Dot with butter and place lime slices over filets. Bake for about 30 minutes or until fish is white and flaky but not over-baked. Serve with fresh quartered limes.

*Lemon cups are great filled with tartar sauce, fruit sherbet, pickle chips or relish and provide a colorful garnish to a fish platter. To make lemon cups, cut lemons crosswise, ream out juice carefully and scoop out pulp lining. Cut a slice from the bottom so that cups will stand upright. Scallop or notch edges as desired.*

# Grouper en Papillote
### Fish in a bag

**May not prepare ahead**                    **4 servings**

4 lunch-size brown paper bags
vegetable oil
1 egg, beaten
½ cup half and half cream
1½ cups toasted buttered
   bread crumbs
½ cup grated Parmesan cheese
lemon pepper to taste
4 grouper filets, about 6 to 8
   ounces each

WINE: Rhine Spätlese or
   Muscadet

Preheat oven to 450 degrees. Open bags and lay on sides. Brush oil on one interior side of each bag.

Combine egg, cream, bread crumbs, cheese and lemon pepper. Divide mixture into 4 equal portions and pat on top of each filet. Place 1 filet on the oiled side of each bag. Tie bags and place directly on rack in oven. Bake 15-20 minutes, depending on thickness. Remove from oven. Carefully cut open with scissors; serve immediately in bags.

# Easy Lemon Fish

**May prepare partially ahead**                    **8 servings**

⅓ cup butter, melted
⅓ cup lemon juice
2 teaspoons seasoned salt
¼ teaspoon pepper
1⅓ cups cooked rice
1 cup shredded sharp cheddar
   cheese
1 10-ounce package frozen
   chopped broccoli, thawed
8 fresh thin fish filets,
   6 to 8 ounces each
paprika

WINE: California Chenin Blanc

Preheat oven to 375 degrees. To make sauce, combine melted butter, lemon juice, seasoned salt and pepper. In medium bowl, mix cooked rice, cheese, broccoli and ¼ cup lemon sauce. Divide among 8 fish filets. Roll up and place seam-side down in a lightly greased 7 x 11-inch baking dish. Top with remaining sauce and paprika. Bake for 25 minutes or until fish flakes with fork.

# Shark with Dilled Hollandaise

May not prepare ahead

6 servings

6 shark filets, about 8 ounces each, preferably blacktip*
2 tablespoons butter, melted

Dilled Hollandaise Sauce:
6 egg yolks
¼ cup fresh lemon juice
½ teaspoon salt
¼ teaspoon paprika
1 teaspoon dried dill weed
1 cup butter, melted and sizzling hot

parsley for garnish

*May substitute swordfish or salmon steaks.

WINE: California or Washington Riesling

Grill shark filets about 3 to 4 minutes on each side, basting with melted butter. Transfer to heated platter.

Combine egg yolks, lemon juice, salt, paprika and dill weed in work bowl of food processor or blender. With machine running, add melted butter slowly but in a steady stream.

Pour a small amount of sauce over each filet; garnish with parsley and serve. Pass remaining sauce in a separate bowl.

# Charbroiled Shark

May not prepare ahead

6 servings

½ cup butter
6 garlic cloves, minced
6 shark filets or steaks, about 8 ounces each, preferably blacktip*

*May substitute swordfish or salmon steaks.

WINE: French Chablis Premier Cru or Swiss Fendant

Melt butter and stir in minced garlic. Grill shark about 3 to 4 minutes on each side, basting frequently with garlic butter. Cooking time will vary with heat of fire and thickness of fish.

# Paella
*Extravagant, but well worth the effort*

May prepare partially ahead                    8 servings

4 skinless, boneless chicken
    breasts
1 pound lobster tails, removed
    from shell, or 8 stone crab
    claws
1 cup olive oil, divided
½ pound Chorizo or Kielbasa
    · sausage, sliced into ¼-inch
    pieces
½ pound mushrooms, halved
2 green peppers, cut into eighths
2 red peppers, cut into eighths
    or pimentos
1 medium zucchini, halved
    lengthwise and cut into
    1-inch pieces
3 large garlic cloves, minced
1 large Spanish onion, minced
1 8-ounce can plum tomatoes,
    drained and finely chopped
2 cups long grain raw rice
¼ cup finely chopped parsley
¼ teaspoon saffron powder
½ teaspoon paprika
3½ cups chicken broth
1 pound shrimp, peeled and
    deveined, leaving tails intact
2 dozen littleneck clams,
    scrubbed well
1 pound grouper, cut into
    ¾-inch chunks
½ pound red snapper, cut into
    ¾-inch chunks

WINE: Sangria

Cut chicken and lobster crosswise into 1-inch chunks. (If using stone crab claws, carefully crack each section of the claw so that it will not be necessary to crack them while eating. Be sure to remove all loose pieces of shell after cracking.) Set aside.

Heat ½ cup olive oil in paella pan (large shallow pan). Sauté chicken and sliced sausage until light streaky brown; remove from pan. Sauté mushrooms, green and red peppers and zucchini until just barely tender; remove from pan. Wash and dry pan.

Add ½ cup olive oil to pan. Heat 1 minute over low flame. Add garlic, onion, tomatoes, rice, parsley, saffron and paprika; stir well. Sauté, stirring constantly, 5 minutes. Add chicken broth, chicken, sausage, peppers, zucchini and mushrooms. Bring to a boil; reduce heat so that liquid merely simmers. Place lobster pieces, shrimp, clams and fish into pan. Simmer slowly, uncovered, tending pan frequently and stirring gently from time to time. Cook until rice is tender and has absorbed all liquid, about 30 to 35 minutes.

Traditionally served with green salad, crusty bread, sangria and, for dessert, flan.

# Snook Supreme

May not prepare ahead

4-6 servings

2 pounds snook* filets
4 tablespoons butter
1½ cups sour cream
½ cup mayonnaise
2 tablespoons chopped chives
2 tablespoons lemon juice
¼ teaspoon salt
¼ teaspoon pepper
sliced lemon

Preheat oven to 350 degrees. Butter a 9 x 13-inch glass baking dish. Place filets in dish and dot with butter. Combine sour cream, mayonnaise, chives, lemon juice, salt and pepper. Pour evenly over filets. Bake for 30 minutes until fish is flaky. Decorate with lemon slices.

*May substitute grouper or haddock.

WINE: Vouvray or Chenin Blanc

# Red Snapper Veracruzana
*Superb is an understatement*

May prepare partially ahead

8 servings

2 garlic cloves, halved
¼ cup vegetable oil
2 medium onions, sliced
3 medium tomatoes, sliced
1 cup chopped parsley
2 lemons, sliced
salt to taste
4 pounds red snapper filets
2 4-ounce cans yellow chilies
    or green chilies in vinegar,
    cut into strips

Preheat oven to 350 degrees. Brown garlic in hot oil; remove garlic and add onions. Fry until tender and well browned. Add tomatoes, parsley, lemons and salt. Cook slightly. Arrange fish in large glass baking dish. Pour onion-tomato mixture over fish. Arrange chili strips on top. Bake for 30 minutes or until fish flakes easily. Serve immediately.

WINE: Spanish Brut Sparkling

# Barbecued Salmon Steaks

Must prepare partially ahead

6 servings

2 pounds salmon steaks*
1 cup dry vermouth
¾ cup vegetable oil
⅓ cup fresh lemon juice
2 tablespoons chopped chives
2 teaspoons seasoned salt
½ teaspoon pepper

*May substitute swordfish or
   shark steaks.

WINE: Moselle Kabinett or
   Qualitätswein

Place salmon steaks in shallow glass baking dish. Combine remaining ingredients. Pour sauce over fish and marinate in refrigerator 4 hours, turning occasionally.

Remove fish and reserve sauce for basting. Place fish on well-greased grill. Cook, about 4 inches from moderately hot coals, 8 minutes. Baste with sauce. Turn and cook 7 to 10 minutes longer or until fish flakes easily.

# Tuna St. Jacques
*Inexpensive and good*

May prepare ahead

6 servings

3 green onions, finely chopped
4 ounces fresh mushrooms,
   chopped
5 tablespoons butter, divided
1 10¾-ounce can cream of
   chicken soup
½ cup dry vermouth
white pepper to taste
2 tablespoons finely chopped
   parsley
2 7-ounce cans solid white
   tuna, drained and broken
   into chunks
2 tablespoons grated Parmesan
   cheese
⅓ cup bread crumbs

Preheat oven to 450 degrees. Sauté onion and mushrooms in 3 tablespoons butter until tender. Remove from heat.

In a saucepan, combine soup and vermouth; bring to a boil. Add ½ of the sauce to onion-mushroom mixture. Spoon into 6 buttered sea shells or ramekins. Top with parsley and chunks of tuna. Spoon on the remainder of sauce. Combine cheese and bread crumbs; sprinkle over each serving. Melt remaining butter and drizzle over crumbs. Heat in oven 10 minutes or until browned.

# Red Snapper with Butter and Shallot Sauce
### *Very elegant*

May prepare partially ahead

2-4 servings

**Crème Fraîche:**
½ cup heavy cream
½ cup sour cream

Whisk together heavy cream and sour cream. Cover loosely with plastic wrap and let stand in reasonably warm spot overnight or until thickened. Cover and refrigerate for 4 hours or until quite thick. Yields 1 cup.

**Sauce:**
⅓ cup raspberry vinegar*
2 tablespoons finely minced shallots
½ pound chilled unsalted butter, cut into small pieces
1 tablespoon crème fraîche

Preheat oven to 400 degrees. Combine vinegar and shallots in a small heavy saucepan. Bring to a boil, lower heat slightly and simmer until vinegar is reduced to about 2 tablespoons. Add butter and 1 tablespoon crème fraîche to sauce. Set aside.

2 red snapper filets, ¾ pound each
⅓ cup fish stock
⅓ cup dry white wine or vermouth
salt to taste
freshly ground pepper to taste

Arrange snapper filets in a shallow baking dish just large enough to hold them without overlapping. Pour the fish stock and the wine over the filets. Season with salt and pepper and set dish on the middle rack of oven. Bake 8 to 10 minutes. Fish should be slightly underdone since it will continue cooking due to residual heat.

3 cups finely shredded fresh spinach

Place raw spinach on a serving platter. Arrange baked fish on spinach. Spoon sauce over fish.

*Raspberry vinegar may be purchased in gourmet or health food stores.

Remaining crème fraîche may be kept in the refrigerator up to ten days. Good as a topping for fruits and desserts.

**WINE: California Chardonnay or Puligny-Montrachet**

# Scalloped Oysters
*Delicious Thanksgiving treat*

May not prepare ahead                    4 servings

1 pint oysters
2 cups medium to coarse saltine
  cracker crumbs
½ cup butter or margarine,
  melted
pepper to taste
¾ cup light cream
¼ cup oyster liquid
¼ teaspoon Worcestershire
  sauce
½ teaspoon salt

WINE: Orvieto Classico or
      Pouilly-Fumé

Preheat oven to 350 degrees. Drain oysters but reserve ¼ cup liquid. Combine crumbs and butter. Spread ⅓ of crumbs in a greased 8-inch round pan. Cover with ½ of the oysters. Sprinkle with pepper. Spread another ⅓ of the crumbs over oysters. Cover with remaining oysters. Sprinkle with pepper. Combine cream, oyster liquid, Worcestershire sauce and salt. Pour over oysters. Top with remaining crumbs. Bake for 40 minutes.

# Crab Casserole

May prepare partially ahead              6 servings

1 6-ounce package frozen
  crabmeat*, thawed
1 cup chopped celery
⅔ cup mayonnaise
¼ cup milk
¼cup finely chopped onion
1 teaspoon Worcestershire
  sauce
3 cups soft white bread crumbs,
  divided
½ teaspoon salt
dash of pepper
¼ cup butter, melted

*May substitute shrimp.

Preheat oven to 350 degrees. Combine crabmeat, celery, mayonnaise, milk, onion, Worcestershire sauce, 1½ cups bread crumbs, salt and pepper. Spoon into a greased 1½-quart casserole. Add remaining bread crumbs to melted butter. Stir until all butter is absorbed. Spread over top of casserole. Bake uncovered for 30 to 35 minutes.

This casserole doubles easily; bake in a 9 x 13-inch pan.

WINE: California Dry Chenin
      Blanc

# Couvie's Kitchen
### An easy Friday night supper

May not prepare ahead

4 servings

4 garlic cloves
½ cup olive oil
48 oysters, drained
1 cup Italian bread crumbs
½ cup butter
juice of 1 lemon
1 tablespoon Worcestershire
  sauce
½ cup grated Parmesan cheese

WINE: White Graves

Preheat oven to 450 degrees. Press garlic into olive oil. Dip oysters into oil mixture, roll in bread crumbs, and lay in buttered individual baking dishes. Mix melted butter with lemon juice and Worcestershire; dribble onto oysters. Sprinkle with Parmesan cheese. Bake for 15 to 20 minutes.

Serve with green salad and French bread.

# Crabmeat au Gratin

May prepare ahead

4 servings

1 medium onion, chopped
2 celery stalks, chopped
½ cup butter
2 tablespoons flour
1 cup + 2 tablespoons half and
  half cream
1 egg yolk
1 pound fresh white crabmeat
8 ounces sharp cheddar cheese,
  grated and divided
salt to taste
pepper to taste

WINE: California Chardonnay
  or White Burgundy

Preheat oven to 350 degrees. Sauté onion and celery in butter. Add flour and blend. Add half and half cream and blend. Remove from heat and add egg yolk, crabmeat, 6 ounces grated cheese, salt and pepper. Put in ungreased individual ramekins or 1-quart casserole. Top with remaining cheese. Bake until heated through, about 30 minutes.

May be held in refrigerator 24 hours before baking.

# Cracked Conch
*A Florida delicacy*

May prepare partially ahead                    **4 servings**

**Batter:**
2 eggs, beaten
⅔ cup milk
1 cup flour
1 teaspoon baking powder
1 teaspoon garlic salt
¼ teaspoon pepper
1 teaspoon vegetable oil

Combine eggs and milk. Stir in flour, baking powder, garlic salt and pepper. Beat in oil. Refrigerate until ready to use.

**Cracked Conch:**
1½ pounds conch
vegetable oil for frying
batter

With a wooden mallet, pound conch until VERY thin. Heat oil to 375 degrees. Coat conch well with batter. Fry until golden brown, about 4 minutes.

**WINE: Soave or Pouilly-Fumé**

Batter is excellent on shrimp or any fish filets.

# Shrimp Kabobs
*Easy, always receives raves*

Must prepare partially ahead                    **4 servings**

2 to 3 pounds large fresh
    shrimp, peeled and deveined
½ pound fresh mushrooms
1 pint cherry tomatoes
2 green peppers, cut into large
    chunks
2 8-ounce bottles Italian salad
    dressing
1 .6-ounce envelope Italian
    salad dressing mix

Early in the day, thread shrimp, mushrooms, tomatoes and green peppers on 12-inch skewers. Place in shallow pan. Pour bottled dressing over kabobs. Sprinkle with salad dressing mix. Refrigerate until ready for grilling.

Remove kabobs from pan; grill over hot coals, approximately 5 minutes. Turn and grill 5 more minutes.

**WINE: Dry Chenin Blanc or
    Riesling Kabinett**

# Gulf Coconut Shrimp
*Incredibly delicate taste*

**May prepare partially ahead**                    **6 servings**

1 medium coconut*
2 tablespoons butter
2 tablespoons vegetable oil
2 pounds large shrimp, peeled
   and deveined
¼ cup chopped onion
1 cup sliced mushrooms
½ cup chopped, seeded
   tomatoes
¼ cup soy sauce
¼ cup dry white wine
salt to taste
freshly ground pepper to taste

*Do not substitute packaged or
   canned coconut!

WINE: California
       Gewürztraminer

Preheat oven to 450 degrees. Drain milk from coconut by piercing the "eyes" with a nail or ice pick. Bake whole coconut 15 minutes, then cool. Wrap in towel and hit with hammer to halve. Separate meat from shell using grapefruit knife or other sharp knife. Pare off brown rind with vegetable peeler. Grate meat coarsely in food processor or by hand.

Melt butter and oil in large heavy skillet over low heat. Add grated coconut and sauté until golden brown, about 8 to 10 minutes. Remove with slotted spoon and save.

Increase heat to medium and add shrimp and onion and cook 4 minutes, stirring occasionally. Add coconut, mushrooms, tomatoes, soy sauce and wine and cook 5 minutes. Season with salt and pepper and serve immediately.

*To devein shrimp, make a shallow cut lengthwise down the back of each shrimp; remove sand vein with point of knife.*

# Hot Seafood Salad
*An easy dish for company*

**May prepare partially ahead**                    **8 servings**

2 pounds raw shrimp, peeled
    and deveined
1 cup finely diced celery
1 cup diced onion
1 cup sliced water chestnuts
1 1-pound can crabmeat
1½ to 2 cups mayonnaise
2 tablespoons lemon juice
4 ounces herb-seasoned
    stuffing mix
½ cup butter, melted

WINE: California Sauvignon
    Blanc

Preheat oven to 325 degrees. Mix shrimp, celery, onion, water chestnuts, crabmeat, mayonnaise and lemon juice. Spread into a greased 9 x 13-inch casserole. Pat stuffing mix on top. Pour melted butter evenly over casserole. Bake uncovered for 1 hour.

May be made ahead and refrigerated until ready for baking.

# Deep Fried Shrimp
*Nice puffy shrimp, very showy*

**May prepare partially ahead**                    **6 servings**

1 cup flour
⅔ cup milk
1½ tablespoons vegetable oil
1 teaspoon baking powder
dash garlic powder or garlic salt
½ teaspoon salt
1 egg
2 pounds fresh unpeeled
    shrimp

WINE: Pinot Grigio or
    California Chablis

Combine flour, milk, oil, baking powder, garlic powder, salt and egg; beat. Peel shells from shrimp leaving last section and tail intact. Butterfly shrimp by cutting almost through at center back without severing ends. Remove vein. Dry shrimp thoroughly between paper towels. Dip into batter and fry in deep hot oil (375 degrees) until golden brown. Drain on paper towels. Serve immediately with lemon wedges and cocktail sauce.

# Mary Lee's Shrimp

**May prepare partially ahead**　　　　　　　　　**4 servings**

**Shrimp Stock:**
1 teaspoon clarified butter
1 stalk celery, quartered
1 medium carrot, quartered
1 small onion, quartered
shrimp shells (from 1 pound
　shrimp)
1 bay leaf
3 sprigs parsley
6 green onion tops, reserving
　white part
3¾ cups water
1 teaspoon salt
½ teaspoon pepper

Pour 1 teaspoon clarified butter into a large saucepan. Stir in celery, carrots and onions; sauté. Stir in remaining shrimp stock ingredients. Bring to a boil. Reduce heat to low and cook 20 minutes. Strain and reserve liquid. Save bay leaf for rice.

**Rice:**
2 tablespoons clarified butter
1 small onion, chopped
1 cup long grain rice
2½ cups shrimp stock
1 bay leaf

Pour clarified butter into a 1½-quart casserole to just cover bottom; stir in onion and cook 2 minutes over medium heat. Stir in rice and shrimp stock. Add bay leaf and cover tightly. Bake at 375 degrees for 30 minutes.

**Cream Sauce:**
white part of 6 green onions,
　chopped
1 tablespoon clarified butter
1 pound medium shrimp,
　peeled and deveined
salt to taste
pepper to taste
¼ cup white wine
1 cup sour cream
1 cup heavy cream

In large skillet over medium heat, sauté onions in clarified butter. Add shrimp and sauté until done. Salt and pepper to taste. Remove shrimp from pan with slotted spoon to colander. Add wine to skillet, bring to a boil, and reduce by at least half. Add sour cream and heavy cream to wine and juices. Simmer, DO NOT BOIL, to desired thickness.

**WINE: Meursault** (Use same
　wine in recipe.)

Just before serving, add shrimp and heat through. Serve over rice.

# Lobster Creole

**May prepare partially ahead**                          **6-8 servings**

4 bacon strips
2 medium onions, chopped
1 cup chopped okra
1 cup tomato sauce
meat from 6 Florida lobsters
1 8-ounce can sliced
    mushrooms, drained
3 tablespoons white wine
salt to taste
pepper to taste
½ teaspoon chopped parsley
⅓ cup bread crumbs
6 to 8 cups cooked rice

WINE: Chilled Beaujolais
          Villages or
          Saint-Amour

Preheat oven to 400 degrees. Fry bacon in skillet and drain; crumble. Set aside. Sauté onions and okra in bacon drippings for 10 to 12 minutes. Add tomato sauce, lobster, mushrooms, wine, salt, pepper and parsley. Place in a greased 2-quart casserole. Cover with bread crumbs and crumbled bacon. Bake 20 minutes. Serve over rice.

# Seafood Kabobs
*A wonderful Gulf Coast recipe*

**Must prepare partially ahead**                          **4 servings**

1 15½-ounce can pineapple
    chunks
¼ cup fresh lemon juice
1 cup soy sauce
3 pounds seafood combination:
    large fresh shrimp, peeled
        and deveined
    scallops
    grouper, cut into chunks
1 pound bacon
1 green pepper, cut into 1-inch
    pieces

WINE: California Chablis

Drain pineapple and reserve juice. Combine pineapple juice, lemon juice, soy sauce and seafood. Cover and marinate in refrigerator for 1 hour or more.

Cut bacon slices in half. Cook until limp but not crisp. Drain and set aside.

Drain seafood. Alternate pineapple chunks, seafood, bacon and green pepper on skewers. Broil until bacon is crisp and seafood is done, turning skewers, about 3 to 5 minutes.

# Oysters in Patty Shells
*Also makes excellent hors d'oeuvres*

**May prepare partially ahead**                    **6 servings**

6 frozen patty shells*
2 dozen oysters
1 cup oyster liquid
4 tablespoons butter
5 tablespoons flour
½ cup chopped onion
½ cup chopped green onions
½ cup chopped celery leaves
½ cup chopped parsley
2 garlic cloves, minced
½ teaspoon salt
¼ teaspoon pepper
¼ teaspoon hot pepper sauce

**WINE: Beaujolais Blanc**

Bake patty shells according to package directions and set aside.

Preheat oven to 425 degrees. Drain oysters, reserving 1 cup liquid. In a large skillet, over medium heat, melt butter and stir in flour until smooth. Cook until dark brown, stirring constantly, about 10 minutes. Lower heat, stir in onions and celery leaves; cook until soft, stirring often. Lower heat to simmer, stir in oyster liquid to blend. Add parsley and garlic, simmer 10 minutes. Cut oysters into fourths and add. Season with salt, pepper and hot pepper sauce. Bring to a boil, simmer 10 minutes. Pour into patty shells and bake for 10 minutes.

Filling may be refrigerated or frozen. Heat before pouring into patty shells.

*For hors d'oeuvres, pour filling into about 48 cocktail patty shells. Bake 5 minutes.

*Freeze fresh fish or shrimp in cold water to retain freshness and lessen odor when cooking.*

# Grilled Shrimp—Scampi Style
### Informal dining with a touch of class

**May not prepare ahead**                               **6 servings**

36 jumbo shrimp
4 garlic cloves
2 teaspoons salt
¾ cup butter
¾ cup olive oil
¼ cup minced parsley
2 tablespoons lemon juice
freshly ground black pepper to
    taste
parsley sprigs

WINE: French Chablis

Preheat broiler. Split the raw un-shelled shrimp through lengthwise to the tail. Leave all the feet on and the shell intact. Remove the sand veins and pat the shrimp dry.

Crush garlic with the salt. To make butter sauce, melt the butter and stir in the garlic and salt, oil, minced parsley, lemon juice and pepper.

Dip shrimp into the butter sauce. Arrange them in a baking dish. They will curl up as they cook. Their tails will "stand up." Broil for 10 to 12 minutes 6 inches from heat. Serve with butter sauce. Garnish with parsley.

# Shrimp Bordelaise
### Good with homemade pilaf

**May not prepare ahead**                               **4-6 servings**

3 tablespoons butter or
    margarine
3 garlic cloves, minced
1 medium onion, chopped
1½ tablespoons lemon juice
½ cup dry white wine
1½ pounds large shrimp, peeled
    and deveined (leave on last
    segment of shell and tail,
    if desired)
2 or 3 tablespoons minced fresh
    parsley

WINE: White Bordeaux

Melt butter in a large frying pan over medium high heat. Add garlic, onion, lemon juice and wine. Bring to a boil. Add shrimp and cook uncovered until shrimp turn bright pink, about 5 minutes. With a slotted spoon, transfer shrimp to a serving dish. Keep warm.

Rapidly boil down cooking liquid until reduced to about ½ cup. Add parsley and pour sauce over shrimp.

# Barbecued Shrimp
*Great informal meal*

**Must prepare partially ahead**                    **8 servings**

**Marinade:**
½ cup bourbon whiskey
½ cup vegetable oil
1 cup soy sauce
1 teaspoon lemon juice
1 to 2 teaspoons seafood
  seasoning

4 pounds unpeeled fresh shrimp

WINE: Egeri Bikavér or Beer

Combine all marinade ingredients; mix thoroughly. Add unpeeled shrimp and marinate in refrigerator 24 hours.

Place large piece of foil on grill, turning up edges to prevent juices from running off. Remove shrimp from marinade and place on foil. Barbecue 3 to 5 minutes or until done. Serve on newspapers.

# Seafood Casserole
*A buffet dinner favorite*

**May prepare partially ahead**                    **8 servings**

1 cup long grain rice
1 pound fresh small shrimp,
  peeled and deveined
1 pound fresh crabmeat
1 4-ounce can sliced
  mushrooms, drained
½ green pepper, finely
  chopped
½ cup chopped onion
1 4-ounce jar pimentos, drained
  and chopped
1 cup chopped celery
1 cup mayonnaise
½ teaspoon salt
1 cup milk
¼ teaspoon pepper
1 tablespoon Worcestershire
  sauce
bread crumbs for garnish

Preheat oven to 375 degrees. Cook rice. Boil shrimp for 3 to 5 minutes until pink. Cool slightly.

In large bowl, mix shrimp, crabmeat, mushrooms, green pepper, onion, pimentos and celery. In a separate bowl, combine mayonnaise, salt, milk, pepper, Worcestershire sauce and cooked rice, mixing well. Combine mayonnaise mixture with shrimp-crab mixture, blending well. Place in a buttered 2-quart casserole. Sprinkle with bread crumbs. Bake for 30 minutes.

May be held in warm oven 15 to 20 minutes.

189

# Shrimp Curry

**May prepare partially ahead**                                    **6 servings**

**Shrimp Stock:**
4 cups water
½ lemon, sliced
½ of a 1¼-ounce jar mixed
   pickling spices
2 teaspoons salt
1 stalk celery with leaves,
   cut into chunks
1 teaspoon whole black
   peppercorns
½ cup white vinegar
2 pounds fresh medium shrimp,
   peeled and deveined


**Curry:**
3 cups shrimp stock
2 chicken bouillon cubes
1 tablespoon curry powder
3 tablespoons butter
3 tablespoons flour
salt to taste
pepper to taste
3 to 4 cups cooked rice
¼ cup peanuts for garnish

**WINE: Riesling Auslese or
   Orvieto Classico**

Bring water to boil in large pot or Dutch oven. Add lemon, pickling spices, salt, celery, peppercorns and vinegar. Simmer covered for 10 to 15 minutes. Add shrimp and simmer 3 to 5 minutes, partially covered, until done. Remove shrimp with slotted spoon; set aside. Strain shrimp stock through cheesecloth, reserving 3 cups liquid. Discard spices, vegetables and any excess liquid.

Heat shrimp stock in medium saucepan; add bouillon cubes and dissolve. Moisten curry powder with a little stock; add to liquid. Blend well. Melt butter in large saucepan and stir in flour. Gradually stir in stock. Cook over low heat until slightly thick and smooth, approximately 20 to 30 minutes. Add salt and pepper if desired. Add shrimp to sauce; heat through. Serve over rice. Garnish with peanuts.

# Scampi with Mustard Sauce

May prepare partially ahead                                    6 servings

**Mustard Sauce:**
3 shallots, chopped
1 garlic clove, minced
2 tablespoons Worcestershire
  sauce
½ cup sherry
½ cup fresh lemon juice
1 pound butter
¾ cup prepared mustard

In large saucepan, mix all ingredients for mustard sauce. Simmer, stirring constantly, until smooth and slightly thickened, about 10 minutes.

**Scampi:**
36 jumbo shrimp, peeled,
  deveined and butterflied
3 tablespoons olive oil
salt to taste
pepper to taste
½ cup fresh bread crumbs
lettuce for garnish
red pepper rings for garnish
lemon wedges for garnish

Arrange butterflied shrimp, split side up, in broiler pan. Brush with oil; season with salt and pepper. Sprinkle with bread crumbs. Broil for about 5 minutes. Place on platter that has been garnished with lettuce, red pepper rings and lemon wedges. Pour ½ cup mustard sauce over shrimp; place remaining sauce in bowl and pass with shrimp.

WINE: Saint-Véran

# Cocktail Sauce

Must prepare ahead                                              1 cup

⅔ cup ketchup
3 tablespoons lemon juice
2 tablespoons prepared
  horseradish
3 tablespoons chili sauce

Mix all ingredients and chill.

# Royal Shrimp

**May prepare partially ahead**       **8-10 servings**

2 10¾-ounce cans cream of
   shrimp soup
½ cup mayonnaise
1 small onion, grated
¾ cup milk
2 tablespoons Morton's
   Nature's Seasons
½ teaspoon garlic powder
⅛ teaspoon cayenne pepper
½ teaspoon ground bay leaf
3 tablespoons minced parsley
3 pounds shrimp, peeled,
   deveined and cooked
1 6½-ounce can crabmeat,
   drained
1 5½-ounce can sliced water
   chestnuts
1½ cups diced celery
1⅓ cups raw long grain rice,
   cooked
paprika
slivered almonds

Blend soup and mayonnaise. Add onion, milk, Morton's Nature's Seasons, garlic powder, pepper, ground bay leaf and parsley. Stir in shrimp, crabmeat, water chestnuts, celery and rice.

Spread into a greased 9 x 13-inch baking dish. Bake at 350 degrees for 30 minutes. Garnish with paprika and almonds.

# Shrimp Sauce

**Must prepare ahead**       **2 cups**

1 cup mayonnaise
¾ cup chili sauce
2 tablespoons Worcestershire
   sauce
2 tablespoons anchovy paste or
   chopped filets
1 teaspoon hot pepper sauce

Combine ingredients and chill. Serve over cold shrimp or as a dip.

May be refrigerated for several days.

breads

# Breads

## MANATEES

*Manatees return to coastal Florida during the winter for the same reason so many human visitors do—the climate. These large and gentle aquatic mammals, an endangered species, have no form of defense and no natural enemies. The entire state of Florida is a manatee sanctuary; the Fort Myers area is a critical manatee wintering refuge.*

# Bite-Size Applesauce Muffins
*Great for a Sunday brunch*

May prepare ahead                                    3½ dozen

**Muffins:**
½ cup butter or margarine,
   softened
½ cup sugar
2 eggs
¾ cup applesauce
1¾ cups all-purpose flour
1 tablespoon baking powder
½ teaspoon salt
½ teaspoon cinnamon

**Topping:**
½ cup sugar
¼ teaspoon cinnamon
½ cup butter or margarine,
   melted

Preheat oven to 425 degrees. Cream butter and gradually add sugar, beating until light and fluffy. Add eggs, one at a time, beating well after each addition. Stir in applesauce. Combine flour, baking powder, salt and cinnamon; add to creamed mixture and stir just until moistened. Spoon batter into lightly greased miniature muffin pans, filling ⅔ full. Bake for 15 minutes. Remove from pans immediately.

Combine sugar and cinnamon. Dip muffins into melted butter, then into sugar-cinnamon mixture.

May freeze.

# Easy Sour Cream Muffins
*Especially good for a large crowd*

May prepare ahead                                    3 dozen

2 cups self-rising flour
1 cup butter or margarine,
   melted
1 8-ounce carton sour cream

Preheat oven to 400 degrees. Mix all ingredients until blended. Drop by teaspoon into ungreased mini-muffin pans. Bake 12 to 15 minutes.

# Blueberry Muffins
### A special treat for the family

**May prepare ahead**                                        **1 dozen**

1¾ cups all-purpose flour
1 teaspoon baking soda
2 teaspoons cream of tartar
¼ cup sugar
1 teaspoon salt
1 egg
milk
⅓ cup butter, melted
1 cup fresh blueberries*

*May substitute unsweetened
  frozen blueberries or canned
  blueberries, drained.

Preheat oven to 400 degrees. In mixing bowl, blend flour, baking soda, cream of tartar, sugar and salt; set aside. Break the egg into a 1-cup measuring cup. Fill cup with milk. Add milk mixture and melted butter to flour mixture; stir lightly with a fork. Fold in the blueberries. Bake in greased or paper-lined muffin pans for 20 to 30 minutes.

# Squash Muffins

**May prepare ahead**                                      **16 muffins**

2 medium yellow squash
  (1 cup cooked)
¾ cup brown sugar
¼ cup molasses
½ cup butter, softened
1 egg, beaten
1¾ cups all-purpose flour
1 teaspoon baking soda
¼ teaspoon salt
¼ cup chopped pecans

Cut squash crosswise into ¼-inch slices. Cook in small amount of boiling, salted water until almost tender, about 8 minutes; drain. Mash until consistency of mashed potatoes. Set aside.

Preheat oven to 375 degrees. Cream sugar, molasses and butter. Add egg and squash; blend well. Mix flour with soda and salt; beat into squash batter. Fold in pecans. Fill greased muffin tins about ½ full. Bake 20 minutes.

# Butter Dips

**May prepare ahead**                    **1 dozen**

½ cup cold butter, divided
2 cups all-purpose flour
1 teaspoon salt
1 tablespoon baking powder
1 cup milk

Preheat oven to 425 degrees. Melt ¼ cup butter in an 8-inch iron skillet. Measure flour into bowl of food processor. Add salt, baking powder and ¼ cup cold butter. Process until mixture looks like fine crumbs. Add milk and process just long enough to mix. Dough will be soft —do not add more flour.

Turn out on a floured board and knead a few turns just until dough forms a ball. Pat out ½-inch thick and cut into 2-inch rounds. Dip the top of each biscuit in the melted butter before turning over. Arrange biscuits in the skillet so that sides of biscuits are touching. Bake 25 minutes.

# Mrs. Edison's Fairy Muffins
*"Old" Fort Myers recipe*

**May prepare ahead**                    **1 dozen**

1 tablespoon shortening
3 tablespoons sugar
2 eggs, separated
1 cup milk
2 cups all-purpose flour
3 teaspoons baking powder
½ teaspoon salt

Preheat oven to 350 degrees. Cream shortening and sugar and add well beaten egg yolks. Add milk, flour, baking powder and salt. Mix well. Fold in egg whites which have been beaten stiff. Spoon into greased muffin tins and bake for 25 minutes.

# Very Moist Bran Muffins

**May prepare ahead**                               **4-5 dozen**

1 10-ounce package bran
   cereal with raisins
5 cups all-purpose flour
3 cups sugar
5 teaspoons baking soda
2 teaspoons salt
1 quart buttermilk
1 cup oil
4 eggs
1 8-ounce package pitted
   dates, chopped, optional

Preheat oven to 400 degrees. In a very large bowl, add dry ingredients, then buttermilk, oil, eggs and dates. Mix well. Pour into greased muffin tins and bake 15 to 20 minutes.

Uncooked batter may be stored in refrigerator for up to 3 weeks.

# Skillet Corn Bread

*A sure way to please the man of the house*

**May not prepare ahead**                          **8 servings**

1 tablespoon vegetable oil
3 tablespoons shortening
½ cup yellow corn meal
½ cup all-purpose flour
½ teaspoon salt
2 teaspoons baking powder
1 tablespoon sugar
1 egg, slightly beaten
½ cup milk

Preheat oven to 400 degrees. Pour 1 tablespoon oil into large iron skillet. Spread around pan evenly. Place skillet in oven to heat.

Melt shortening; set aside. Mix dry ingredients. Add egg to milk. Pour milk mixture and melted shortening into dry ingredients. Blend with a fork. Pour mixture into hot iron skillet and bake 20 minutes or until brown.

# Mamaw's Good Ol' Biscuits with Sausage Gravy
### *Real country-style breakfast*

**May not prepare ahead**                    **8-10 servings**

**Biscuits:**
4 heaping tablespoons
  shortening
3 cups self-rising flour
1½ cups milk

Preheat oven to 450 degrees. Cut shortening into flour until small dough pieces form and all flour mixture is blended. Slowly stir in milk and blend thoroughly. Form into large ball. Turn out onto lightly floured surface and knead a few turns. Do not overknead. Form 8 to 10 individual biscuits in cup of hands; place in greased 10-inch pie plate. Bake 12 to 15 minutes.

**Sausage Gravy:**
1 pound seasoned bulk sausage
1 tablespoon sausage drippings
5 tablespoons sifted all-purpose
  flour
4 cups milk
½ teaspoon coarsely ground
  pepper

Brown broken-up sausage in large skillet. Drain off excess grease, leaving about 1 tablespoon. Sprinkle flour over sausage and stir until flour disappears. Slowly add milk, stirring constantly. Add pepper and simmer for 20 minutes. Serve over biscuits.

# Blueberry Coffee Cake

**May prepare ahead**                                      **15 servings**

**Topping:**
¼ cup all-purpose flour
¼ cup brown sugar
½ cup chopped pecans
3 tablespoons butter or
   margarine

Combine flour, sugar and pecans. Cut in butter until mixture resembles coarse meal. Set aside.

**Cake:**
1 cup margarine, softened
1 cup sugar
2 eggs
1 cup sour cream
1 teaspoon vanilla extract
2 cups all-purpose flour
1 teaspoon baking powder
1 teaspoon baking soda
1 21-ounce can blueberry*
   pie filling

*May substitute any fruit
 pie filling.

Preheat oven to 375 degrees. Cream margarine and gradually add sugar, beating thoroughly until light and fluffy. Add eggs one at a time, beating well after each addition. Stir in sour cream and vanilla. Combine dry ingredients; gradually add to sour cream mixture, beating thoroughly after each addition. Spread ½ of batter in greased 9 x 13-inch pan; spread with pie filling. Top with remaining batter and sprinkle with topping. Bake for 45 minutes.

# Chocolate Chip Coffee Cake
*Unbeatable way to start the morning*

**May prepare ahead**                                    **16 servings**

2 cups all-purpose flour
1½ teaspoons baking powder
1 teaspoon baking soda
¼ teaspoon salt
½ cup margarine or butter, softened
1 cup sugar
2 eggs
1 teaspoon vanilla extract
1 cup sour cream
6 ounces chocolate chips
¾ cup brown sugar
1½ teaspoons cinnamon
3 to 4 ounces chopped walnuts, optional

Preheat oven to 350 degrees. Mix flour, baking powder, baking soda and salt. Set aside. In a separate bowl, cream butter and sugar until fluffy. Add eggs and vanilla; beat well. Alternately blend in sour cream and flour mixture, beginning and ending with flour. Stir in chocolate chips; set aside.

Combine brown sugar, cinnamon and walnuts; set aside. Spoon ½ of batter into a greased and floured 10-inch Bundt pan. Sprinkle in ½ of the cinnamon mixture. Repeat process with remaining batter and cinnamon mixture. Bake for 40 to 45 minutes or until done. Cool in pan for 10 minutes; remove from pan and cool completely.

*The shelf life of white flour is 1 to 2 years. To store it, transfer to a tightly closed container to prevent moisture absorption. Keep in a cool, dark spot.*

*Nonwhite flours should be used within 3 to 4 months. To keep high fat flours such as whole wheat, wheat germ, oatmeal and soy fresh, store in the freezer.*

# Banana Bread
*Easy and yummy*

**May prepare ahead**                                              **1 loaf**

¹/₄ lb. butter, cut in pieces
1 cup sugar
2 eggs
4 VERY ripe bananas
2 cups all purpose flour
1 teaspoon baking powder
1 teaspoon baking soda
¹/₄ teaspoon salt

Place butter, sugar and eggs in food processor. Process until ingredients are blended. Add bananas and process again. Combine flour, baking powder, and salt and add to food processor. Turn machine on and off and push mixture down from the sides of the bowl. Process until flour disappears. Spoon mixture into a greased 9x5x3 loaf pan. Bake in a preheated 350 degree oven for 1 hour. Can be made with a mixer also. Freezes well if wrapped in foil while still warm.

# Strawberry Tea Bread

**May prepare ahead**                                              **2 loaves**

3 cups all-purpose flour
1 teaspoon baking soda
1 teaspoon salt
1 tablespoon cinnamon
2 cups sugar
4 eggs, beaten
1¹/₄ cups butter, melted
2 pints strawberries*, cleaned
   and coarsely chopped
1¹/₄ cups chopped pecans

*May use 2 10-ounce packages frozen, sweetened strawberries, thawed, but decrease sugar to 1½ cups.

Preheat oven to 350 degrees. Combine flour, soda, salt, cinnamon and sugar, mixing well; set aside. Combine eggs, butter, strawberries and pecans; add to dry ingredients, blending well. (This may be done in a food processor, but do not over process.)

Pour batter into 2 greased and floured 5 x 9-inch loaf pans. Bake 1 hour. Cool in pans 10 minutes before turning out.

Serve at room temperature with honey and cream cheese.

# Cinnamon Bread

*Terrific toasted lightly and buttered*

May prepare ahead                                    6-8 servings

1½ tablespoons cinnamon
1⅓ cups sugar, divided
½ cup butter or margarine,
   softened
2 eggs
1 cup sour cream
2 cups all-purpose flour
1 teaspoon baking powder
1 teaspoon baking soda
½ teaspoon salt
1 teaspoon vanilla extract

Preheat oven to 350 degrees. Grease a 5 x 9-inch loaf pan. Mix cinnamon and ⅓ cup sugar; set aside. Cream butter with remaining sugar. Add eggs and sour cream, mixing well with electric beater. Sift together flour, baking powder, soda and salt. Slowly add flour mixture to batter, blending well. Stir in vanilla. Pour ⅓ batter into loaf pan and sprinkle with ⅓ cinnamon-sugar mixture. Repeat twice, ending with cinnamon on top (3 layers). Bake 50 to 60 minutes. Cool in pan 2 minutes. Remove from pan.

# Cheese-Onion Bread

*Great with chili or spaghetti*

May prepare ahead                                    6-8 servings

½ cup chopped onion
3 tablespoons melted butter or
   margarine, divided
1 egg, beaten
½ cup milk
1½ cups Bisquick or similar
   baking mix
1 cup grated sharp cheese,
   divided
1 tablespoon poppy seeds

Preheat oven to 350 degrees. Sauté onion in 1 tablespoon butter or margarine until tender, but not clear. Combine egg and milk; add to Bisquick and stir only until dry ingredients are moist. Stir in onion and ½ cup cheese. Place in greased 9 x 9-inch baking dish; top with remaining cheese, poppy seeds and remaining melted butter or margarine. Bake 30 minutes. Cut into squares.

# Cranberry Orange Bread
*Outstanding holiday bread*

**Must prepare ahead**  **6-8 servings**

1 egg
1 cup sugar
grated rind of 1 orange
juice of 1 orange (¾ cup)
2 tablespoons melted
   shortening
2 cups all-purpose flour
½ teaspoon salt
½ teaspoon baking soda
1½ teaspoons baking powder
½ cup chopped pecans or
   walnuts
1½ cups halved raw cranberries
1 cup golden raisins, optional

Preheat oven to 325 degrees. Beat egg and sugar. Add orange rind, orange juice and melted shortening. Sift flour, salt, baking soda and baking powder. Add to egg-sugar mixture. Stir in nuts, cranberries and raisins. Pour into greased and floured 5 x 9-inch loaf pan. Bake for 1 hour. Invert at once (do not allow to cool). Wrap securely in aluminum foil and refrigerate 24 hours before serving. May freeze.

# Zucchini Bread
*Coconut makes this unique*

**May prepare ahead**  **2 loaves**

3 eggs, well beaten
2 cups sugar
3 cups grated zucchini
1 cup vegetable oil
2 teaspoons vanilla extract
3 cups all-purpose flour
1 teaspoon salt
1 teaspoon baking soda
1 teaspoon baking powder
1 teaspoon cinnamon
1½ cups chopped nuts
1½ cups coconut
¼ cup raisins, optional

Combine eggs, sugar, zucchini and oil; mix well. Add vanilla, flour, salt, soda, baking powder and cinnamon; stir until well blended. Stir in nuts, coconut and raisins. Pour into 2 lightly greased and floured 5 x 9-inch loaf pans. Bake at 325 to 350 degrees for 1 hour.

# Raw Apple Bread

May prepare ahead

12 servings

½ cup butter
1 cup sugar
2 eggs
1 teaspoon vanilla extract
2 cups all-purpose flour
½ teaspoon salt
½ teaspoon baking soda
1 teaspoon baking powder
2 teaspoons cinnamon
2 tablespoons buttermilk
1 cup chopped tart apples
½ cup chopped walnuts

Preheat oven to 350 degrees. Cream butter and sugar until light. Beat in eggs and vanilla; set aside. Combine flour, salt, soda, baking powder and cinnamon in a separate bowl. Blend dry ingredients into batter alternately with buttermilk. Stir in apples and nuts. Pour into a greased and floured 5 x 9-inch loaf pan. Bake 50 to 60 minutes. Cool in pan 10 minutes. Remove from pan and cool completely on wire rack.

May be made in food processor. Freezes well.

# Spicy Pumpkin Bread
*Guaranteed compliments*

May prepare ahead

1 loaf

1½ cups sugar
1 teaspoon baking soda
2 eggs, well beaten
½ cup vegetable oil
½ cup water
¼ teaspoon baking powder
¾ teaspoon salt
2 teaspoons cinnamon
1 teaspoon ground cloves
2 teaspoons nutmeg
1 cup canned pumpkin
1⅔ cups sifted all-purpose
    flour

Preheat oven to 325 degrees. Mix all ingredients. Pour into a greased 5 x 9-inch loaf pan. Bake 1½ hours.

# Food Processor—Three Grain Loaf

**Must prepare partially ahead**                                    **1 loaf**

1 ¼-ounce package dry yeast
1 cup warm water
3 tablespoons brown sugar
2¾ cups bread flour
½ cup whole wheat flour
¼ cup rye flour
¼ cup corn meal
1½ teaspoons salt
¼ cup non-fat dry milk powder
1 egg, room temperature
2 tablespoons corn oil

Mix yeast and warm water according to package directions. Stir in brown sugar and let stand until mixture foams. Combine flours, corn meal, salt and dry milk in food processor. Add egg and oil. With machine running add yeast mixture. Run about 30 seconds or until dough forms a ball. Turn dough out into a greased bowl. (May spray bowl with a vegetable cooking spray.) Cover with a clean dish towel and let rise in a warm place, about 1 hour.

Generously butter a 5 x 9-inch loaf pan and dust with corn meal. Punch down and shape dough into a loaf and place in pan. Let rise again until doubled, 35 to 45 minutes.

Bake in a preheated 375 degree oven about 35 minutes. Bread is done if it sounds hollow when tapped.

*A bowl of warm water on the bottom shelf of a cold oven and the dough bowl on the top shelf works very well as a place to let dough rise.*

desserts

# Desserts

*Found elsewhere in the book.

## BURROUGHS HOME

*At the dawn of the twentieth century, Fort Myers, with 943 residents, experienced a "building boom." The Burroughs Home, an elaborate Victorian two and one-half story home located at the foot of the Edison Bridge, set the standard. The largest and most ornate nineteenth century residence in Fort Myers, it is now the property of the City of Fort Myers.*

# Apple Walnut Squares
*Compliments of Donna Lou Askew, former First Lady of Florida*

**May prepare ahead**                                    **1½ dozen**

4 cups coarsely chopped,
  peeled apples
2 cups sugar
2 eggs, slightly beaten
½ cup vegetable oil
2 cups all-purpose flour
2 teaspoons baking soda
2 teaspoons cinnamon
½ teaspoon salt
1 cup black walnut pieces

Preheat oven to 350 degrees. Combine apples and sugar and let stand until sugar is absorbed, about 45 minutes. Beat eggs and oil with wire whisk. Sift flour, baking soda, cinnamon and salt together. Stir alternately the egg mixture and flour mixture into the apple-sugar mixture. Stir in black walnut pieces.

Spread into a greased and floured 9 x 13-inch pan. Bake 1 hour.

# Clarizen Cookies
*Quick, easy and no flour*

**May prepare ahead**                                    **3 dozen**

½ cup butter or margarine
1½ cups quick-cooking oats
1 egg
½ cup light brown sugar
1 teaspoon vanilla extract
½ teaspoon cinnamon

**Optional:**
½ cup nuts
½ cup raisins
½ cup chocolate chips

Preheat oven to 350 degrees. Melt butter in a large saucepan and add oats. Cook 3 minutes, stirring occasionally. Remove from heat. Beat egg and sugar in a medium-sized bowl; mix in vanilla and cinnamon. Add cooked oats and mix thoroughly. Add any one or two of the optional ingredients, but no more than two as batter becomes too thick. If adding chocolate chips, let batter cool first. Drop by teaspoonfuls on greased cookie sheet and bake 15 minutes or until browned. Cool on rack.

# Drei Augen Cookies
### *Elegant and delicate*

**Must prepare partially ahead**                    2½-3 dozen

1¼ cups unsalted butter,
  softened
⅔ cup sugar
2½ cups all-purpose flour
1 teaspoon cinnamon
1 cup ground unblanched
  almonds
confectioners' sugar
1 10-ounce jar currant jelly

Cream butter. Gradually beat in sugar; stir in flour, cinnamon and almonds. Divide dough in half. Roll each piece between wax or parchment paper to ⅛-inch thickness. Leave in paper; place on cookie sheets and refrigerate until firm, at least 4 hours or overnight.

Preheat oven to 325 degrees. Line cookie sheet with parchment paper. Remove ½ of chilled dough and carefully peel paper from top. Cut dough into 1½-inch circles. In ½ of the circles, cut a ¾-inch hole in the center. Place all the circles on prepared cookie sheets. Repeat this process with the remaining chilled dough. Bake about 15 minutes. Do not let cookies brown too much as the ground nuts will naturally color them due to their oil content. Cool cookies on cookie sheet 1 minute; transfer to rack and cool completely. Generously dust cookies with holes with confectioners' sugar. Warm currant jelly until smooth and liquefied. Spread about ½ teaspoon jelly over each solid cookie. Carefully top each jellied cookie with a powdered cookie.

May freeze dough; cookies may be held in airtight containers for up to 3 weeks.

# Pecan Dreams

May prepare ahead                    4 dozen

1 cup butter or margarine,
  softened
4 tablespoons sugar
2 teaspoons vanilla extract
2 cups all-purpose flour
2 cups finely chopped nuts
confectioners' sugar

Preheat oven to 300 degrees. Cream butter and sugar; add vanilla, flour and nuts, mixing well. Roll into small balls and place on ungreased cookie sheet. Bake 30 to 45 minutes. Remove from oven and roll in confectioners' sugar. Let cool and roll in confectioners' sugar again.

# Heavenly Hash Brownies
*Delicious*

Must prepare ahead                    4 dozen

**Brownies:**
½ cup margarine, softened
1 cup sugar
4 eggs
1 16-ounce can chocolate
  syrup
1 teaspoon vanilla extract
1 cup all-purpose flour
1 teaspoon baking powder

**Topping:**
1 10-ounce bag miniature
  marshmallows
1 cup chopped pecans
3 1-ounce squares unsweetened
  chocolate
1 cup margarine
1 teaspoon vanilla extract
2 eggs
3 cups confectioners' sugar

Preheat oven to 350 degrees. Cream margarine and sugar until light. Add eggs, one at a time, beating well after each. Add chocolate syrup and vanilla; mix well. Sift flour and baking powder into the batter, beating well. Pour batter into a foil-lined and greased 9 x 13-inch pan. Bake 30 minutes.

After removing brownies from oven, immediately cover with marshmallows and pecans. Melt chocolate with margarine; cool. Add vanilla; beat in eggs and confectioners' sugar until smooth. Pour or spoon on brownies. Refrigerate until icing is set. Cut into small bars to serve.

# Butterscotch Brownies

May prepare ahead                                    2 dozen

½ cup margarine
1 1-pound box light brown
   sugar
2 eggs
2 cups all-purpose flour
2 teaspoons baking powder
½ teaspoon vanilla extract
½ teaspoon maple flavoring
1 cup chopped nuts
1 6-ounce package chocolate
   chips, optional

Preheat oven to 350 degrees. Cream margarine and brown sugar. Add remaining ingredients and mix well. Mixture will be stiff. Spread into greased 9 x 13-inch baking pan. Bake 35 minutes.

# Whiskey Cookies

Must prepare partially ahead                          5 dozen

1 pound butter
2 eggs
1 1-pound box brown sugar
½ cup white sugar
5½ cups all-purpose flour
4 tablespoons whiskey
   (enough to make dough stiff)
1 cup chopped pecans

Cream butter until light. Add eggs, mixing well. Add brown and white sugars alternately, mixing well. Add flour, alternating with whiskey, and blend well. Stir in pecans. Chill dough 1 hour. Shape into four 2 x 8-inch rolls and wrap in wax paper. Return rolls to refrigerator and chill at least 24 hours. Slice ⅛-inch thick and bake in a preheated 350 degree oven for 10 minutes or until light brown.

May freeze dough and/or cookies for 2 to 3 months.

# Walnut Squares

May prepare ahead                    **12-16 bars**

½ cup sugar
½ cup butter or margarine,
  softened
2 egg yolks
1 cup all-purpose flour
½ teaspoon baking powder
pinch of salt
½ teaspoon vanilla extract
2 egg whites
1 cup brown sugar
½ cup chopped walnuts

Preheat oven to 350 degrees. Cream sugar, butter and egg yolks. Add flour, baking powder, salt and vanilla, blending well. Spread into an ungreased 8 x 8-inch pan. Beat egg whites until stiff; stir in brown sugar and walnuts. Spread on top of first layer. Bake 20 minutes or until brown. Cut into squares when cool.

# Delicate Lemon Squares
*Rich and yummy*

May prepare ahead                    **2 dozen**

**First Layer:**
1 cup all-purpose flour
¼ cup confectioners' sugar
½ cup butter

Preheat oven to 350 degrees. Stir flour and sugar with a fork until blended. Cut in butter until mixture clings together. Pat into an ungreased 8 x 8-inch baking pan. Bake 10 to 12 minutes.

**Second Layer:**
2 eggs
¾ cup sugar
3 tablespoons freshly squeezed
  lemon juice
2 tablespoons all-purpose flour
½ teaspoon baking powder
confectioners' sugar

Beat eggs in mixing bowl; add sugar and lemon juice. Beat until slightly thick and smooth. Stir together flour and baking powder; add to egg mixture. Blend just until moistened. Pour over baked layer. Bake 20 to 25 minutes. Sift confectioners' sugar over top. Cool and cut into squares.

# German Chocolate-Caramel Layer Squares

**Must prepare ahead**                                    **4 dozen**

1 14-ounce bag caramels
⅔ cup evaporated milk, divided
1 18½-ounce package German chocolate cake mix
¾ cup butter or margarine, softened
1 cup chopped nuts
1 6-ounce package semi-sweet chocolate chips

Preheat oven to 350 degrees. Combine caramels and ⅓ cup evaporated milk in top of double boiler. Heat, stirring constantly, until caramels are melted completely. (Caramels may also be melted on high in microwave for 4 minutes, stirring frequently.) Remove from heat and set aside.

Combine cake mix, ⅓ cup evaporated milk and butter. Beat with electric mixer until mixture holds together. Stir in nuts. Press ½ of mixture into a well-greased 9 x 13-inch pan. Bake 6 minutes.

Sprinkle chocolate chips over crust and cover evenly with caramel mixture. Crumble remaining cake mixture on top. Bake 15 to 18 minutes. Cool and chill. Cut into small squares.

*Pack cookies for mailing by using popcorn to cushion plastic bags containing cookies.*

# Zucchini Brownies
*An unusual brownie*

May prepare ahead                                    1½ dozen

**Brownies:**
2 cups all-purpose flour
½ cup sugar
½ teaspoon salt
1½ teaspoons baking soda
2½ tablespoons cocoa
⅓ cup vegetable oil
1 teaspoon vanilla extract
2 cups finely grated zucchini
½ cup chopped pecans or
  walnuts

Preheat oven to 325 degrees for glass pan or 350 degrees for metal pan. Mix flour, sugar, salt, soda and cocoa. Add oil, vanilla, zucchini and nuts. Mix well. Pour into greased and floured 9 x 13-inch pan. Bake 20 minutes. Cool. Frost with chocolate frosting.

**Frosting:**
2 1-ounce squares semi-sweet
  or unsweetened chocolate
¼ cup butter or margarine
2 tablespoons milk
2 cups sifted confectioners'
  sugar
⅛ teaspoon salt
½ teaspoon vanilla extract

Melt chocolate in top of double boiler over boiling water. Blend in butter and milk. Remove from heat. Add sugar, salt and vanilla. Blend until smooth. If necessary, thin with a few drops of milk.

# Grandma's Sugar Cookies

May prepare ahead                                    3 dozen

½ cup shortening
1 cup sugar
1 egg
1 teaspoon vanilla extract
1½ cups all-purpose flour
1 teaspoon baking powder
½ cup chopped nuts, optional
milk

Preheat oven to 350 degrees. Mix shortening, sugar, egg, vanilla, flour, baking powder and nuts; roll into small balls. Place on greased cookie sheet and press flat with fork dipped in milk. Bake 10 to 15 minutes. Remove from pan at once.

# Sunday Brownies

May prepare ahead                                           3 dozen

**Brownies:**
½ cup margarine
1 cup sugar
4 eggs, well beaten
1 teaspoon vanilla extract
1 16-ounce can chocolate syrup
1 cup + 1 tablespoon all-
    purpose flour
½ teaspoon baking powder
½ cup chopped pecans

Preheat oven to 350 degrees. Cream margarine, sugar, eggs, vanilla and chocolate syrup. Blend in flour and baking powder. Stir in pecans. Pour into a well-greased 10 x 15 x 2-inch baking pan. Bake 30 minutes. Frost immediately. Cool and cut into squares.

**Frosting:**
6 tablespoons butter
6 tablespoons milk
1½ cups confectioners' sugar
½ cup chocolate chips
½ cup chopped pecans

In a saucepan, blend butter, milk and sugar; bring to a boil and cook 30 seconds. Remove from heat; add chocolate chips and pecans. Stir well until frosting begins to thicken.

# Greek Wedding Cookies
*Brings health and luck to the marriage*

May prepare ahead                                           3 dozen

1 cup butter, softened
½ cup shortening
1 cup confectioners' sugar
3 cups all-purpose flour
1 teaspoon vanilla extract
1 cup chopped toasted almonds
confectioners' sugar for dusting

Preheat oven to 350 degrees. Cream butter with shortening; add sugar and beat until mixture is creamy. Add flour, vanilla and almonds, mixing well. Drop on cookie sheet by teaspoonfuls. Bake about 20 minutes. Sprinkle with confectioners' sugar while hot. May be frozen up to 6 months.

# Crème de Menthe Brownies
*A colorful and delectable brownie*

Must prepare ahead                    2 dozen

**Brownies:**
1 cup sugar
½ cup butter
4 eggs, beaten
1 cup sifted all-purpose flour
½ teaspoon salt
1 16-ounce can chocolate syrup
1 teaspoon vanilla extract
½ cup chopped pecans or
  walnuts

Preheat oven to 350 degrees. Cream sugar, butter and eggs until light. Add flour and salt, mixing by hand. Stir in syrup, vanilla and nuts; blend until smooth. Pour into a greased 9 x 13-inch pan. Bake 30 minutes. Cool.

**Frosting:**
2 cups sifted confectioners'
  sugar
½ cup butter, softened
2 tablespoons crème de menthe

Mix sugar, butter and crème de menthe with electric mixer. Frost cooled brownies.

**Glaze:**
6 ounces chocolate chips
6 tablespoons margarine

Melt chocolate chips and margarine in the top of a double boiler. Pour over brownies (will be slightly runny). Refrigerate.

# Chewies

May prepare ahead                    20 bars

1½ cups all-purpose flour
1 teaspoon baking powder
1 teaspoon salt
2 cups firmly packed dark
  brown sugar
½ cup butter, melted
4 eggs, slightly beaten
2 cups chopped nuts
2 cups pitted dates, cut into
  quarters

Preheat oven to 350 degrees. Combine flour, baking powder, salt and brown sugar. Add butter to eggs and mix with dry ingredients. Stir in nuts and dates. Pour into a greased 9 x 13-inch pan and bake 30 minutes. These will keep in a cookie tin for at least a week.

# Cherry Squares

**May prepare ahead**                                          **18 bars**

**Crust:**
1/4 cup butter, softened
1/4 cup brown sugar
1 cup all-purpose flour

**Topping:**
2 eggs, well beaten
1 cup brown sugar
1 teaspoon vanilla extract
1/4 cup all-purpose flour
1/2 teaspoon baking powder
1/4 cup milk
1 cup shredded coconut
1 cup chopped candied cherries

Preheat oven to 375 degrees. Mix butter, brown sugar and flour; pat into a greased 9 x 13-inch pan.

Mix topping ingredients and spread over crust. Bake 25 minutes or until brown. Do not overbake. It will harden when cool.

# Jim's Crispy Extra-Chocolaty Chip Cookies
*A+*

**May prepare ahead**                                          **4 dozen**

3/4 cup butter or margarine,
   softened
6 tablespoons sugar
6 tablespoons brown sugar
3/4 teaspoon vanilla extract
2 egg whites
1 cup + 2 tablespoons
   all-purpose flour
1/2 teaspoon baking soda
1 8-ounce package chocolate
   chips
1/2 cup chopped nuts, optional

Preheat oven to 375 degrees. Cream butter and sugars. Stir in vanilla and egg whites. Gradually stir in flour and soda. Add chocolate chips and, if desired, nuts. Drop by rounded teaspoonfuls onto greased cookie sheets. Bake about 10 minutes.

# Raspberry Walnut Shortbread Bars

May prepare ahead                                                18 bars

**Shortbread:**
1¼ cups sifted all-purpose flour
½ cup sugar
½ cup butter

Preheat oven to 350 degrees. Combine flour and sugar. Cut in butter until mixture is like fine meal. Press over bottom of a lightly greased 7 x 11-inch baking pan. Bake 20 minutes or just until edges become slightly brown. Remove from oven.

**Topping:**
½ cup raspberry jam
2 eggs
½ cup brown sugar
1 teaspoon vanilla extract
2 tablespoons all-purpose flour
⅛ teaspoon salt
⅛ teaspoon baking soda
1 cup chopped walnuts
confectioners' sugar, optional

Spread raspberry jam over shortbread. Beat eggs with brown sugar and vanilla until well blended. Stir in flour mixed with salt and soda; add walnuts. Spoon over jam and spread to corners of pan. Return to oven and bake 15 minutes, or until top is set. Cool in pan; cut into bars. May dust with confectioners' sugar, if desired.

*A 1-pound box of brown sugar yields 2¼ cups firmly packed brown sugar.*

# Goody Cake Bars
*Good to serve at a coffee*

**May prepare ahead**                                    **2 dozen**

**Crust:**
1 18¼-ounce package yellow cake mix
½ cup margarine, melted
1 egg, beaten

Combine cake mix, margarine and egg; mix with a fork. Press into 9 x 13-inch pan.

**Topping:**
1 8-ounce package cream cheese, softened
2 eggs, beaten
1 1-pound box confectioners' sugar
1 teaspoon lemon juice
small amount grated lemon rind

Preheat oven to 350 degrees. Combine cream cheese, eggs and sugar, reserving a little of the sugar to sprinkle on top of bars. Add lemon juice and grated rind. Pour over crust. Bake 30 to 40 minutes. While hot, sprinkle with sugar.

# Toffee Squares

**May prepare ahead**                                    **2 dozen**

1 cup butter, softened
1 cup packed dark brown sugar
2 cups all-purpose flour
1 egg yolk
1 8-ounce solid chocolate candy bar, broken into pieces
½ cup chopped nuts

Preheat oven to 350 degrees. Combine butter, brown sugar, flour and egg yolk, mixing well. Press into a 9 x 13-inch pan and bake 18 minutes.

Sprinkle chocolate candy bar pieces on top of warm cookie layer; let chocolate melt and spread gently. Sprinkle chopped nuts on top. Cut into squares. Keep in refrigerator if day is warm.

# Bourbon Balls

Must prepare ahead                                    5 dozen

½ cup + 3 tablespoons butter
2 1-pound boxes confectioners'
  sugar
¾ cup bourbon (no more)
1½ cups chopped pecans
1 8-ounce package semi-sweet
  chocolate
1 8-ounce package
  unsweetened chocolate
chunk of paraffin, about
  ½ x 4 inches

Cream butter and sugar; add bourbon and pecans. Refrigerate several hours. Roll into 1-inch balls. If the mixture is too thin to form into balls, add a bit more sugar. Refrigerate again for a short time. Melt chocolates and paraffin in a double boiler over simmering, not boiling, water. Using a toothpick, dip each ball in chocolate. After dipping, put balls on a cookie sheet covered with wax paper and place in refrigerator to set before wrapping them in plastic wrap.

# Caramel Corn
*A wonderful non-sticky treat*

Must prepare ahead                                    6 quarts

2 cups popcorn kernels
1 cup margarine
2 cups firmly packed light
  brown sugar
½ cup dark corn syrup
1 teaspoon baking soda
pinch of cream of tartar

Preheat oven to 200 degrees. Pop kernels, without salt, and set aside. In a 1-quart saucepan, combine margarine, brown sugar and syrup. Boil 5 minutes; remove from heat. Stir in baking soda and cream of tartar. Pour mixture over popcorn and toss. Place on a cookie sheet or 9 x 13-inch baking pan. Bake 1 hour, stirring every 15 minutes. Cool and store in an airtight container. Will stay fresh up to 2 weeks.

# Easy Chocolate Candy
*Quick, easy and so good*

May prepare ahead                           3 dozen

1 12-ounce package chocolate
   chips
1 14-ounce can sweetened
   condensed milk
1 teaspoon vanilla extract
1 cup chopped pecans

Melt chocolate chips over low heat. Remove from heat. Add milk. Put back over low heat and stir a couple of minutes. Add vanilla, mixing well. Stir in pecans. Remove from heat. Drop by teaspoon on foil-lined cookie sheet. Refrigerate at least 30 minutes before serving.

# Microwave Fudge

May prepare ahead                     1½-2 dozen

½ cup butter
¼ cup milk
1 1-pound box confectioners'
   sugar
¼ cup cocoa
1 tablespoon vanilla extract
1 cup chopped nuts

Combine butter, milk, sugar, cocoa and vanilla in large glass bowl. Microwave on high 3 minutes. Beat with wire whisk until smooth. Stir in nuts. Pour onto buttered plate. Cool.

# Chocolate Balls

Must prepare ahead                         3 dozen

1 14-ounce can sweetened
   condensed milk
1 cup chocolate chips
1 cup coconut
½ teaspoon baking soda
confectioners' sugar

Preheat oven to 350 degrees. Mix milk, chocolate chips, coconut and soda. Spread in a greased 9 x 9-inch baking pan. Bake about 30 minutes. When partially cooled, cut into 36 squares. Shape into balls then roll in confectioner's sugar. Refrigerate.

# Katim's Candy
*Scrumptious*

Must prepare ahead

2-3 dozen

1 12-ounce package chocolate
  chips
¾ cup chunky peanut butter
1 8-ounce chocolate candy bar
  with almonds
½ cup chopped nuts
1½ cups miniature
  marshmallows

Melt chocolate chips in a double boiler over low heat. Add peanut butter, candy bar and nuts, mixing well. Pour ½ of the mixture into a greased 8-inch square pan. Cover with marshmallows. Spread the remaining batter over the marshmallows. Refrigerate. Cut into squares before serving. May be frozen up to 6 months.

# Fudge Cake

May prepare ahead

12-15 servings

Cake:
2 cups sugar
3 tablespoons cocoa
¼ teaspoon salt
⅔ cup shortening
2 eggs
1 tablespoon vanilla extract
⅓ cup boiling water
⅔ cup sour milk or 1 cup
  buttermilk
2 cups all-purpose flour
1 teaspoon baking soda

Preheat oven to 325 degrees. Combine sugar, cocoa, salt, shortening, eggs and vanilla; mix thoroughly. Add water and buttermilk. Mix with electric mixer until well blended. Add flour and soda, mixing well. Pour into greased and floured 9 x 13-inch pan. Bake 45 minutes. Frost cake while "just warm."

Chocolate Mocha Frosting:
3 tablespoons butter, softened
3 tablespoons brewed coffee,
  room temperature
3 teaspoons cocoa
2 cups confectioners' sugar
1 teaspoon vanilla extract

Combine all ingredients and blend until smooth.

# Brownie Cake
*A brownie lover's delight*

**May prepare ahead**                                    **16 servings**

1 cup butter, softened
2 cups sugar
4 eggs
1 teaspoon baking powder
1 teaspoon baking soda
2½ cups all-purpose flour
1 cup milk
2 teaspoons vanilla extract
1 16-ounce can chocolate syrup
pecan halves, optional
whipped cream, optional

Preheat oven to 350 degrees. In a large bowl, cream butter and sugar. Add eggs and beat. Add baking powder, baking soda, flour, milk, vanilla and chocolate syrup. Beat at medium speed until batter is well mixed and even in color, approximately 3 minutes. Generously grease and flour a large tube pan. If desired, place pecan halves in bottom of pan. Pour in batter. Bake 60 minutes or until inserted toothpick comes out clean. Cake needs no frosting but a dab of whipped cream is nice.

# Avocado Holiday Cake
*An unusual fruit cake*

**May prepare ahead**                                    **24 servings**

1 egg, slightly beaten
½ cup mashed avocado
½ cup buttermilk or sour milk
1 cup chopped pecans
1 cup chopped candied cherries
1 cup chopped candied
    pineapple, optional
2 cups sifted all-purpose flour
¾ cup sugar
½ teaspoon baking soda
½ teaspoon baking powder
¼ teaspoon salt

Preheat oven to 350 degrees. Mix egg, avocado, buttermilk, pecans, cherries and pineapple. Sift together remaining ingredients into a large bowl. Pour avocado mixture into flour mixture. Mix only until flour is moistened. Do not overblend. Pour into a well-greased 9 x 13-inch pan or 3 small 4 x 7-inch loaf pans. Fill slightly more than ½ full. Bake 1 hour, or 45 minutes if using small pans. Cool on rack.

# Sour Cream Cake

May prepare ahead                                    12-16 servings

1 cup butter, softened
3 cups sugar
6 egg yolks
3 cups all-purpose flour
¼ teaspoon baking soda
1 cup sour cream
1 teaspoon almond extract
1 teaspoon vanilla extract
6 egg whites, stiffly beaten

Preheat oven to 300 degrees. Cream butter and sugar until light; add egg yolks, one at a time, beating well after each addition. Sift flour 3 times. Add baking soda to sour cream and stir. Add flour and sour cream alternately to butter mixture, blending well after each addition. Add almond and vanilla extracts; fold in egg whites. Pour into well-greased, lightly floured large tube pan; bake 1 hour and 30 minutes.

# Case's Orange Pound Cake
*First to sell at any bake sale*

May prepare ahead                                    16 servings

Cake:
1 cup butter, softened
2 cups sugar
6 eggs
2 cups all-purpose flour
½ teaspoon orange extract
3 tablespoons orange juice
1 tablespoon lemon juice
zest of 2 oranges*

Preheat oven to 350 degrees. Cream butter and sugar. Add eggs, one at a time, and beat well after each. Gently beat in remaining ingredients. Bake in a greased and floured tube pan 45 minutes or until tester comes out clean. Cool in pan 10 minutes, turn out, and place top side up. Pour glaze over warm cake, if desired.

Orange Glaze, optional:
2 cups confectioners' sugar
4 tablespoons orange juice
½ teaspoon orange extract

Combine all ingredients and pour over warm cake. As cake cools, occasionally spoon glaze over the top and sides.

*The term "zest" refers to finely grating the outer layer of a whole orange, lemon or lime.*

# Best-Ever Chocolate Cake
*A chocolate lover's dream*

**May prepare ahead**                                        **12 servings**

**Cake:**
2 cups all-purpose flour
2 cups sugar
1 cup margarine
4 tablespoons cocoa
1 cup cold water
½ cup buttermilk
1 teaspoon vanilla extract
1 teaspoon cinnamon
¼ teaspoon salt
1 teaspoon baking soda
2 eggs

Preheat oven to 375 degrees. Sift together flour and sugar; set aside. In a saucepan, bring to a boil margarine, cocoa and water; remove from heat. In a large bowl, mix remaining cake ingredients. Add flour mixture and cocoa mixture, stirring well. Bake in a greased and floured 9 x 13-inch pan 20 to 30 minutes.

**Frosting:**
½ cup margarine
4 tablespoons cocoa
5 tablespoons evaporated milk
1 teaspoon vanilla extract
1 cup chopped pecans
1 1-pound box confectioners'
  sugar

Ten minutes before cake is done, prepare frosting. Place margarine, cocoa and milk in saucepan; bring to a boil. Remove from heat and add remaining ingredients. Beat until smooth. Frost cake as soon as it comes out of the oven.

*Use cocoa instead of flour when preparing pan for chocolate cake.*

# Easy Piña Colada Cake
*Always a hit*

**Must prepare ahead**                                    **12 servings**

**Cake:**
1 18½-ounce package
   yellow cake mix
⅔ cup light rum*
3 eggs
½ cup butter or margarine,
   softened

**Sauce:**
1 15-ounce can cream
   of coconut
⅓ cup light rum, optional

**Frosting:**
1 7-ounce package shredded
   coconut
1 8-ounce can crushed
   pineapple, drained well
1 12-ounce container frozen
   whipped topping, thawed

*May substitute juice from
 drained pineapple and enough
 water to make ⅔ cup.

Preheat oven to 350 degrees. Grease and flour a 9 x 13-inch pan. Mix all cake ingredients; beat with an electric mixer for 5 minutes. Pour into prepared pan and bake 35 minutes.

While cake is still warm, poke holes in top with a large fork. Mix cream of coconut and rum; pour over warm cake. Cool in pan.

Fold coconut and pineapple into whipped topping. Frost cake. Place in refrigerator and chill 2 to 3 hours before serving. Cake keeps well for a week in the refrigerator.

# Coconut Cake
*Moist, rich and easy*

**May not prepare ahead**                    **12 servings**

**Cake:**
4 eggs
2 cups sugar
1 cup vegetable oil
1 cup buttermilk
2 cups self-rising flour
1 7-ounce package coconut
2 teaspoons coconut flavoring

**Topping:**
1 teaspoon coconut flavoring
½ cup sugar
¼ cup water

Preheat oven to 350 degrees. Beat eggs and sugar; add oil and mix well. Alternately mix in buttermilk and flour. Blend in coconut and coconut flavoring. Pour batter into a well-greased and floured Bundt pan. Bake 45 minutes. Let cool 10 minutes; remove from pan and immediately pour on topping. Best if served warm.

Mix topping ingredients in small saucepan. Bring mixture to a boil and let boil 1 minute. Remove from heat.

Cover cake with plastic wrap to keep moist.

# Self-Filled Cupcakes
*Kids love these*

**May prepare ahead**                    **24-30 cupcakes**

1 18¼-ounce package white
   or yellow cake mix
⅓ cup sugar
1 8-ounce package cream
   cheese, softened
1 egg
pinch of salt
1 cup chocolate chips

Preheat oven to 350 degrees. Prepare cake mix according to package directions. Fill paper cupcake liners ⅔ full.

Cream sugar with cream cheese; beat in egg and salt. Stir in chocolate chips. Drop a rounded teaspoon of cream cheese mixture onto each cupcake. Bake as directed on cake mix box.

# Carrot Cake

May prepare ahead                                    16. servings

**Cake:**
1¼ cups vegetable oil
2 cups sugar
4 eggs
3 cups grated raw carrots
1 cup chopped nuts
1 8-ounce can crushed
   pineapple, drained
2 teaspoons vanilla extract
2 cups sifted all-purpose flour
1 teaspoon salt
2 teaspoons baking soda
2 teaspoons cinnamon

Preheat oven to 350 degrees. Combine oil, sugar and eggs. Beat well. Stir in grated carrots, nuts, pineapple and vanilla. Add flour, salt, soda and cinnamon; beat well. Pour into a greased and floured 9-inch Bundt pan. Bake 1 hour and 15 minutes. Let cool before frosting.

May be baked in microwave on medium power 15 to 20 minutes. Rotate dish once during baking time.

**Cream Cheese Nut Frosting:**
1 8-ounce package cream
   cheese, softened
½ cup butter or margarine,
   softened
1 1-pound box confectioners'
   sugar
2 teaspoons vanilla extract
1 cup chopped nuts

Mix cream cheese and butter. Add sugar and vanilla. Beat until smooth. Stir in nuts.

*If your frosting is creamy, layer cakes should be stored loosely covered with aluminum foil, plastic wrap or under a large inverted bowl.*

*If your frosting is fluffy, it should be served the day it is made. If it must be stored, lift cover slightly so the container is NOT airtight.*

# Raw Apple Cake

May prepare ahead | 16 servings

2 cups sugar
2 eggs
1½ cups vegetable oil
3 cups all-purpose flour
1 heaping teaspoon cinnamon
½ teaspoon salt
1⅛ teaspoons baking soda
3 cups peeled and diced apples
1 cup chopped pecans
¾ cup chopped candied
   cherries, optional
¾ cup coconut
2 teaspoons vanilla extract

Preheat oven to 300 degrees. Cream sugar and eggs. Add oil slowly and beat well. Combine flour, cinnamon, salt and baking soda; add to sugar mixture and mix well. Add remaining ingredients and mix thoroughly. Pour into a greased and floured tube pan. Bake 1 hour and 20 minutes.

# Orange Cake

May prepare ahead | 9-12 servings

**Cake:**
2¼ cups sifted cake flour
1 teaspoon baking soda
½ teaspoon salt
½ cup butter, softened
1 cup sugar
2 eggs, slightly beaten
1 teaspoon vanilla extract
grated peel of 1 orange
1 cup raisins
½ cup chopped walnuts
1 cup sour milk

**Glaze:**
1 cup sugar
⅓ cup orange juice

Preheat oven to 350 degrees. Sift together flour, baking soda and salt. Cream butter, gradually blending in sugar. Beat in eggs. Stir in vanilla, orange peel, raisins and walnuts. Add flour mixture alternately with milk. Pour into well-greased 9-inch square pan. Bake 40 minutes. Remove from oven and spread with glaze.

Mix ingredients for glaze.

# Hummingbird Cake

May prepare ahead                                    **16 servings**

**Cake:**
3 cups all-purpose flour
2 cups sugar
1 teaspoon salt
1 teaspoon cinnamon
1 teaspoon baking soda
3 eggs, beaten
1½ cups vegetable oil
2 cups chopped bananas
1 8-ounce can crushed
    pineapple, undrained
1 cup chopped pecans
1½ teaspoons vanilla extract

Preheat oven to 350 degrees. Sift flour, sugar, salt, cinnamon and baking soda together. Add eggs and oil, stirring until moistened. Do not beat. Stir in bananas, pineapple, pecans and vanilla. Pour into large greased and floured tube pan. Bake 1 hour and 10 minutes. Cool.

**Cream Cheese Frosting:**
½ cup butter, softened
1 8-ounce package cream
    cheese, softened
1 1-pound box confectioners'
    sugar
1 teaspoon vanilla extract

Cream butter and cream cheese. Add sugar, beating until light and fluffy. Stir in vanilla. Frost cooled cake.

# Mom's Pound Cake

May prepare ahead                                    **16 servings**

½ cup shortening
¾ cup butter, softened
3 cups sugar
5 eggs
1 cup milk
3 cups all-purpose flour
½ teaspoon baking powder
½ teaspoon almond extract
1 tablespoon vanilla extract

Preheat oven to 325 degrees. Cream shortening and butter, gradually adding sugar. Add eggs, one at a time, beating well after each egg is added. Gradually add milk, flour and baking powder. Stir in almond and vanilla extracts. Pour into greased and floured large tube pan or Bundt pan. Bake 1 hour and 25 minutes.

# Chocolate Cake and Frosting

*This cake is a hit wherever it's taken*

**Must prepare ahead**                    **12 servings**

**Cake:**
2 cups all-purpose flour
2 cups sugar
½ cup butter
½ cup shortening
4 tablespoons cocoa
1 cup water
½ cup buttermilk
1 teaspoon baking soda
2 eggs
2 teaspoons vanilla extract

**Frosting:**
½ cup margarine
4 tablespoons cocoa
6 tablespoons buttermilk
1 1-pound box confectioners'
   sugar
2 teaspoons vanilla extract
1 cup chopped nuts
1 cup coconut, optional

Preheat oven to 350 degrees. Sift flour and sugar into a large mixing bowl and set aside. In a saucepan, combine butter, shortening, cocoa and water; bring to a boil. Pour over flour and sugar. Mix buttermilk and soda; add to mixture in the bowl. Add eggs and vanilla. Mix well. Pour into a lightly greased and floured 9 x 13-inch baking pan. Bake 35 minutes. Cool on wire rack.

In a saucepan, combine margarine, cocoa and buttermilk; bring to a boil. Add sugar, vanilla, nuts and, if desired, coconut. Cool and pour over cake.

*Frosting will not stick to wax paper if you butter the paper lightly before wrapping.*

# Prune Spice Cake

May prepare ahead                                    20-24 servings

**Cake:**
2 cups sugar
1 cup vegetable oil
2 cups all-purpose flour
1 teaspoon baking soda
2 eggs
1 cup buttermilk
1 cup cooked, chopped prunes
1 cup chopped pecans
1 teaspoon cinnamon
1 teaspoon nutmeg
1 teaspoon allspice
1 teaspoon vanilla extract

Preheat oven to 350 degrees. Combine all cake ingredients, mixing well. Pour into greased and floured 9 x 13-inch pan. Bake 45 minutes or until cake tests done. Cool cake in pan.

**Glaze:**
1 cup sugar
1 cup buttermilk
1 teaspoon baking soda
1 tablespoon light corn syrup
6 tablespoons butter

In large saucepan, mix sugar, buttermilk, baking soda and corn syrup. Cook over medium heat, stirring constantly until it turns caramel brown. Add butter and cook 2 to 3 minutes longer. Pour glaze over cooled cake.

# Dump Cake
*Easy*

May prepare ahead                                    8-10 servings

1 22-ounce can cherry pie
   filling
1 16-ounce can crushed
   pineapple, drained
1 18¼-ounce package
   yellow cake mix
1 cup butter, melted
1 cup chopped pecans
whipped cream or vanilla
   ice cream, optional

Preheat oven to 350 degrees. In order listed, layer ingredients in a greased 9 x 13-inch pan. Bake 50 minutes.

May serve with whipped cream or vanilla ice cream.

# Pumpkin Date Cake with Bourbon Eggnog Sauce

May prepare ahead                                    12 servings

**Cake:**
2 cups sugar
1½ cups vegetable oil
3 teaspoons cinnamon
1 teaspoon allspice
1 teaspoon salt
2 cups canned pumpkin
2 teaspoons baking soda
2 teaspoons baking powder
4 eggs
2 cups all-purpose flour
1 cup pitted, chopped dates
1 cup raisins
1 cup chopped nuts

**Bourbon Eggnog Sauce:**
½ cup butter, softened
1 cup sugar
1 egg
1 cup heavy cream
¾ ounce bourbon

Preheat oven to 300 degrees. Grease and flour a large tube pan. Cream sugar and oil; add cinnamon, allspice, salt, pumpkin, baking soda and baking powder. Mix well. Add eggs, one at a time, beating well after each addition. Roll dates, raisins and nuts in part of flour; add to pumpkin mixture along with remaining flour. Mix well. Pour into prepared pan; bake 1 hour and 40 minutes. Serve with Bourbon Eggnog Sauce.

Cream butter and sugar; add egg and beat well. Add cream; put into double boiler, stirring constantly over medium heat until thick. Remove from heat; add bourbon.

To serve, slice cake and spoon sauce over each slice. Sauce keeps several days in refrigerator.

# Ruth's Surprise Cake
*Very rich*

May prepare ahead                                    **16 servings**

**First Layer:**
⅔ cup butter
¼ cup packed brown sugar
1 cup all-purpose flour

Preheat oven to 350 degrees. Mix butter, brown sugar and flour until well blended. Press into ungreased 9 x 9-inch pan.

**Second Layer:**
1½ cups packed brown sugar
2 tablespoons all-purpose flour
1 cup coconut
¾ cup chopped walnuts or
    pecans
¾ cup currants
¼ teaspoon baking powder
½ teaspoon salt
1 teaspoon vanilla extract
2 eggs

Mix all ingredients for second layer and spread on top of first layer. Bake 30 minutes.

**Frosting:**
1 cup confectioners' sugar
1 tablespoon butter,
    softened
½ teaspoon vanilla extract
1 tablespoon boiling water

Mix all ingredients for frosting. Frosting will be thin. Spread on hot cake.

# Fresh Blueberry Pie
*Quick and different*

Must prepare ahead                                    **8 servings**

1 9-inch pie shell, baked
1 pint fresh blueberries
1 8-ounce jar red currant jelly
1 cup sour cream

Wash and drain blueberries and pour into baked crust. Melt jelly over low heat; pour over berries. Spread sour cream on top. Refrigerate 3 to 4 hours before serving.

# Best Chocolate Pie
### Excellent, light and easy

**Must prepare ahead**                                    **8 servings**

1 cup butter, softened
1 cup sugar
2 1-ounce squares unsweetened
  chocolate, melted
2 teaspoons vanilla extract
4 eggs
1 9-inch pie shell, baked
1 cup heavy cream, whipped

Combine butter, sugar, chocolate and vanilla; beat well. Add eggs one at a time, beating after each addition for 3 minutes. Pour into pie shell. Top with whipped cream. Refrigerate.

# Triple Crown Pie

**May prepare ahead**                                    **8 servings**

¾ cup semi-sweet chocolate
  chips
1 9-inch unbaked pie shell
¼ cup butter or margarine,
  melted
2 eggs, slightly beaten
¼ cup packed light brown
  sugar
½ cup sugar
½ cup + 1 tablespoon light
  corn syrup
1½ teaspoons all-purpose flour
½ teaspoon vanilla extract
1½ ounces bourbon or rum
¾ cup chopped nuts
whipped cream for garnish

Preheat oven to 350 degrees. Spread chocolate chips evenly over bottom of pie shell. Combine remaining ingredients and mix well. Pour mixture over chips. Bake 40 to 50 minutes. Serve cold or warm. Top with whipped cream, if desired.

# Grasshopper Pie
*Cool, pretty and delicious*

**Must prepare ahead**                                    **6-8 servings**

**Crust:**
1¼ cups chocolate wafer
   crumbs
⅓ cup butter, melted

Combine chocolate wafer crumbs and butter; press into an 8-inch pie plate. Chill well.

**Filling:**
⅔ cup milk
24 large marshmallows
¼ cup green crème de menthe
2 tablespoons white crème de
   cacao
1 cup heavy cream, whipped
chocolate wafer crumbs,
   optional

Combine milk and marshmallows in a heavy saucepan; cook over low heat, stirring often, until marshmallows melt. Cool to room temperature. Fold liqueurs and whipped cream into marshmallow mixture. Spoon into pie shell. Garnish with chocolate wafer crumbs, if desired. Freeze 4 to 6 hours.

# Citrus Chiffon Pie
*Fast, easy and good*

**Must prepare ahead**                                    **8 servings**

1 3-ounce package cream
   cheese, softened
1 14-ounce can sweetened
   condensed milk
½ cup citrus juice (lime,
   lemon or calamondin*)
1 8-ounce carton frozen
   whipped topping, thawed
1 9-inch pie shell, baked

Beat cream cheese, milk and citrus juice until well blended. Fold in whipped topping. Pour into baked pie shell. Refrigerate.

*Calamondin is a small, round citrus fruit grown in South Florida and is generally in season from November through March.*

# Buttermilk Pie

**Must prepare ahead**                                    **6 servings**

½ cup butter, melted
3 eggs, beaten
¼ cup all-purpose flour
1¾ cups sugar
½ teaspoon salt
½ cup buttermilk
½ teaspoon vanilla extract
1 9-inch unbaked pie shell

Preheat oven to 350 degrees. Mix butter and eggs; add flour, sugar, salt, buttermilk and vanilla; beat lightly to mix. Pour into pie shell and bake 45 minutes. Cool pie 1 hour before serving. It is best served at room temperature.

# Nana's Chocolate Pie
*So good and easy to prepare*

**Must prepare ahead**                                **8-10 servings**

**Filling:**
1 cup sugar
2 rounded tablespoons cocoa
2 tablespoons all-purpose flour
2 cups milk
3 egg yolks, beaten well

1 9-inch pie shell, baked

Preheat oven to 325 degrees. Mix sugar, cocoa and flour in a saucepan. Combine milk and beaten egg yolks. Add to the saucepan a little at a time, mixing thoroughly after each addition so that it will not lump. Cook over medium heat, stirring constantly, until it thickens. Pour into pie crust.

**Meringue:**
3 egg whites
5 tablespoons sugar

Beat egg whites until they hold a peak. Gradually add sugar while continuing to beat. Spread onto pie, sealing edges. Bake approximately 25 minutes or until meringue is golden brown. Refrigerate.

# Joyce's Egg Custard Pie

**Must prepare ahead**                                    **8 servings**

1 cup half and half cream
1 cup milk
1 cup sugar
4 eggs
½ teaspoon salt
1½ teaspoons vanilla extract
1 9-inch unbaked pie shell
nutmeg

Preheat oven to 350 degrees. Mix cream, milk and sugar in a saucepan. Heat only to scalding point. Beat egg; add salt. Add heated milk mixture SLOWLY to eggs, stirring constantly to keep eggs from cooking too quickly. Add vanilla. Pour into unbaked pie shell. Sprinkle nutmeg liberally on top. Bake 35 to 45 minutes or until knife inserted 1 inch from edge comes out clean. Pie should be set, but do NOT overbake. Cool, then refrigerate.

# Florida Pecan Pie

*A traditional Southern treat combined with
the sunny taste of Florida oranges*

**May prepare ahead**                                    **8 servings**

3 eggs, beaten
½ cup sugar
1 cup dark corn syrup
1 tablespoon grated orange
   rind
⅓ cup fresh orange juice
1 tablespoon all-purpose flour
¼ teaspoon salt
1¼ cups chopped pecans
1 9-inch unbaked deep dish
   pie shell
¾ cup pecan halves
whipped cream for topping

Preheat oven to 350 degrees. Combine eggs, sugar, corn syrup, orange rind, orange juice, flour and salt. Beat with electric mixer at medium speed until blended. Stir in chopped pecans. Pour mixture into pie shell. Arrange pecan halves on top of pie. Bake 55 to 60 minutes. Serve topped with whipped cream.

May be frozen.

# Kay's Coconut Pie

**Must prepare ahead**                                    **6-8 servings**

2 cups milk
1¾ cups sugar
½ cup Bisquick
4 eggs
¼ cup butter or margarine
1½ teaspoons vanilla extract
1 7-ounce package flaked
  coconut

Combine milk, sugar, Bisquick, eggs, butter and vanilla in blender. Blend on low for 3 minutes. Stir in coconut. Pour into a greased 9-inch pie pan. Let stand 5 minutes before baking. Bake at 350 degrees for 40 minutes. Serve at room temperature or cold.

# Key Lime Pie
*Easy and very Floridian*

**Must prepare ahead**                                    **6-8 servings**

**Filling:**
4 egg yolks
1 14-ounce can sweetened
  condensed milk
¼ cup key lime juice*
1 9-inch baked pie shell or
  graham cracker crust

Preheat oven to 350 degrees. Blend egg yolks and milk until well mixed. Slowly add lime juice, mixing well. Custard will thicken as you add lime juice. Pour into baked crust. Top with meringue.

**Meringue:**
4 egg whites
½ teaspoon cream of tartar
8 tablespoons sugar

*May substitute twice the
  amount of Persian lime juice.

Beat egg whites with cream of tartar until stiff. Slowly add sugar while beating. Whip until whites hold stiff peaks. Top pie filling. Bake 10 minutes or until meringue is delicately browned. Serve chilled.

NEVER add green food coloring. If it is green, it is not key lime pie!

*Freeze key lime juice in ice cube trays while key limes are plentiful. When frozen, place cubes in freezer bags and keep frozen until ready to use.*

# Kahlúa Pecan Pie

May prepare ahead

8 servings

1 9-inch unbaked deep dish
   pie shell
3 eggs
¾ cup sugar
1 cup dark corn syrup
1 teaspoon vanilla extract
¼ cup butter, melted
1 tablespoon Kahlúa or other
   coffee liqueur
1 cup pecan halves

Preheat oven to 350 degrees. Beat eggs; add sugar and beat well. Stir in syrup, vanilla, butter and Kahlúa. Arrange pecan halves in bottom of pie shell and pour syrup mixture over them. (Pecans will come to the top.) Bake 40 to 45 minutes or until center is set. If crust begins to brown too much, protect with strips of foil.

# Turtle Pie

Must prepare ahead

8 servings

Crust:
1½ cups crushed chocolate
   wafers*
2 tablespoons butter, melted
Filling:
1 cup marshmallows
1 cup chocolate chips
1¼ cups evaporated milk
1 quart vanilla ice cream,
   softened
1 cup heavy cream, whipped,
   optional

*These are often found near the ice cream section of the grocery store.

Combine crushed cookies and melted butter; press into a 9-inch pie plate.

In a saucepan, combine marshmallows, chocolate chips and milk. Boil until mixture coats a spoon. Let cool.

Fill chocolate shell with ½ of the softened ice cream, freeze until solid. Spread with chocolate filling, and then remaining ice cream. Freeze several hours before serving. Top with whipped cream, if desired.

# Cranberry Pie

**Must prepare ahead**                    **9-12 servings**

2 cups chopped fresh
  cranberries
1 large banana, diced
⅔ cup sugar
2 cups crushed vanilla wafers,
  divided
½ cup butter or margarine,
  softened
1 cup confectioners' sugar
2 eggs
½ cup chopped pecans
1 cup heavy cream, whipped

Mix cranberries, banana and sugar; set aside. Place 1½ cups of crushed vanilla wafers in bottom of an 8 x 8-inch glass baking dish or large pie plate. Cream butter and confectioners' sugar. Add eggs and beat well. Spread mixture over crumbs. Top with cranberry-banana mixture and sprinkle with pecans. Spread whipped cream over top. Sprinkle with remaining crushed vanilla wafers. Chill 4 hours or overnight.

# Key Lime Chiffon Pie

**Must prepare ahead**                    **8 servings**

1¼ cups sugar, divided
2 egg yolks, slightly beaten
¼ teaspoon salt
½ cup key lime juice, divided
1 tablespoon unflavored gelatin
½ cup cold water
1 teaspoon grated lime rind
2 egg whites, stiffly beaten
1 cup heavy cream, whipped
1 9-inch graham cracker crust
  or pie shell, baked

Combine 1 cup sugar, egg yolks, salt and ¼ cup lime juice; cook over boiling water in double boiler, stirring constantly until thickened (do not worry about a few lumps). Soften gelatin in cold water. Add hot lime mixture, stirring until thoroughly dissolved. Add rind and remaining lime juice. Cool in refrigerator until mixture begins to gel. Fold ¼ cup sugar into beaten egg whites. Slowly fold egg white mixture into cooled lime mixture until well blended. Fold in whipped cream and spoon into pie shell. Chill 3 to 6 hours before serving.

# Island Key Lime Pie

**Must prepare ahead**                              **6-8 servings**

**Pie:**
1½ cups sugar
1½ cups water
6 tablespoons cornstarch
½ cup key lime juice
3 egg yolks, slightly beaten
1 9-inch pie shell, baked

In a heavy saucepan, bring sugar and water to a boil. Meanwhile, combine cornstarch and lime juice in a bowl; mix until cornstarch is dissolved. Gently blend yolks into lime mixture until thoroughly mixed. Pour lime-egg yolk mixture into boiling sugar and water, stirring constantly just until mixture comes to a boil again. Remove immediately and cool 15 minutes. Pour into pie shell. Spread meringue on top. Bake at 400 degrees until lightly browned.

**Meringue:**
3 egg whites
6 tablespoons sugar

Beat egg whites until stiff but not dry. Gradually beat in sugar a tablespoon at a time. Spread on pie.

# Million Dollar Pie

**Must prepare ahead**                              **2 pies**

1 cup chopped nuts
¼ cup lemon juice
1 14-ounce can sweetened
   condensed milk
1 12-ounce container frozen
   whipped topping, thawed
1 15¼-ounce can crushed
   pineapple, slightly drained
2 9-inch pie shells, baked
coconut or almonds for garnish,
   optional

Mix nuts, lemon juice, condensed milk, whipped topping and pineapple; blend well. Pour into pie shells. Top with coconut or almonds, if desired. Refrigerate.

# Peanut Butter Pie

**Must prepare ahead**                                      **6-8 servings**

3 heaping tablespoons peanut
   butter (smooth or crunchy)
1 8-ounce package cream
   cheese, softened
1¾ cups confectioners' sugar
1 teaspoon vanilla extract
1 8-ounce container frozen
   whipped topping, thawed
1 9-inch graham cracker crust

Blend peanut butter, cream cheese, sugar and vanilla in food processor until smooth. Fold in whipped topping. Pour into graham cracker crust and chill at least 6 hours.

# Peanut Butter Banana Cream Pie

**Must prepare ahead**                                      **6-8 servings**

⅓ cup creamy peanut butter
¾ cup confectioners' sugar
1 9-inch pie shell, baked
⅓ cup all-purpose flour
½ cup sugar
dash of salt
2 cups milk
2 egg yolks, slightly beaten
2 teaspoons butter or
   margarine
1 teaspoon vanilla extract
1 banana, sliced
½ cup heavy cream

Mix peanut butter and confectioners' sugar until crumbly. Reserve 2 tablespoons of the mixture and spread the remainder on the bottom of the baked pie shell.

Mix flour, sugar, salt, milk and egg yolks in a saucepan and cook, stirring constantly, until it comes to a rolling boil. Remove filling from heat and add butter and vanilla. Arrange banana slices over the peanut butter mixture. Pour filling over bananas and let cool. Chill in refrigerator several hours.

Whip cream and spread over filling. Sprinkle 2 tablespoons of reserved peanut butter crumbs on top of whipped cream.

# Lemon Pie with Blueberry Sauce
*Light and simple to prepare*

**Must prepare ahead**

**8 servings**

**Crust:**
1 cup all-purpose flour
½ cup butter
2 tablespoons sugar
¼ teaspoon salt

**Filling:**
2 egg whites
⅔ cup sugar
¼ cup fresh lemon juice
2 teaspoons grated lemon peel
1 cup heavy cream, whipped

**Sauce:**
⅔ cup sugar
1 tablespoon cornstarch
⅔ cup cold water
2 cups fresh blueberries

Preheat oven to 375 degrees. In a food processor mix flour, butter, sugar and salt until crumbly. Place ⅓ cup of the crumb mixture in a small baking dish; press remaining mixture into a greased and floured 9-inch pie plate. Bake both 12 to 15 minutes; cool.

Combine egg whites, sugar and lemon juice; beat to stiff peaks. Fold lemon peel and whipped cream into egg white mixture. Turn entire mixture into pie shell. Top with baked crumbs. Chill. Serve with blueberry sauce.

In a saucepan combine sugar and cornstarch. Add water; cook and stir until thick. Cook 2 minutes more. Add blueberries. Return mixture to boiling. Remove from heat. Chill.

The pie freezes well. Do not freeze sauce.

*For any fresh fruit pie, it is better to brown crust a bit prior to filling and baking.*

*Make pie crusts ahead in large batches. Form balls large enough for one crust; place individual balls into freezer bags. These will keep 3 or 4 months.*

pies

# Pumpkin Pie

**May prepare ahead**                    **6-8 servings**

2 cups pumpkin
1 cup brown sugar
1 cup sugar
2 eggs
1 cup evaporated milk
1 teaspoon ginger
1 teaspoon cinnamon
1 teaspoon pumpkin spice
1 teaspoon salt
1 9-inch unbaked pie shell

Preheat oven to 350 degrees. Mix pumpkin, sugars, eggs, milk and spices in a large bowl with electric mixer until very well mixed. Pour into pie shell. Bake 1 hour or until set in center.

# Sour Cream Apple Pie
*Good warm or cold*

**May prepare ahead**                    **6-8 servings**

Pie:
2 tablespoons all-purpose flour
⅛ teaspoon salt
¾ cup sugar
1 egg
1 cup sour cream
½ teaspoon vanilla extract
2 cups peeled and chopped
  apples
1 10-inch unbaked pie shell

Preheat oven to 425 degrees. Mix flour, salt and sugar. Add egg, sour cream and vanilla, beating until smooth. Stir in apples. Pour mixture into pie shell. Bake 15 minutes, then reduce heat to 350 degrees and continue baking 30 minutes longer. Remove from oven.

Topping:
⅓ cup sugar
¼ cup margarine
1 teaspoon cinnamon

Mix topping ingredients until crumbly. Sprinkle over pie and bake 10 minutes at 425 degrees.

whipped cream, optional

Serve with whipped cream if desired.

# Fresh Peach Pie with Crusty Topping
*Fast and easy*

**May prepare ahead**                    **6 servings**

6 to 8 fresh peaches, peeled
  and halved
1 9-inch pie shell, partially
  baked
1 cup sugar
⅓ cup margarine
⅓ cup all-purpose flour
1 egg, beaten
¼ teaspoon vanilla extract

Preheat oven to 425 degrees. Place peach halves in pie shell with cavity sides down. Cream sugar and margarine. Add flour, egg and vanilla, mixing well. Spread mixture over peaches. Bake 15 minutes; reduce heat to 325 degrees and bake 60 minutes, or until peaches are done.

# Strawberry Meringue Pie
*Superb with Florida strawberries*

**Must prepare ahead**                    **8 servings**

**Meringue Shell:**
4 egg whites at room
  temperature
½ teaspoon cream of tartar
¼ teaspoon salt
1 cup sugar
1 teaspoon vanilla extract

**Pie:**
½ cup butter or margarine,
  softened
2 cups confectioners' sugar
4 egg yolks
½ teaspoon shredded lemon
  peel
1 tablespoon lemon juice
1 quart fresh strawberries,
  cleaned and hulled
1 cup heavy cream, whipped

Preheat oven to 275 degrees. Combine egg whites, cream of tartar and salt; beat until frothy. Add sugar gradually and beat until stiff peaks form. Fold in vanilla. Form into a shell in a 10-inch pie pan. Bake approximately 1 hour until meringue is firm and dry. Cool.

Cream butter and sugar; add egg yolks. Beat in lemon peel and lemon juice. Mix well and pour into meringue shell. Arrange whole or halved strawberries in a pattern around the custard filling. Cover with plastic wrap and refrigerate several hours or overnight. Serve with whipped cream.

# Strawberry Pie

**Must prepare ahead**                                    **6 servings**

1 9-inch deep dish pie shell,
  baked
1¼ cups water
½ cup sugar
2 tablespoons cornstarch
1 3-ounce package strawberry
  gelatin
1½ pints fresh strawberries,
  hulled and cleaned, or
  1 16-ounce package
  unsweetened frozen
  strawberries, thawed*
1 cup heavy cream, whipped

*May substitute sweetened
  frozen strawberries, but
  decrease sugar to ¼ cup or less.

Boil water, sugar and cornstarch until clear. Add gelatin. Put strawberries into pie shell. Pour liquid over strawberries. Refrigerate at least 2 hours. Top with whipped cream.

# Fruit Mousse

**Must prepare ahead**                                    **4 servings**

1 1-ounce envelope unflavored
  gelatin
¼ cup + ½ teaspoon boiling
  water
½ cup heavy cream
4 ounces frozen sweetened
  strawberries, raspberries
  or blueberries
fresh fruit, optional
whipped cream, optional

Dissolve gelatin in boiling water. Place gelatin mixture, cream and fruit into a blender; blend until thick, about 2 minutes. Pour into small parfait glasses. Refrigerate at least 20 minutes. Garnish with fresh fruit or whipped cream, if desired.

# Amaretto Chocolate Mousse Dessert

**Must prepare ahead**                                    **12 servings**

1 6-ounce package semi-sweet
 chocolate chips
18 whole blanched almonds
½ cup Amaretto
2 1-ounce envelopes
 unflavored gelatin
¼ cup water
4 egg yolks
⅓ cup sugar
2 cups milk
4 egg whites, stiffly beaten
2 cups heavy cream, whipped
2 3-ounce packages
 ladyfingers, split

Place chocolate in bowl. Place bowl in another bowl of hot water. Stir until chocolate is melted. Dip bottom half of almonds into chocolate and put on wax paper. Chill until firm. Gradually stir Amaretto into remaining chocolate. Set aside.

In a saucepan, combine gelatin and water. Stir in egg yolks, sugar and milk. Stir over low heat until mixture thickens slightly and coats a spoon. Stir in chocolate mixture. Chill until mixture mounds. Fold in egg whites. Remove 1 cup of the whipped cream and set aside for decorating top. Fold remaining cream into chocolate mixture. Chill until mixture mounds. Line the bottom and sides of an ungreased 9-inch springform pan with split ladyfingers. Pour in chocolate mixture. Chill until firm.

When ready to serve, remove sides of pan. Spoon reserved whipped cream into pastry bag; pipe rosettes around outer edge of cake. Press a chocolate almond into each rosette. Chill until ready to serve.

*Egg whites should be at room temperature before beating.*

# Amaretto Coconut Cream Dessert
*Fabulous*

**Must prepare ahead**                          **12 servings**

**Crust:**
1 cup graham cracker crumbs
¼ cup sugar
4 tablespoons butter, melted

**Filling:**
1¼ cups shredded coconut
1 cup sugar
4 eggs
2 1-ounce envelopes
  unflavored gelatin
⅓ cup cold water
½ cup Amaretto
⅛ teaspoon almond extract
4 cups heavy cream, whipped
12 fresh strawberries for
  garnish

Grease bottom of a 10-inch spring-form pan. Combine all crust ingredients and press evenly into bottom of pan.

Preheat oven to 350 degrees. Spread coconut on baking sheet. Toast in oven 5 minutes or until golden; stir often.

Beat sugar and eggs until fluffy. Sprinkle gelatin into cold water in glass measuring cup or bowl; let stand 5 minutes. Then set cup in pan of hot water over heat until gelatin is dissolved. Fold gelatin, Amaretto and almond extract into egg mixture. Let stand until slightly thickened. Fold in coconut, reserving small amount for garnish. Fold in whipped cream. Pour into pan. Chill.

To serve, sprinkle with reserved coconut and garnish with strawberries.

*Beaten egg whites are stiff enough if they do not slide when the bowl is turned upside down.*

# Angel Food Chocolate Dessert
*For those who love chocolate*

**Must prepare ahead**                    **14-16 servings**

1 12-ounce package chocolate
  chips
2 tablespoons sugar
3 egg yolks, beaten
3 egg whites, stiffly beaten
2 cups heavy cream, whipped
8 ounces angel food cake
½ cup sliced almonds

Melt chocolate chips and sugar in double boiler or microwave. Remove from heat and add beaten egg yolks slowly. Cool 5 minutes. Fold in stiffly beaten egg whites and whipped cream. Break cake into bite-size pieces. Layer ½ of the cake on bottom of a buttered 8 x 12-inch dish. Spread with ½ of chocolate mixture. Repeat layers. Sprinkle sliced almonds on top. Chill overnight. Cut into small squares before serving.

# Lemon Dainty

**May prepare ahead**                    **4-6 servings**

1 cup sugar
⅓ cup all-purpose flour
2 egg yolks
juice of 1 lemon
grated rind of 1 lemon
1 cup milk
2 egg whites, beaten
1 cup heavy cream, whipped

Preheat oven to 350 degrees. Mix sugar and flour; add egg yolks, lemon juice and rind. Stir thoroughly until creamy and well-mixed; add milk. Fold in egg whites. Pour into 1½-quart square dish. Place dish in pan of lukewarm water and bake for about 45 minutes. Serve warm or cold with whipped cream.

# Apple Crisp
*A nice family-style dessert for the cooler weather*

**May prepare ahead**                                    **6 servings**

**Apple Layer:**
6 tart apples, peeled and
   thinly sliced
½ cup sugar
2 teaspoons lemon juice
½ teaspoon cinnamon
¼ teaspoon ground cloves

**Topping:**
¾ cup sifted all-purpose flour
½ cup sugar
dash of salt
6 tablespoons butter or
   margarine
¼ cup chopped walnuts

Place prepared apples in a bowl; add sugar, lemon juice, cinnamon and cloves. Toss lightly to make sure all apple slices are coated. Transfer apple mixture to a well-greased 2½-quart baking dish. Set aside.

In a separate bowl (or in a food processor) combine flour, sugar, salt and butter until crumbly. Stir in walnuts and sprinkle topping mixture over apples. Bake in a preheated 350 degree oven 45 minutes or until apples are tender.

Serve warm with whipped cream or vanilla ice cream. May be prepared early in the day and reheated before serving.

# Mango Ice Cream

**Must prepare ahead**                                    **4 servings**

⅔ cup sweetened condensed
   milk
½ cup milk
2 cups puréed mango pulp*
¼ cup confectioners' sugar
1 cup heavy cream
1 teaspoon lime or lemon juice
pinch of salt

*May substitute peaches.

Blend condensed milk and milk thoroughly. Add mango pulp and sugar; mix well. Add cream, lime or lemon juice and salt, mixing well. Freeze in ice cream freezer.

# Chocolate Glazed Marble Cheesecake

*Takes a long time to prepare, but good things come to those who wait*

**Must prepare ahead**                                    **16 servings**

**Crust:**
1 cup graham cracker crumbs
2 tablespoons cocoa
2 tablespoons sugar
¼ cup butter, melted

Preheat oven to 350 degrees. Combine crust ingredients in a small bowl and blend well. Press mixture into the bottom of a 9-inch greased springform pan. Bake 10 minutes. Remove from oven.

**Cake:**
4 8-ounce packages cream
   cheese, softened
1¾ cups sugar
2 tablespoons all-purpose flour
1 teaspoon vanilla extract
¼ teaspoon almond extract
4 eggs
2 1-ounce squares unsweetened
   chocolate, melted and cooled

Beat cream cheese until smooth; beat in sugar, flour, vanilla and almond extracts. Add eggs, one at a time, beating well after each. Pour ⅓ of the batter into a small bowl; add chocolate, mixing until smooth. Alternately place large spoonfuls of white batter and small spoonfuls of chocolate batter over the crust. Bake cake in the bottom third of the oven for 1 hour and 45 minutes. Cake should be golden brown; top may have several cracks. Cool to room temperature.

**Glaze:**
4 tablespoons cocoa
3 tablespoons water or brewed
   coffee
2 tablespoons butter or
   margarine
2 tablespoons light corn syrup
1¼ cups sifted confectioners'
   sugar

Combine cocoa, water or coffee, margarine and corn syrup; cook over very low heat until mixture is smooth, about 5 minutes. Gradually stir in confectioners' sugar. Glaze cake. Refrigerate 5 to 6 hours before serving.

# Chocolate Yogurt Sour Cream Cheesecake

**Must prepare ahead**                                    **12 servings**

**Nut Crumb Crust:**
½ cup butter, softened
⅓ cup sugar
1 cup all-purpose flour
½ teaspoon salt
½ cup chopped nuts

Preheat oven to 350 degrees. Mix all crust ingredients until well blended. Press firmly onto bottom of well-greased 8-inch springform pan. Bake 30 minutes. Remove from oven and reduce heat to 300 degrees.

**Cheesecake:**
2 8-ounce packages cream cheese, softened
1 cup sugar
3 eggs, room temperature
1 teaspoon vanilla extract
1 teaspoon almond extract
6 1-ounce squares semi-sweet chocolate, melted and cooled
1 cup plain yogurt
1 cup sour cream

In a large bowl, beat cream cheese and sugar until smooth. Beat in eggs, vanilla and almond extracts. Stir in chocolate, yogurt and sour cream until well blended. Pour over prepared crust. Place a pan of water on bottom rack of oven; place cheesecake on middle rack. Bake 50 to 60 minutes or until edges of cake pull away slightly from sides of pan. Do not open door during baking. Turn off heat; let cake cool in oven with door ajar. Run thin blade between cake and pan; carefully remove sides of pan. Place on serving plate. Chill before glazing.

**Chocolate Glaze:**
3 1-ounce squares semi-sweet chocolate
2 tablespoons butter
1 tablespoon corn syrup
½ teaspoon vanilla extract

In small saucepan over low heat, stir chocolate, butter, corn syrup and vanilla until mixture is smooth. Remove from heat; cool slightly before using. Spread glaze on top of cheesecake, creating pattern with back of spoon. Chill several hours or overnight.

**Garnish:**
nuts
whipped cream
rose, optional

Garnish with nuts or whipped cream. You may also garnish with a rose for an elegant touch!

# Gloria's Cheesecake
*The creamiest ever*

**May prepare ahead**                    **10-12 servings**

**Crust:**
1 6-ounce box zwieback toast
1 tablespoon sugar
¼ cup butter, melted

Preheat oven to 350 degrees. Crush zwieback toast in food processor with steel blade until crumbs form. Add sugar and melted butter, mixing well. Line sides and bottom of a well-buttered 9-inch springform pan.

**Filling:**
5 8-ounce packages cream cheese, softened
1¾ cups sugar
3 tablespoons all-purpose flour
1½ teaspoons grated lemon rind
1 tablespoon lemon juice
½ teaspoon vanilla extract
7 eggs
½ cup heavy cream
kiwi slices for garnish
strawberry halves for garnish

Blend cream cheese, sugar, flour, lemon rind, juice and vanilla. Add 5 whole eggs, one at a time, beating lightly after each. Add 2 egg yolks; beat lightly after each. Fold in heavy cream. Pour into pan. Bake 1 hour. Shut off oven, open door slightly and let sit in oven another hour. Chill. Garnish with kiwis and strawberries.

Cheesecake may be frozen several weeks.

*Grated rind of 1 lemon yields approximately 1½ teaspoons.*

*Grated rind of 1 orange yields approximately 1 tablespoon.*

*Juice of 1 lemon yields approximately 3 tablespoons.*

*Juice of 1 orange yields approximately 8 tablespoons.*

# Mini Cheesecakes
*Wonderful for parties or teas*

**Must prepare ahead**                                    **3 dozen**

12 ounces cream cheese,
   softened
½ cup sugar
2 eggs
¾ teaspoon vanilla extract
36 mini muffin paper cups

**Topping:**
1 cup sour cream
¼ cup sugar
½ teaspoon vanilla extract
strawberry or pineapple
   preserves

Preheat oven to 300 degrees. Cream the cheese and sugar thoroughly. Add eggs, one at a time, beating after each. Add vanilla; beat until smooth and creamy. Place paper cups in mini muffin pans and fill each ⅔ full. Bake 20 to 25 minutes. Cool 10 minutes. Cakes will cave in slightly in the center.

In a small bowl, thoroughly mix sour cream, sugar and vanilla. Place about ½ teaspoon of the topping mixture on each cake, spreading well. Top each with a small amount of preserves. Return the pans to the oven and bake an additional 10 minutes. Refrigerate.

# Easy Lemon-Chess Tarts
*Quick and easy*

**May prepare ahead**                                    **10 tarts**

½ cup butter or margarine,
   melted
1½ cups sugar
3 eggs, slightly beaten
1 teaspoon vanilla extract
2 to 3 tablespoons lemon juice
10 unbaked tart shells

Preheat oven to 300 degrees. Mix butter, sugar, eggs, vanilla and lemon juice with a wooden spoon. Fill unbaked tart shells. Bake 1½ hours. Serve warm or at room temperature.

# Flan

*Spectacular ending to a meal*

**Must prepare ahead**                                    **8 servings**

**Syrup:**
**¾ cup sugar**

Carefully heat sugar in large heavy skillet, cooking over medium heat until sugar melts and forms a light brown syrup. Immediately pour syrup into heated 9-inch round, shallow baking dish or cake pan. Turn pan to coat bottom and sides. Set aside.

**Custard:**
**2 cups milk**
**2 cups light cream**
**6 eggs, slightly beaten**
**½ cup sugar**
**½ teaspoon salt**
**2 teaspoons vanilla extract**
**⅓ cup brandy**
**boiling water**

Preheat oven to 325 degrees. In medium saucepan, heat milk and cream just until bubbles form around edge of pan. In large bowl, combine eggs, sugar, salt and vanilla. Gradually stir in hot milk mixture and brandy. Pour into prepared dish. Set dish in shallow pan; pour boiling water to ½-inch depth around dish. Bake 35 to 40 minutes or until knife inserted in center comes out clean. Let custard cool; refrigerate 4 hours or overnight.

**2 tablespoons brandy, heated**

To serve, run small spatula around edge of dish to loosen. Invert on shallow serving dish, shaking gently to release. The caramel acts as a sauce. Carefully ignite heated brandy; pour over caramel flan and serve flaming.

# Grapefruit Sorbet
*Refreshing*

**Must prepare ahead**                                              **6 servings**

¾ cup sugar
2¼ cups grapefruit sections*,
   about 3 large grapefruit
1 cup fresh grapefruit juice
2 tablespoons Kirsch, optional
1 egg white

*May substitute pink
 grapefruit and a dash
 of grenadine.

Place sugar in food processor or blender and run on high 30 seconds; remove and set aside. Purée grapefruit sections in food processor or blender; remove and set aside.

In medium saucepan, combine sugar, juice and Kirsch; bring to a boil, stirring until sugar is dissolved. Reduce heat and simmer 5 minutes. Cool. Blend in grapefruit purée. Pour into shallow baking dish and freeze until solid. Remove from freezer and let stand until slightly softened. Spoon into processor or blender and mix until smooth. Add egg white and mix until satiny. Pour into bowl or individual serving dishes and return to freezer until firm, at least 3 hours. Soften several minutes prior to serving. The sorbet will keep 2 weeks in freezer if wrapped tightly in plastic wrap.

*When whipping cream, the greatest volume and lightest texture are obtained by using well chilled cream and a bowl and beater that have been chilled in the freezer for at least 45 minutes.*

# Trifle

*An easy variation of the traditional English dessert*

**Must prepare ahead**  **8 servings**

1 6⅛-ounce box vanilla
  instant pudding
1 10-inch prepared round angel
  food cake, split horizontally
½ cup apricot or peach brandy
1 10-ounce jar seedless
  raspberry jam, warmed
1 16-ounce can sliced peaches,
  drained
2 cups heavy cream, whipped

Prepare pudding according to package directions. Place ½ of angel food cake in a large glass bowl with flat bottom and straight sides. Pour ¼ cup brandy over cake. Layer ½ the warmed jam, ½ the sliced peaches and ½ the pudding onto cake. Repeat layers and top with whipped cream. Refrigerate at least 4 hours before serving.

# Melons and Blueberries in Rum-Lime Sauce

**Must prepare ahead**  **8 servings**

1 cantaloupe
1 small honeydew melon
⅛ small watermelon
1 cup fresh blueberries

**Rum-Lime Sauce:**
⅔ cup sugar
⅓ cup water
1½ teaspoons grated lime rind
6 tablespoons lime juice
½ cup light rum
mint sprigs, optional

Cut the cantaloupe and honeydew melons in half; remove seeds. With a melon scoop, form fruit into small balls. Repeat with watermelon, working around seeds. Pile melon balls and blueberries into a serving bowl; chill.

In a small saucepan, mix sugar with water; bring to a boil. Reduce heat and simmer 5 minutes. Add lime rind; let cool to room temperature. Stir in lime juice and rum. Pour sauce over fruit. Cover and chill for several hours.

To serve, decorate with sprigs of mint and add additional rum, if desired.

# Peppermint Ice Cream Freeze
*A dessert all ages enjoy*

**Must prepare ahead**                    **18 servings**

**Crust:**
6 tablespoons butter, melted
1 12½-ounce box vanilla
  wafers, crushed
**Filling:**
½ cup butter, softened
2 cups confectioners' sugar
3 eggs, separated
2 1-ounce squares semi-sweet
  chocolate, melted
½ cup chopped pecans
  or walnuts
2 quarts peppermint ice cream,
  softened

Combine butter and vanilla wafer crumbs, reserving a small amount of crumbs for topping. Press into 9 x 13-inch pan. Freeze.

Cream butter with sugar; add egg yolks and blend well. Beat in melted chocolate; cool. Beat egg whites until stiff. Fold into sugar mixture; add nuts. Spread over crust. Freeze. Spread softened ice cream over chocolate mixture. Sprinkle with reserved crumbs. Freeze until firm. Cut into squares to serve.

# Banana Boats
*Have everyone participate in making their own*

**May not prepare ahead**                    **6-8 servings**

6 to 8 large firm bananas
tin foil
1 12-ounce package mini
  chocolate chips
1 10½-ounce package mini
  marshmallows
ice cream

Lay each banana on a 12 x 18-inch piece of foil. Hollow out a ½-inch deep trough in each banana. Sprinkle chocolate chips and marshmallows into the troughs. Be careful not to let any chips or marshmallows fall onto the foil as they will burn. Fold the foil over the bananas to form a loose tent; seal foil. Grill banana boats over low heat until marshmallows and chocolate melt, approximately 4 to 6 minutes. Serve with your favorite ice cream.

# Special Chocolate Dessert

**Must prepare ahead**                    **8-10 servings**

**Layer 1:**
½ cup butter, softened
1 cup all-purpose flour
½ cup chopped pecans

Preheat oven to 350 degrees. Grease a 9 x 13-inch pan. Mix butter, flour and pecans; spread over bottom of pan. Bake 20 minutes. It should appear creamy and pale—not browned. Let cool. (A brownie mix may be substituted. Follow package directions, but decrease cooking time by 7 minutes.)

**Layer 2:**
1 8-ounce package cream cheese, softened
1 cup confectioners' sugar
1 12-ounce container frozen whipped topping, thawed

Combine cream cheese with sugar. Add ½ the container of whipped topping, mixing well. Spread over first layer.

**Layer 3:**
1 4⅛-ounce package instant chocolate pudding mix
1 3½-ounce package instant vanilla pudding mix
3 cups milk

In a large bowl, combine pudding mixes and milk. Beat on low speed until thick. Pour over second layer.

**Layer 4:**
1 1.45-ounce chocolate candy bar

Spread the remaining whipped topping over third layer. Grate candy bar over top. Refrigerate at least 3 hours.

 *Frozen chocolate is easier to shave. Use a potato peeler to shave chocolate bars or to make chocolate curls.*

# Triple Chocolate Dessert
*Rave reviews*

**Must prepare ahead**                    **8-10 servings**

**Crust:**
1¼ cups graham cracker
  crumbs
3 tablespoons sugar
3 tablespoons unsweetened
  cocoa
⅓ cup butter, melted

Preheat oven to 350 degrees. Combine crumbs, sugar and cocoa in 9-inch pie plate; add butter and stir until well coated. Press mixture into bottom and sides of pan. Bake 8 minutes. Cool slightly.

**Cheese Layer:**
12 ounces cream cheese,
  softened
¾ cup sugar
2 eggs
1 tablespoon vanilla extract
1 tablespoon Kahlúa
8 ounces sour cream
1 to 2 ounces semi-sweet
  chocolate, grated

In large mixing bowl or food processor, cream the cheese and sugar until light and fluffy; add eggs, one at a time, and continue beating until well mixed. Stir in vanilla and Kahlúa. Pour mixture into pie crust. Bake 30 minutes. Cool exactly 10 minutes. Spread sour cream evenly over baked cheese layer. Sprinkle on grated chocolate. Refrigerate.

**Chocolate Layer:**
1½ teaspoons instant coffee
2 tablespoons boiling water
4 ounces semi-sweet chocolate
4 eggs, separated
⅓ cup sugar
½ teaspoon vanilla extract
2 tablespoons rum, divided

Dissolve coffee in boiling water. Add chocolate and melt, stirring until smooth. In small bowl, beat egg yolks until thick and lemon colored; gradually add sugar and continue beating until light yellow. Stir in chocolate mixture, vanilla and 1 tablespoon rum until well mixed. Beat egg whites to stiff peaks. Stir ¼ of egg whites into chocolate mixture. Gently fold chocolate mixture into remaining egg whites. Refrigerate mixture until cheese layer is chilled. Evenly spread chocolate mixture over cheese layer; chill.

1 cup heavy cream
shaved chocolate

To serve, whip cream; fold in 1 tablespoon rum. Spread over chocolate layer. Sprinkle with shaved chocolate.

# Pots de Crème

**Must prepare partially ahead**                          **4 servings**

**Filling:**
1 6-ounce package semi-sweet chocolate chips
1 egg
1 teaspoon vanilla extract
1 teaspoon instant coffee
1 tablespoon brandy
dash of salt
1 tablespoon butter
⅔ cup light cream, scalded

Melt chocolate chips in top of double boiler or in microwave on low power. Add egg, vanilla, coffee, brandy, salt and butter. Pour into a blender. Blend on high, pouring in hot cream in a steady stream. Blend 1 minute. Pour into dessert glasses, custard cups or pots de crème. Chill 3 hours or until set.

**Topping:**
1 cup heavy cream
4 tablespoons confectioners' sugar
shaved chocolate

Just before serving, whip cream with confectioners' sugar. Top each pot with whipped cream and chocolate shavings.

# Hot Fudge Sauce
*Thickens when poured over ice cream*

**May prepare ahead**                          **8 servings**

2 1-ounce squares unsweetened chocolate
1 tablespoon butter
⅓ cup boiling water
1 cup sugar
2 tablespoons corn syrup
3 tablespoons bourbon
½ cup chopped walnuts or pecans, optional

Melt chocolate in double boiler. Add butter and let melt. Stir. Add water and blend well. Stir in sugar and corn syrup. Place pan over direct heat and boil gently for 8 minutes. Do NOT stir. Just before serving, stir in bourbon and nuts.

May be made ahead and reheated over boiling water.

# Praline Cheesecake

Must prepare ahead                                            12 servings

**Crust:**
1 cup graham cracker crumbs
3 tablespoons sugar
3 tablespoons butter, melted

**Filling:**
3 8-ounce packages cream
  cheese, softened
1¼ cups packed dark brown
  sugar
2 tablespoons all-purpose flour
3 eggs
1½ teaspoons vanilla extract
½ cup finely chopped pecans
1 tablespoon maple syrup
pecan halves for top decoration

Preheat oven to 350 degrees. Combine crumbs, sugar and butter. Press into the bottom of a 9-inch greased springform pan. Bake 10 minutes.

In a large bowl, combine cream cheese, brown sugar and flour. Beat at medium speed until well blended. Add eggs, one at a time; beat well. Add vanilla and chopped pecans. Pour mixture over crust. Bake 50 to 55 minutes. Cool. Loosen cake and chill. Brush top with maple syrup and garnish top with pecan halves.

# Chocolate Sauce

May prepare ahead                                                 3 cups

½ cup unsweetened cocoa
¼ cup butter or margarine
1¾ cups sugar
½ cup milk
½ teaspoon vanilla extract
2 tablespoons light corn syrup
dash of salt

Combine all ingredients in a saucepan. Bring to a boil over medium heat. Cook to 234 degrees F. on a candy thermometer or until a small amount just holds its shape when dropped into a cup of cold water. Sauce may be refrigerated and reheated.

restaurants

# CAPTIVA INN

*Home of the "seven course gourmet dinner" served in style and grace in an intimate home setting.*

## Shrimp Boat

**May prepare partially ahead**          **6 servings as an appetizer**

6 puff pastry shells
2½ cups dry white wine
1 pound small shrimp, peeled
    and deveined
4 tablespoons butter
2 tablespoons flour
1 tablespoon tomato paste*
salt to taste
pepper to taste
¼ cup heavy cream
½ teaspoon freshly grated
    nutmeg
1 tablespoon fresh lemon juice

*May substitute lobster stock.
 (Boil lobster shells with onion,
 celery, salt, pepper and 1 cup
 lobster meat.)

Prepare your favorite puff pastry shells. Set aside.

Bring wine to a boil. Carefully place shrimp in wine; boil very gently 10 minutes. Remove shrimp, reserving 2 cups liquid. In a separate pan make a roux with the butter and flour. Gradually add reserved liquid and cook until slightly thickened. Stir in tomato paste. Season with salt and pepper. Add cream, nutmeg, lemon juice and shrimp. Cook until shrimp are heated. Spoon shrimp and sauce into prepared pastry shells.

### TROPICAL FOLIAGE

*The beautiful hibiscus, with over 1,000 named varieties, comes in almost every color imaginable. It is the rare Southwest Florida garden that is not graced by at least one hibiscus. The sea-grape, a Florida native, is distinguished by its large, broadly rounded, red-veined leaves. It is salt-resistant and grows well in seaside locations. The ripe fruit is used to make a delicious jelly.*

 Château Robert

*Elegant surroundings styled after a classical French palace. Modern French cuisine presented with elegance.*

## Lobster Bisque

**May prepare partially ahead**　　　　　　　　**12 servings**

1 cup white wine
½ cup brandy
1 gallon water
3 2-pound lobsters
1 carrot
1 stalk leek
2 stalks celery
3 bay leaves
1 tablespoon tarragon
1 teaspoon thyme
1 tablespoon peppercorns
8 ounces tomato purée
10 ounces white roux
2 cups heavy cream
2 ounces sherry
salt to taste
pepper to taste

In a small stock pot add wine, brandy and water. Bring to a boil. Add lobster; cook 12 minutes. Remove from liquid. Remove all meat from lobster; place shells back into poaching liquid. Add vegetables, seasonings and tomato purée. Simmer 1 hour; strain. Place liquid back on fire. Add white roux while whipping it into liquid using wire whip. Simmer 45 minutes; strain. Stir in heavy cream and sherry. Correct seasoning with salt and pepper. Garnish bisque with diced lobster meat.

# Flora and Ella's Restaurant

*A LaBelle tradition since 1935 which has gained an international as well as an area and national reputation as a friendly home town restaurant serving some of the best family style meals anywhere.*

## Peanut Butter Meringue Pie

**May prepare ahead**                                    **8 servings**

½ cup confectioners' sugar
¼ cup peanut butter
1¼ cups sugar
1 13-ounce can evaporated
  milk
1 13-ounce can water, divided
1 teaspoon vanilla extract
1 tablespoon butter or
  margarine
pinch of salt
5 egg yolks
5 tablespoons corn starch
1 9¼-inch pie shell, baked

Combine confectioners' sugar and peanut butter with a fork until it resembles coarse meal. Measure out ½ cup peanut butter mixture, reserving remainder.

In a medium saucepan combine ½ cup peanut butter mixture, sugar, milk, ½ can water, vanilla, butter and salt. Bring to a boil over medium to medium-high heat, stirring occasionally.

Meanwhile, mix remaining ½ can water with corn starch and egg yolks. Blend with a fork until smooth. Pour quickly into boiling mixture, stirring constantly until thickened. Pour into pie shell and top with meringue. Sprinkle on reserved peanut butter mixture. Bake at 350 degrees for 25 minutes.

**Meringue:**
5 egg whites
½ teaspoon vanilla extract
¼ teaspoon corn starch
¼ teaspoon cream of tartar
pinch of salt
½ cup sugar

Combine egg whites, vanilla, corn starch, cream of tartar and salt in a large mixing bowl. Beat until frothy. Gradually add sugar and continue beating until stiff peaks form. Spoon over pie.

*Featuring a fresh new approach to steak and seafood with the most beautiful panoramic view of the Gulf of any restaurant on Sanibel.*

## Chicken Morgan

**May prepare partially ahead**                    **8 servings**

3 ounces butter
1 garlic clove, minced
1 shallot clove, minced
½ pound ham, finely chopped
½ pound Swiss cheese, finely
   chopped
1 bunch green onions, finely
   chopped
1 medium red pepper, finely
   chopped
4 large mushrooms, finely
   chopped
½ pound spinach leaves,
   stems removed
1 ounce Worcestershire sauce
1 ounce Dijon mustard
8 ounces bread crumbs
1 teaspoon salt
1 tablespoon pepper
8 6-ounce skinless, boneless
   chicken breasts, thinly
   pounded

Heat pan to 300 degrees. Add butter and allow to cook until foam subsides. Add garlic and shallot; sauté until very lightly browned. Stir in ham, Swiss cheese, onions, pepper, mushrooms and spinach leaves. Cook 5 minutes until tender. Add Worcestershire sauce, mustard and bread crumbs. Set aside.

Salt and pepper chicken breasts. Place an equal amount of ham-mushroom mixture on each breast. Roll lengthwise. Place each breast on a greased cookie sheet. Butter each. Bake at 350 degrees for 20 minutes until firm.

Serve with fettuccine and your favorite vegetable.

*Offers one of the largest selections of fresh seafood in Southwest Florida in a greenhouse dining room.*

# Conch Salad

**Must prepare ahead**                                      **16 servings**

2½ pounds fresh or frozen conch

Chop conch in food processor or by hand.

**Marinade:**
1 cup lime juice
½ cup white vinegar
½ cup vegetable oil
1 tablespoon Worcestershire sauce

Combine all marinade ingredients. Marinate conch in refrigerator for 24 hours.

**Salad:**
2 cups coarsely chopped red onions
5 jalapeño peppers, chopped
2 cups coarsely chopped green peppers
2 cups coarsely chopped celery
2 cups coarsely chopped tomatoes

Drain marinade from chopped conch. Toss conch with salad ingredients. Refrigerate.

Serve chilled on a bed of lettuce.

*Created in an authentic turn-of-the-century southern residence with a stunning garden-courtyard which features "Southern hospitality with a touch of New Orleans."*

## Strawberry Fruit Soup

**Must prepare ahead**                                    **1 quart**

**2 10-ounce packages frozen
    strawberries, thawed**
**1 pint fresh strawberries,
    hulled and washed**
**½ cup sour cream**
**¼ cup lemon juice**
**1 tablespoon cinnamon**
**1 cup heavy cream**
**strawberry slices for garnish**
**whipped cream for garnish**

Blend all ingredients in a food processor or blender. Chill 3 hours. Garnish with a strawberry slice on a dollop of whipped cream.

# ACKNOWLEDGMENTS

The Junior League of Fort Myers, Inc. would like to thank its members and their friends who contributed so much to this book. Each recipe has been tested for accuracy and excellence. We do not claim that all the recipes are original, only that they are our favorites. We deeply regret that we were unable to include many recipes which were submitted, due to similarity or lack of space.

Kathy Adams
Lori Anderson
Karen Appleby
Larry Appleby
Sam Arnall
Donna Lou Askew
Deborah Backes
Kay Bailey
Jane Ball
Vickie Banks
Peggy Barrett
Connie Bartholomew
Joan Baugher
Kathleen Belcastro
Debbie Blue
Colleen Brett
Brenda Brunk
Ella Burchard
Jo Carlson
Dorry Christy
Maxine Crispi
Peg Crittendon
Linda DeCarlo
Judy Dees
Kathy Delorio
Jean deTarnowsky
Emma Lou Dressler
Barb Dunlap
Barbara Dunphy
Paula Edenfield
Susan Erickson
Julia Estabrook
Kate Evans
Ann Fink
Debby Focht
Jan Foster
Marty Friedman
Nicky Frierson
Beverly Fuller
Leslie Galinski
Mary Ann Galloway
Saundra Garner
Darbi Gillingham
Barbara Anne Goede
Carolyn Gora
Judy Gore
Jeananne Grace
Susan Grace
Patricia Graddy
Nancy Green
Tallulah Gregory
Audrey Gwennap
Caroline Halgrim

Sue Hamilton
Ellen Hanish
Chef Pete Harmon
Margaret Harrison
Susan Harrison
Gordon Harrison
Becky Hartman
Bill Haverfield
Eve Haverfield
Susan Henderson
Betty Hendry
Juanita Hermes
Kay Higgins
Lyn Hill
Paula Himschoot
Debby Hobe
David Hobe
Fran Holmes
Robbie Howes
Andrea Horowitz
Johanna Hudson
Judi Hughes
Dottie Hummel
Betty Hyde
Bob Jacobs
Maureen Jividen
Barbara Johnson
Connie Jones
Kathy Jones
Sandy Johnson
Karen Judah
Liz Kagan
Judy Kash
Jack Kaune
Donna Kaye
Babs Kendziorski
Carolyn Keyes
Alene Kiesel
Ruth Kiesel
Pat King
Liz Kinsey
Angela Kirby
Sue Kitchens
Gay Kunkle
Susan Kyle
Sandi Lambros
Kit Latell
Susan Mahlman
Ann McCaughan
Betty McEwen
Mary McFadden
Diana McGee

Judy McIver
Gene McKenzie
Maggi McKenzie
Mary McKenzie
Beverly McNew
Mary Lee Mann
Kate Metke
Diana Migliore
Joan Mikkus
Josie Mills
Linda Moorey
Suzanne Moore
Mildred Morehouse
Sara Morrison
Annette Morroni
Karin Murray
Bob Muzio
Laura Muzio
Karen Nathan
Jim Nathan
Sandy Nelson
Betty Nevans
Marilyn Niederman
Dee Olitsky
Dorothy Olitsky
Cheryl Osborne
Dianne Ostendorf
Anna Pack
Velma Parham
Candy Parnell
Sue Parsons
Chef Joseph Percevault
Julie Peters
Beverly Pierce
Dee Pisaris
Peter Pisaris
Mimi Potts
Sarah Prather
Gwyn Raney
Maggie Reese
Carole Richardson
Barbara Riester
Teta Roberts
Carol Ruke
Bobbi Sanders
Helen Sanders
Michael Schleig
Diann Seals
Susan Seeley
Diane Seidenstein
Sara Sharpe
Jim Sherfey
Betteann Sherman

Rhonda Shook
Mary Shorack
Joy Sicks
Mary Kay Sidell
Anna Siemen
Susan Siler
Joyce J. Simmons
Mary Jo Simpson
Annie Bea Sisler
Nancy Skalko
Mary Smalley
Marilyn Smith
Nanette Smith
Ruth Smith
Ann Smoot
Barbara Snyderman
Jackie Speas
Mary Squires
Betty Squires
Charlotte Staton
Carol Steinberg
Jeannine Sterckx
George Sterckx
Delores Taschner
Freda Taschner
Marie Taschner
Mary Ten Broeck
Bunny Terry
Orpah Travis
Mary Kay Tressler
Helen Turnell
Linda Uhler
Tom Uhler
Peggy Van Voorhis
Joann Waugh
Barbara Weber
Diane Weiss
Susan Welborn
Anna Belle Womack
Jan Whited
Connie Whiteside
Dot Williams
Kay Williams
Trish Winrow
Kathy Wolfe
Martha Wolfe
Maryann Wyner
Linda Yaeger
Ruth Young
Judith Zeterberg

# INDEX

*Variation

*Variation

*Variation

*Variation

277

*Variation

*Variation

*Variation

*Variation

*Variation

*Variation